HOKUSAI

HOKUSAI

ANN YONEMURA

Contributions by

NAGATA SEIJI

KOBAYASHI TADASHI

ASANO SHŪGŌ

TIMOTHY CLARK

NAITŌ MASATO

FREER GALLERY OF ART AND ARTHUR M. SACKLER GALLERY,
SMITHSONIAN INSTITUTION, WASHINGTON, D.C.

Copyright 2006 Smithsonian Institution

Published by the Freer Gallery of Art and the Arthur M. Sackler Gallery
on the occasion of an exhibition held at the Arthur M. Sackler Gallery,
Smithsonian Institution, Washington, D.C., March 4–May 14, 2006.

Hokusai is co-organized by the Freer Gallery of Art and the Arthur M.
Sackler Gallery, Smithsonian Institution, and the Nihon Keizai
Shimbun, Inc., in cooperation with the Tokyo National Museum.

COVER Detail, cat. 131. FRONTISPIECE Detail, cat. 138. PAGES VIII-IX Detail,
cat. 60. PAGE X Detail, cat. 64. PAGE 8 Detail, cat. 142. PAGE 16 Detail, cat. 119.
PAGE 26 Detail, cat. 88. PAGE 40 Detail, cat. 89.

PHOTOGRAPHIC CREDITS
© Réunion des Musées Nationaux, Art Resource, NY, 105; © Rijksmuseum
Amsterdam, 54; © the Trustees of The British Museum, 9, 10, 14, 24, 61, 62,
66, 80, 116, 122, 137, 164; John Deane, 52, 96; Richard Goodbody, 21, 93, 94;
Katya Kallsen, 69; Robert Lifson, 6, 13, 58; Mel McLean, 46; Photograph ©
1991 The Metropolitan Museum of Art, 134; Photograph © 1994 The
Metropolitan Museum of Art, 100; Photograph © 2006 Museum of Fine
Arts, Boston, 11; Photography © The Art Institute of Chicago, 22, 92, 103, 106,
109–12, 157; V & A Picture Library, V & A Images/Victoria and Albert
Museum, 3, 4.

Library of Congress Cataloging-in-Publication Data

Yonemura, Ann, 1947–
    Hokusai / Ann Yonemura; contributions by Nagata Seiji … [et al.].
    p.   cm.
    Includes bibliographical references and index.
    ISBN 0-934686-02-5 (978-0-934686-02-0)
1. Katsushika, Hokusai, 1760–1849 — Catalogues raisonnés.
2. Katsushika, Hokusai, 1760–1849 — Criticism and interpretation.
I. Katsushika, Hokusai, 1760–1849. II. Nagata, Seiji. III. Arthur M. Sackler
Gallery (Smithsonian Institution). IV. Freer Gallery of Art. V. Title.
N7359.K37A4 2006a
760.092 — dc22   2006002841

The paper used in this publication meets the minimum requirements of
the American National Standard for Information Science — Permanence
of Paper for Printed Library Materials, ANSI Z39.48-1984.

HEAD OF DESIGN, PUBLICATIONS,
AND DIGITAL MEDIA Dennis Kois
HEAD OF VISUAL DESIGN John Gordy
EDITOR Mariah Keller
DESIGNER Rebecca Rivas-Rogers
PRODUCTION MANAGER Rachel Faulise
TYPEFACES Minion and Interstate

THE EXHIBITION IS GENEROUSLY SUPPORTED BY

Fidelity Investments through
the Fidelity Foundation
The Anne van Biema Endowment Fund
Asahi Glass Co. Ltd.
Astellas Pharma, Inc.
All Nippon Airways Co., Ltd.
CANON U.S.A., INC.
Mitsubishi Corporation
NEC Corporation
Panasonic Corporation of America
Toyota Motor Corporation
Robert and Betsy Feinberg
with additional support from
the Blakemore Foundation, and
the Mary Livingston Griggs and
Mary Griggs Burke Foundation.

Smithsonian
*Freer Gallery of Art and
Arthur M. Sackler Gallery*

CONTENTS

PREFACE

This volume contains four essays and catalogue entries for all works in the exhibition *Hokusai* held at the Arthur M. Sackler Gallery, Smithsonian Institution. The exhibition follows a related show held at the Tokyo National Museum in 2005. The essays were written for publication in both exhibition catalogues; however, edited versions with added citations and cross-references as well as minor revisions by the authors are included in this volume. The catalogue entries were all written specifically for this publication and are not translations of the entries found in the Tokyo catalogue. For objects exhibited in both venues, the Tokyo catalogue is cited for reference, but the individual views of authors writing for this volume have been respected and should not be assumed to be identical to the opinions of other authors.

The essay by Nagata Seiji, guest curator of the Tokyo National Museum exhibition and a renowned authority on Katsushika Hokusai (1760–1849), presents a detailed account of Hokusai's life and work and identifies areas for future research. Kobayashi Tadashi, a leading scholar of Japanese painting of the Edo period (1615–1868), discusses Hokusai and his work in the context of Edo cultural life and the artistic schools of the period. My essay describes the remarkable expansion of Hokusai's influence and reputation in the West in the half-century after his death in 1849, and reveals how Charles Lang Freer (1854–1919) formed his unparalleled collection of paintings and drawings by Hokusai between 1898 and 1907. Asano Shūgō presents a detailed analysis of Hokusai's subjects and his signatures and seals, based on research that he, Timothy Clark, and Naitō Masato conducted at the Freer gallery in 2004. Those three scholars contributed detailed entries on the paintings in the catalogue section. I wrote the entries on drawings, prints, and printed books. Carol Morland translated the Japanese essays, and Alfred Haft translated Mr. Naitō's catalogue entries, with the advice of John T. Carpenter on translations of inscriptions. Tim Clark translated Mr. Asano's catalogue entries, edited the translations of Japanese catalogue entries, supplied references, and provided valuable editorial advice. I am also indebted to Roger Keyes, Sebastian Izzard, and Joan Mirviss for sharing their knowledge and experience, and to many colleagues at the Tokyo National Museum for their support of our first cooperative exhibition.

The contributions of the authors, all distinguished scholars with demanding schedules, are gratefully acknowledged. The translators worked diligently to meet the compressed production schedule for this volume. I am especially indebted to Mariah Keller, who provided essential and experienced editorial guidance for a complex manuscript. In the museum's department of design, publications, and digital media, Dennis Kois, John Gordy, Reid Hoffman, Rebecca Rivas-Rogers, Victoria Dawson, Rachel Faulise, Adina Brosnan-McGee, Nancy Hacskaylo, and Edna Jamandre all devoted their time and skills to this publication. John Tsantes, Neil Greentree, and Corey Grace ably coordinated photography and image management. My gratitude is also due to the staff of the Freer Gallery of Art and Arthur M. Sackler Gallery Library, Smithsonian Institution Libraries, especially Reiko Yoshimura and Kathryn Phillips; David Hogge and Linda Ravitz of the Freer and Sackler Archives; and the Freer collections managers, Susan Kitsoulis, Tim Kirk, and Christina Popenfus, who responded to numerous requests from the authors and staff throughout this project. Finally, I would like to acknowledge the invaluable assistance of Takako Sarai, who provided excellent research support and liaison with the authors, and Kyoko Arakawa, who managed object data, photography requests, and permissions in coordination with registrar Alan Francisco.

The authors are indebted to the many scholars who have contributed to the advancement of our understanding of Hokusai and of the enduring significance of his work from his own lifetime to the present day. Exhibitions of Hokusai's printed and painted images at museums throughout the world continue to surprise us with new insights into his artistic world and creative spirit. We hope that this show, the first international exhibition to include a substantial number of paintings collected a century ago by Charles Lang Freer, will inspire others to continue the research that we have begun and set forth here.

Ann Yonemura
Senior Associate Curator of Japanese Art
Freer Gallery of Art and Arthur M. Sackler Gallery

NOTE TO THE READER

The detailed catalogue entries in this volume are organized chronologically within major periods of Hokusai's career. In each section, brush drawings, prints, and printed books follow paintings. Descriptive data for each object includes provenance (if known) in reverse chronological order from most recent source through previous collections. Literature citations include the most relevant works consulted by each author. The author's initials are given at the end of each article. Cross-references to volume one catalogue numbers are provided for each entry. A concordance of volume one to volume two numbers is provided on page 108.

NAMES, TITLES, AND DATES

All Japanese names in this volume are given family name first. Romanization of Japanese words follows the convention of minimal hyphenation and word division, except where such division assists the reader in understanding pronunciation—for example in the four-syllable word *ukiyo-e*. In compound words, *n* before *m*, *b*, and *p*, does not change to *m*, thus Rinpa rather than Rimpa. Exceptions are made for citations of published proper names in which alternate spelling is customary. Romanization of Chinese follows the *pinyin* system. Titles of works are given English translation first, followed by romanized Japanese title. If the work is untitled, a descriptive title in English is provided.

The lunar calendar was in use during the Edo period, thus, numbers designate months, and the "first month" does not correspond to January in the solar calendar. Dates, if precisely known, are given in descending order: year, month, and day. Occasionally cyclical dates based on an East Asian system consisting of two sequences of ten and twelve signs respectively are cited; the identical combination of two signs recurs at sixty-year intervals. The Japanese *nengō* system, often cited in historical records, designates eras within larger historical periods. The *nengō* that encompass Hokusai's lifetime are:

Hōreki	1751–64
Meiwa	1764–72
An'ei	1772–81
Tenmei	1781–89
Kansei	1789–1801
Kyōwa	1801–04
Bunka	1804–18
Bunsei	1818–30
Tenpō	1830–44
Kōka	1844–48
Kaei	1848–54

Hokusai often included his age in the inscriptions around his signatures, especially in his late works. Traditionally, age was expressed as one year at birth. Therefore, in Western terms, Hokusai's paintings stating his age as "ninety" may generally be understood to indicate an age of one year less, or eighty-nine. Unless noted, the Japanese system for designating age is used here.

HOKUSAI'S NAMES, SIGNATURES, AND SEALS

Hokusai's signatures and seals appear on many of his works, and together with other documentation, they often provide evidence for establishing an approximate date of production. Hokusai changed his art names many times during his career. His major name changes signified important turning points in his artistic life, but he also used many other names and variants. Some of Hokusai's names appear mainly as pen names for his poetry and writings. He became so famous as Hokusai that he often preceded his later names such as Taito and Iitsu with the notation "*saki no Hokusai*," meaning "formerly Hokusai." The term *aratame* (changed to) also appears in many signatures. Some signatures are followed by terms such as *hitsu* (literally, "brush," meaning "painted by"), or *ga* ("picture," also meaning "by"). In this volume, full transcriptions of signatures are given with translations if the inscriptions are lengthy or contain other than standard and frequently repeated terms. Readings of Hokusai's seals are given if known.

JAPANESE PRINT FORMATS AND DIMENSIONS

In this catalogue, terms that describe the formats of Japanese prints precede the dimensions in centimeters. Approximate dimensions for each term are given below.

> *chūban*, midsize print, 25.0 x 18.0 cm
> *hashira-e*, pillar print, 66.7 x 12.1 cm
> *hosoban*, narrow print, 33.5 x 15.5 cm
> *koban*, small print, 12.0 x 9.0 cm to 19.0 x 13.0 cm
> *nagaban*, long print, 47.0 x 17.0 to 52.0 x 25.0 cm
> *ōban*, large print, 39.0 x 26.0 cm
> *shikishiban*, square print, 21.5 x 19.0 cm
> *surimono*, small-edition prints, privately printed or commissioned; formats vary.

ESSAYS

HOKUSAI'S ARTISTIC CAREER AND TOPICS FOR RESEARCH
NAGATA SEIJI

Katsushika Hokusai (1760–1849) entered the art world during the latter part of the Edo period (1615–1868) as a designer of ukiyo-e (pictures of the floating world). However, he was much more: an indefatigable artist who, during the latter half of a seventy-year career, made a unique place for himself in that world, and, unconfined to the category of ukiyo-e, regularly sought challenges in new areas of art. Intending to live more than one hundred years in order to perfect his art, Hokusai conducted his life on a truly grand scale.

Viewing his career as a whole, it is clear that he was, as one might imagine, very different from the ordinary artist. The style of his work changed throughout his lifetime, and in conjunction with those changes, he accumulated a long list of artistic names. In the *Collection of Correspondence by Kyokutei [Bakin] (Kyokutei raikanshū)*, Hokusai's close acquaintance Kyokutei Bakin (1767–1848) wrote "there was no man who changed his name so often."[1] Indeed, it is difficult to understand such a varied and complex life.

Research on Hokusai and a reassessment of his career as an artist constitute an active area of study in the field of early modern (Edo period) painting and prints. Studies of Hokusai have been concerned not only with his work, but also with many aspects of his life. Building on these studies, the following is a reexamination of the changes in Hokusai's work as well as an exploration of topics for which further research is necessary.

THE ARTIST'S BEGINNINGS
The color prints known as *nishiki-e* (brocade prints) first appeared two hundred forty years ago in 1765 (Meiwa 2), a year that ushered in a new age of prosperity for the Edo art world. At the time, Hokusai was a six-year-old boy called Tokitarō who delighted in drawing everything he saw.

According to existing records, Tokitarō was born into the Kawamura family on the twenty-third day of the ninth month of 1760 (Hōreki 10) in Honjo Warigesui, Shimōsa,[2] and the artist himself records his birth date in the inscription to his painting of Daikoku (1844).[3] In a supplement to the *Compendium of Ukiyo-e Artists (Ukiyo-e ruikō)*, Shikitei Sanba (1776–1822) wrote that Hokusai "was a native of Honjo."[4] It is likely that Hokusai was born into the Kawamura family. The name "Mr. Kawamura" appears on Hokusai's gravestone, and when a female child believed to be his younger sister died in 1766 (Meiwa 3), a Kawamura Ichirōemon was recorded as head of the household in the death registry of the family temple at Seikyōji.[5] Also, in the *Map of Honjo (Honjo ezu;* preserved in Sumida ward) of 1798 (Kansei 10), two houses in Warigesui are designated as belonging to a Kawamura. Whether or not either of these bore any relationship to Hokusai is still unclear.

Records also indicate that at some point Hokusai's uncle Nakajima Ise, a mirror smith to the Bakufu, adopted him and changed his name to Tetsuzō.[6] That Hokusai was indeed Nakajima's adopted son is confirmed in a memo appended to the *Kyokutei raikanshū* stating that Nakajima Ise intended Hokusai would succeed him as mirror smith to the shogun.[7]

Little is known, however, about Hokusai's life from the time he was born until his appearance as an artist. In the first volume of *One Hundred Views of Mount Fuji (Fugaku hyakkei;* cat. 162), published in 1834 (Tenpō 5), Hokusai described how, from the age of six, he enjoyed making sketches.[8] Beyond that, there is no record of what his early life was like. *Katsushika Hokusai den* (1893), by Iijima Kyoshin (1841–1901), states that Hokusai was an assistant in a book rental business, but no other records corroborate this.[9] Asakura Musei has noted that some years later, around the age of sixteen, Hokusai worked as a carver of woodblock prints. According to Asakura (quoting Ishizuka Hōkaishi [1779–1861]), Hokusai said that he had carved the blocks for the last six albums of *Courtesans' Lattice (Gakujō gōshi)*, that he had been a carver from ages sixteen to nineteen, and that, after giving up the craft, he had become an artist. Asakura also revealed that the *Gakujo gōshi* actually comprised eighteen volumes, and that the style of carving in volumes one through twelve is distinctly different from that seen in volumes thirteen through eighteen.[10] Bakin's *Kyokutei raikanshū* also states that after abandoning woodblock carving, Hokusai studied art with Katsukawa Shunshō (1726–92).[11] It thus seems reasonably certain that Hokusai worked as a woodblock carver during his teens.

Before changing his name to Shunrō and entering the art world, Hokusai must have had some art training. In the preface to the first volume of the art manual *(edehon) Illustrated Manual on Color (Ehon saishiki tsū;* cat. 164), published in 1848, he described how from the age of six to the age of eighty-eight, he continuously drew and painted.[12] This indicates that from an early age, when he was fervently making sketches from life, Hokusai had already started on the path to becoming an artist.

THE "SHUNRŌ" PERIOD: HOKUSAI'S APPRENTICESHIP

As Ishizuka described in the *Gakujō gōshi*, Tetsuzō left his job as a woodblock carver at the age of nineteen and, determined to become an artist, entered the studio of Katsukawa Shunshō.[13] Shunshō conferred the name Shunrō on him, and three extant prints of kabuki actors in the *hosoban* format published in 1779 (An'ei 8), constitute Shunrō's debut: the depiction of the actor Segawa Kikunojō III as the daughter of Masamune from the *New Tale of Usuyuki (Shin Usuyuki monogatari)* performed at the Ichimura Theater; *The Actor Iwai Hanshirō IV as Kashiku* in a performance of *Revenge, Kashiku the Enemy (Katakiuchi adana Kashiku)* at the Nakamura Theatre; and *Ichimura Monnosuke as Komamonoya Rokusaburō*.[14] Yasuda Gōzō suggests a fourth print, *The Actor Nakamura Rikō as the Wife of Fukusei,* should be included as a debut work, but this has not been substantiated.[15] An anonymous scholar kindly told me some time ago of the existence of another early work, one produced by Hokusai when he was nineteen years old, but this too has not been proven. Therefore, the three above-mentioned prints are considered to be Hokusai's first published works. The prints are signed "Katsukawa Shunrō ga," and the fifteen years or so after their publication is known as the "Shunrō" period. This period can be divided into four subperiods corresponding generally to changes in Hokusai's style.

1779 (An'ei 8)–Circa 1784 (Tenmei 4)

The first subperiod comprises the five or so years when Shunrō made his entrance into the art world. Generally, until around 1781, he was no better than an imitator of his teacher Shunshō, and a certain stiffness is evident in his portrayals of the figures. In 1780 (An'ei 9), his first illustrations for the type of popular novels called yellow covers (*kibyōshi*) were published, and afterward, he tried his hand at illustrations for "smart" books (*sharebon*) and collections of humorous stories (*hanashibon*), thereby greatly broadening the range of his artwork.

By 1782 or 1783 (Tenmei 2 or 3), Shunrō had developed a style with some individual characteristics. His color prints included not only actor prints (*yakusha-e*), but also a number of pictures of beauties (*bijinga*) and genre pictures (*fūzokuga*). Under the influence of Torii Kiyonaga (1752–1815), Hokusai began to draw women with fuller, rounder features, and he also completed book illustrations, including the *sharebon* titled *Viewing Fukagawa (Fukagawa haiken)* in which his depictions of men and women are infused with poetic beauty.[16] By the beginning of 1784 (Tenmei 4), the aesthetic qualities of Hokusai's book illustrations became more striking, and one finds in the yellow-covers ideas in accord with those seen in later illustrated books. Yasuda Gōzō ascribes to Shunrō a picture of a beauty done around 1782 (Tenmei 2) and signed "Mari," but this attribution needs further investigation.[17]

1785 (Tenmei 5)–Circa 1786 (Tenmei 6)

Significant differences between Hokusai's illustrations for yellow-covers and other publications characterize this two-year subperiod, indicating an important change in his circumstances. This change is reflected not only in Hokusai's style, but also in his artistic name. His signature in a yellow cover from 1785 (Tenmei 5) reads "Shunrō aratame Gunbatei ga," meaning "by Gunbatei, formerly Shunrō," and one done the following year is signed "Gunbatei ga." At the same time, a *hosoban* color print entitled *Teahouse at Ryōgoku (Ryōgoku mizuchaya)* is signed "Shunrō aratame Gunbatei."[18] Rejecting the name given by one's teacher was a very serious affair, and it is believed that the change to Gunbatei indicates a temporary break with the Katsukawa school. Whether true or not, this name change is the great puzzle of the "Shunrō" period, and an investigation of the circumstances behind it is an important subject for future research.

1787 (Tenmei 7)–1792 (Kansei 4)

The five or so years after Hokusai reverted to the name Shunrō are the most satisfying of the entire period. Especially as one moves into the Kansei era (1789–1801), there is a sudden increase in the number of works and a style that is immediately recognizable as Shunrō's. There is also a change in the types of themes, with great expansion in the range of subject matter. All the while, Shunrō was advancing his standing and solidifying his position as a central artist of the Katsukawa school.

1793 (Kansei 5)–1794 (Kansei 6)

Shunshō died on the eighth day of the twelfth month of 1792 (Kansei 4). Almost immediately afterward, in the first month of 1793 (Kansei 5), Hokusai published a picture calendar (*egoyomi*) for the Year of the Ox entitled *Ox-drawn Cart (Gyūsha)*, which bears the signature "Kusamura Shunrō ga."[19] The use of this family name was probably not Hokusai's idea: The artists Toyomaru (fl. 1785–97), Kunimaro (fl. late eighteenth century), and Kanro used the name Kusamura, and there is an actor print in the Katsukawa style depicting Ichikawa Omezō by the artist Kusamura Kumeharu.[20] The meaning of this name for Hokusai is unclear, but Kusamura is attached to a group of his works in a similar style, and one can suppose that the change in name is related to his break from the Katsukawa school.

There is a significant transformation in the works from this subperiod. Beginning with *Water Seller (Reisui uri;* cat. 12), Shunrō began designing *surimono* around the summer of 1793 (Kansei 5), and these lavishly produced prints as well as the picture calendars from this period are so unlike his previous work that one might think they are from the hand of another artist altogether. In part, they anticipate the style of the following "Sōri" period, which can be seen in the Chinese-style fan *The Gods Ebisu and Daikoku Performing a Manzai Dance (Ebisu to Daikokuten no manzai)* and in the painting *Shōki and Demon (cat. 1)*.[21] Expanding into new areas, Shunrō began to produce illustrations for *kyōka ehon* (albums combining pictures and *kyōka*, a form of comic verse), including *A Kyōka Competition and Critique of Women (Kyōka tsurane awase onna shinasadame).*[22] Noted for displaying this new direction are *egoyomi*, as well as *surimono*-style works containing *kyōka* in the style of the subsequent "Sōri" period such as *Handball and Battledore (Temari to Hagoita zu).*[23] Thus, this last part of the "Shunrō" period can be seen as an era of transition to the following "Sōri" period.

Incidentally, some prints from this era have a strong connection to *haikai*, in which one can discern Hokusai's movement from the picture calendars mentioned above to the world of *kyōka*.

THE "SŌRI" PERIOD: DEVELOPMENT OF THE "SŌRI" STYLE

The last known work from the "Shunrō" period is a *surimono* published around the eighth month of 1794 (Kansei 6) entitled *Fulling Cloth (Kinuta uchi zu).*[24] Two picture calendars for the following New Year, *Firing a Canon (Ōzutsu uchi no zu)* and *Manzai Dance in a Residence (Zashiki manzai),* are signed "Sōri."[25] The Sōri signature also appears on the print *New Year's Greeting (Nenrei no zu)* in a New Year *kyōka* album entitled *New Year* Kyōka: *Edo Murasaki (Saitan kyōka Edo Murasaki).*[26] Since picture calendars and *kyōka* albums are printed media, the name change to Sōri must have occurred sometime after the eighth month but before the end of 1794 (Kansei 6). Hokusai subsequently handed the Sōri name over to his pupil Sōji, and around the autumn of 1798 (Kansei 10), adopted the name Hokusai Tokimasa, signaling his identity as an independent artist. Although he later changed his name again to Gakyōjin Hokusai, works in the "Sōri" style continued to be published until 1806 or 1807 (Bunka 3 or 4). With the advent of the Bunka era (1804–18), however, one sees a gradual shift of Hokusai's focus and energy to illustrations for historical novels (*yomihon*). Thus, at least provisionally, the second half of the "Sōri" period lasted roughly through the preceding Kyōwa era (1801–04). While Hokusai's style during this time is fairly consistent, it can be useful to divide the period into two parts, before and after the artist's assertion of his independence.

The circumstances behind the change from Shunrō to Sōri are unclear. The name Sōri is taken from Tawaraya Sōri (fl. ca. 1764–80), whose name was given to the school of artists that brought the Rinpa style to Edo and later acted as an important influence on artists such as Sakai Hōitsu (1761–1822) and others. However, the lineage is unclear: The artist considered to be the first-generation Sōri came from the Sumiyoshi school of Yamato-e painting, and even now it is uncertain from which line Shunrō inherited the name. The Tawaraya school was deeply involved with *haikai*, and one can make the point that Shunrō was identifying with that aspect of the school when he took the name Sōri. There are, in fact, works related to *tentori* (point-scoring) haiku that date from the "Kusamura Shunrō" period, and, as recent research has discovered, many *suri-*

mono incorporating *haikai* by poets such as Ōshima Kanrai (1748–1817) and Iwanami Goshin (d. 1817) were produced during the "Sōri" period. The relationship with *haikai* is another topic that requires further consideration.

At any rate, works completed during Hokusai's "Sōri" period are unlike those created earlier. Not one commercially published color print, not even an actor print, is extant from this period, and, except for a single work, none of the yellow-covers attributed to Sōri are signed, indicating that Hokusai was distancing himself from standard ukiyo-e. What he focused on instead was the production of privately commissioned *surimono* with *kyōka* and *haikai*, and on designs for calendar prints and *kyōka* albums. Illustrations that rank with those of popular artists such as Kitao Shigemasa (1739–1820) and Kitagawa Utamaro (d. 1806) fill this period. They include the previously mentioned *Saitan kyōka Edo Murasaki, Spring in Every Quarter (Yomo no haru), Dawn in Spring (Haru no akebono), Willow-silk (Yanagi no Ito), Mists of Sandara (Sandara kasumi;* cat. 22), *Elegance of Spring (Haru no miyabi), Men's New Year Ceremonial Dance (Otoko tōka), Warbler in the Deep Mountains (Miyama uguisu;* cat. 24), and *Album of Springtime Diversions (Shunkyō-jō).*[27] Hokusai drew all nine illustrations of the one-volume *Shikinamigusa* (cat. 23) in 1796 (Kansei 8), rather than sharing the commission with other artists, indicating that he was already highly regarded in this field.

Paintings, rare during the "Shunrō" period, abruptly increased during this time: at present, close to twenty extant works can be securely attributed to Hokusai. All depart from the Katsukawa mode and display the individuality characteristic of the "Sōri" style. One can only be astounded at such a quick transformation. Most likely, Hokusai acquired painting skills through studying the techniques of various schools during the latter half of the "Shunrō" period.

By the autumn of 1798 (Kansei 10), Sōri had established himself as an independent artist, changed his name to Hokusai Tokimasa, and embarked on a new phase of his career. He concentrated on *surimono* and *kyōka* albums, focused on painting, and also worked again on color prints. With a few notable exceptions, actor prints, which were published regularly throughout the "Shunrō" period, do not reappear during this phase of Hokusai's oeuvre. Works representative of the period include the large-scale *ōban* series *Fashionable Seven Habits (Fūryū nakute nanakuse;* cats. 51 and 52). The title indicates that the set would have had seven sheets, but only two are extant today (one other is known to have existed, but it was destroyed in the great Kantō earthquake and fire of 1923). Each print portrays two beauties, and both works are noteworthy for their mica embellishments. As close-up views, with only the head and shoulders shown, they are unprecedented and therefore especially valuable. *Eight Views of Traveling Lovers from* Jōruri *Plays (Michiyuki hakkei),* also from this period, is a *chūban* print set imbued with a rich poetic atmosphere characteristic of the "Sōri" style. The prints all depict *michiyuki* (on-the-road) scenes from *sewa-jōruri* plays ("domestic" dramas performed by puppets), and though small in size, each work is expressive of the artistic sentiment that characterizes the period. Another print series that should be mentioned here is the *Newly Published Perspective Pictures of* Chūshingura (*Shinpan uki-e Chūshingura*), an ambitious work comprising eleven sheets.[28]

Interestingly, the color print series from this period are all signed "Kakō." The signature "Gakō Kakō" appears on the only yellow-cover inscribed by Hokusai during the "Sōri" period, the *History of Japanese Ghosts (Bakemono Yamato honsō),* published for the New Year of 1798 (Kansei 10).[29] It was under the Kakō name, incidentally, that Hokusai entered the world of popular fiction. The signature "Tokitarō Kakō" appears on the yellow-cover, *The Book of Tactics of General Oven (Kamado Shōgun kanryaku no maki),* published in 1800 (Kansei 12), for which Hokusai wrote the text and completed the illustrations.[30]

THE KATSUSHIKA HOKUSAI PERIOD: FOCUS ON ILLUSTRATIONS FOR *YOMIHON*

With the start of the Bunka era, Hokusai gradually turned from *surimono* and *kyōka* albums, a genre with which he gained much popularity, to illustrations for full-length novels known as *yomihon,* which were then coming into vogue. Year after year, especially from 1805 (Bunka 2) on, he worked without pause, greatly contributing to the popularity of the genre. On the other hand, the number of his *surimono* and especially *kyōka* markedly decreased, as he primarily concentrated on *yomihon* illustrations and paintings.

Hokusai's first *yomihon,* published at the beginning of 1803 (Kyōwa 3) by Maruya Jin'emon, was titled *Ancient and Modern Curious Tales Left by Fishermen (Kokon kidan ama no sutegusa).*[31] It comprised six volumes of text and an equal number of illustrations. The author was Ryūgasō Hirozumi, the same Hirozumi whose poems were included in *Warbler in the Deep Mountains.* That Hokusai chose to supply illustrations for this work may be related to the fact that one of his pupils had also illustrated a *yomihon* by Hirozumi several years before. The pupil was Teisai Hokuba (1770–1844), and the work was the four-volume *Brocade of Rain (Ame no nishiki),* which was published in the first month of 1800 (Kansei 12).[32] One would not expect a pupil to venture into this field before his teacher, and that the same person wrote the text is particularly interesting. Did Hokuba inspire Hokusai? Or did Hokuba perhaps act as mediator? The circumstances surrounding Hokusai's involvement in *yomihon* warrants further investigation.[33] *Kokon kidan ama no sutegusa* is a short collection of seven stories and is rather different in character from later, full-scale *yomihon,* such as *Love Story: Joined Family Crests (Shōsetsu hiyoku mon),* which was done in collaboration with Bakin and was published in the first month of the following year.[34]

In any case, beginning with the publication of the first of six volumes of the *Illustrated New Edition of* The Water Margin (*Shinpen suiko gaden shohen shochitsu*) two years later, Hokusai's rate of production began to increase, with a sharp rise especially from 1807 (Bunka 4) onward.[35] The numbers are astonishing: Nine novels were printed in 1807 (Bunka 4), ten were printed in 1808 (Bunka 5), and seven *yomihon* were published in 1809 (Bunka 6). Since Hokusai continued to produce illustrations for *yomihon* throughout his lifetime, the total number of these illustrations easily exceeds one thousand, an indication of the concentrated attention he focused on this genre.

Despite Hokusai's intense activity in the field of *yomihon,* he also produced paintings at a rate comparable to that of his later years. Works that display the particular characteristics of this period include *Woman Reading a Letter (Ensō no bijin zu;* cat. 33), which depicts a close-up view of a woman with delicately drawn features within a circular format. It is a fine painting and a good example of Hokusai's continuing divergence from the "Sōri" style. *The Tanabata Festival (Tanabata zu)* dates from around the same time and has long been highly valued. The robes are depicted in strong, variegated brushstrokes, and supreme confidence is conveyed in the way the ink seems to flow across the paper.[36] In her facial features and physique, the woman in *Beauty Becoming Inebriated (Suiyo bijin zu;* cat. 41) constitutes a complete departure from the "Sōri" style. A kind of glossy elegance is prominent in this painting, and although small in size, it displays the characteristics typical of this period. The collaborative work entitled *Seven Gods of Good Fortune (Shichi fukujin)* of 1810 (Bunka 7) makes an especially interesting topic of study, first because we know exactly when it was created, and second, because of the novel make-up of the group of artists who participated in its creation.[37] *Gathering Shellfish at Ebb Tide* (cat. 40), which was completed around the same time, displays an amazing blend of disparate techniques, as Hokusai brilliantly fused the lyrical atmosphere unique to his work with Western laws of perspective. Here, the earthen bank in the foreground is depicted in ink with Chinese-style brushwork, while Mount Fuji, the mountains in the distance, the clouds, and the sky are represented using chiaroscuro and oil painting techniques. This outstanding painting shows definitively the extent to which Hokusai had mastered a wide range of techniques derived from traditional Japanese, Chinese, and Western painting.

Gracing the end of the period is the painting entitled *Tametomo and the Inhabitants of Onoshima Island (Chinzei Hachirō Tametomo;* cat. 66). It celebrated the completion of the *yomihon, Chinzei Hachirō Tametomo, Strange Tales of the Bow Moon (Chinzei Hachirō Tametomo gaiden chinsetsu yumiharizuki),* a work that Hokusai as illustrator and Bakin as author jointly produced, which comprised twenty-eight books in twenty-nine volumes and took four years to finish. Created at the request of the publisher Hirabayashi

Shōgorō (late eighteenth–mid-nineteenth century) in 1811 (Bunka 8), the painting can surely be counted as one of Hokusai's masterpieces on the warrior theme.[38]

While *nishiki-e* from this period are surprisingly rare, the prints represent a wide variety of subjects, including Western-style landscapes, caricatures (*toba-e*), warrior pictures, and sets depicting stations on the Tōkaidō road.

THE "TAITO" PERIOD: THE ERA OF *EDEHON*

After the age of fifty, Hokusai moved away from the production of *yomihon* and instead concentrated his energies on publishing art manuals (*edehon*). His career took a definitive turn after 1812 (Bunka 9) or so, and with the publication of the first volume of *Random Sketches by Hokusai* (*Hokusai manga*; cat. 73) in 1814 (Bunka 11), he became fully involved in art manuals. Why would Hokusai pour his talents into this genre? As the number of his pupils increased, so did the demand for copybooks, and printing large quantities of his manuals in woodblock form was a practical and timesaving solution. Also, Hokusai was ambitious, and he was intent on disseminating the "Katsushika" style to his many devotees scattered throughout the country. Another reason was that collections of his designs were in demand by craftsmen in various media who used the illustrations as models.

Hokusai's first art manual, titled *Foolish One's Nonsense Picture Dictionary* (*Onoga bakamura mudajie zukushi*), was published by Tsutaya Jūzaburō in the first month of 1810 (Bunka 7), a time when Hokusai was primarily producing *yomihon*.[39] The manual illustrates *moji-e*, pictures that cleverly incorporate the Japanese syllabary. Since it was issued at the beginning of 1810, the preparatory sketches must have been completed in 1809 (Bunka 6), the year in which Hokusai turned fifty. Advertisements at the end of volume one for three types of *edehon*—*Quick Reference of Abbreviated Drawings* (*Ryakuga haya-jibiki*), *Illustrated Models for Wisdom* (*Ehon chie no hinagata*), and *Kasaki Linked Pictures* (*Kasaki renga*)—indicate that by this time Hokusai was already planning future publications. The following year, an advertisement for *A Quick Lesson in Simplified Drawings* (*Ryakuga Hayaoshie*) appeared in another Tsutaya publication; the manual itself was issued in the first month of 1812 (Bunka 9).[40]

In the fall of 1812, Hokusai, traveling on business, spent six months in Nagoya. He stayed at the home of a pupil, Maki Bokusen (1775–1824), and there he made more than three hundred detailed sketches for woodblock prints. Two years later, in the first month of 1814 (Bunka 11), the Nagoya publisher Eirakuya Tōshirō issued the first volume of those drawings as *Hokusai manga*. It is likely that the publisher and Hokusai's pupils such as Bokusen pushed to get the manual printed, but Hokusai's own strong will and ambition were probably important driving forces as well. With the publication of the *Hokusai*

manga, *edehon* production moved into full swing. Hokusai continued to be very active in this genre well into the latter part of his career, though the intensity of his focus declined after 1829 (Bunsei 12) or so. The *Illustrated Album of Three Styles of Painting* (*Santai gafu*; cat. 72), which portrays the same subject in three styles—formal, semicursive, and cursive—and the *One-brushstroke Picture Book* (*Ippitsu gafu*; cat. 116), a collection of sketches done with a brush dipped only once into ink, are among Hokusai's most distinctive manuals.

Hokusai also produced many compilations of designs for craftsmen, including the three-volume *Modern Designs for Combs and Tobacco* (*Imayō sekkin hinagata*) of 1823 (Bunsei 6), which contains designs for combs and the type of long-stemmed tobacco pipe known as a *kiseru*, and the *Notebook of New Patterns for Textiles* (*Shingata komon-chō*) of 1824 (Bunsei 7), which provides a variety of motifs for textile dyers.[41] From around this time until the end of his career, Hokusai also illustrated practice books used by children, beginning with manuals for those of elementary school age. These no doubt performed a very valuable service.

Hokusai did not concentrate solely on *edehon* during this period, but was active in the production of a variety of *ehon* and illustrated books. One finds few *nishiki-e*, but masterful examples of *surimono* in series such as the *Genroku Shell Match* (*Genroku kasen kai awase*; cat. 92), which was designed to fit the small, square *shikishiban* format, and *Horses of Every Fashion* (*Umazukushi*; cats. 93 and 94) are extant. Paintings are also rare; those that do survive primarily depict plants and animals.

THE "IITSU" PERIOD: THE ERA OF *NISHIKI-E*

The years from approximately 1830 (Tenpō 1) to 1833 (Tenpō 4) are generally considered to be the era of color prints (*nishiki-e*). Indeed, Hokusai worked constantly during this period publishing multicolored prints, and, in the process, gained worldwide renown as an artist of woodblock print landscapes.

Hokusai's art during this period was quite varied. Looking in terms of broad thematic categories and beginning with sets of prints, one finds landscapes, including *Thirty-six Views of Mount Fuji* (*Fugaku sanjūrokkei*; cats. 96–100), *Traveling around the Waterfalls in the Provinces* (*Shokoku taki meguri*; cats. 101 and 102), *Unusual Views of Famous Bridges in Various Provinces* (*Shokoku meikyō kiran*),[42] and *One Thousand Pictures of the Ocean* (*Chie no umi*; cats. 110–12); *meisho-e* (pictures of famous places), such as *Eight Views of Edo* (*Edo hakkei*), *Snow, Moon, and Flowers in Landscape* (*Shōkei setsugekka*), *Snow, Moon, and Flowers* (*Setsugekka*), and *Eight Views of the Ryūkyū Islands* (*Ryūkyū hakkei*);[43] works based on Japanese and Chinese classics, including *True Mirrors of Chinese and Japanese Poetry* (*Shiika shashin kyō*; cats. 108 and 109); and pictures of ghosts and apparitions such as *One Hundred Ghost Tales* (*Hyaku monogatari*; cats. 103 and 104). There are also bird-and-flower prints, bird's-eye views, depictions of warriors, caricatures, toys, and prints on round fans — a vast range of subjects and formats. Of the many works from this period, *Thirty-six Views of Mount Fuji* warrants further discussion.

This series was generally thought to have been issued around 1832 (Tenpō 3). According to a detailed study by Suzuki Jūzō, however, an advertisement for *Thirty-six Views of Mount Fuji* first appeared in 1831 (Tenpō 2) in a publication issued by Nishimuraya Yohachi. Suzuki thus believes that the series was issued in that year, and some other scholars support this date.[44] While publication may have occurred in 1831, the original issue date of the prints is unknown as is the publication date of the entire set of forty-six. Recent research on the use of Prussian (Berlin) blue in the prints from the series also suggests the possibility that publication may have begun as early as 1829.[45] Publication appears to have continued even in 1834 (Tenpō 5), the year Hokusai changed his name to Gakyō rōjin Manji. Nishimuraya issued an advertisement for the series that year.[46] A number of prints in the set have no publisher's seal, and there are some with color tones quite different from the shades of indigo blue characterizing the earlier works. One can thus imagine that publication of the entire series took a long time. That so many questions about the *Thirty-six Views of Mount Fuji* remain unanswered is surprising.

THE "GAKYŌ RŌJIN MANJI" PERIOD: HOKUSAI'S LAST YEARS

In the third month of 1834 (Tenpō 5), Hokusai published the first volume of *One Hundred Views of Mount Fuji* (*Fugaku hyakkei;* cat. 162). Up until that time, he had been using the name Iitsu, but he signed this work "Gakyō rōjin Manji," meaning "Old man mad about painting," followed by the propitious *manji* symbol.

Except for a few works such as *One Hundred Poets, One Verse Each, as Explained by the Nurse* (*Hyakunin isshu uba ga etoki;* cats. 150–61), Hokusai was not involved in designing color prints, and, little by little, he also stopped producing pictures of contemporary life. Instead, he turned to the world of painting, wielding his brush to depict scenes from Japanese and Chinese classical literature and popular legend, representations of plants and animals, and works with religious themes. It is difficult to understand what he was thinking at the time, but he seems to have been driven by a strong sense of

purpose as he brushed painting after painting, adding his age to his inscriptions on virtually every work from the time he turned eighty years old. A glimpse of Hokusai's state of mind in his final years is essential to any understanding of the works from this period. The artist's own words are helpful in this regard. In his postscript to *One Hundred Views of Mount Fuji,* he wrote:

> From the time I was six, I was in the habit of sketching things I saw around me, and around the age of fifty (half-way to one hundred), I began to work in earnest, producing numerous designs. It was not until after my seventieth year, however, that I produced anything of significance. At the age of seventy-three, I began to grasp the underlying structure of birds and animals, insects and fish, and the way trees and plants grow. Thus, (if I keep up my efforts), I will have even a better understanding when I am eighty, and by ninety will have penetrated to the heart of things. At one hundred, I may reach a level of divine understanding, and if I live a decade beyond that, everything I paint — every dot and line — will be alive. I ask that the god of longevity grant me a life long enough to prove this true.[47]

In an inscription written at the end of the art manual titled *New Designs for Craftsmen* (*Shin hinagata*), published in 1836 (Tenpō 7), Hokusai stated that

> When one is old, one's skill quickly declines. Fortunately, however, I am not bound by these long-established ways of thinking. In making my pictures, I may regret last year or even be ashamed of what I did yesterday, but I continue on my own path, alone. Now I am close to eighty, but the strength of my brush is unchanged — it is like that of a young man's. Therefore, I ask for the perseverance to live to one hundred, to keep trying until I reach what I judge as perfection.[48]

Finally, from his postscript to the art manual, the *Illustrated Manual on Color* (*Ehon saishiki tsū,* cat. 164), he wrote: "Speaking from my heart, I say that at ninety I will change my style once again, and after the age of one hundred, I will take my art in a new direction."[49] When we look at Hokusai's artwork from this final period, we would do well to remember that it is this ideal that lies at its center.

Translated by Carol Morland

1. Kokuritsu Kokkai Toshokan 1982, 12:40.

2. Iijima 1999, 31, 173.

3. Ibid., 31.

4. Yura 1979, 142.

5. Iijima 1999, 170.

6. Kokuritsu Kokkai Toshokan 1982, 12:40.

7. Ibid.

8. Katsushika Hokusai. Postscript to *One Hundred Views of Mount Fuji.* English translation in Smith 1988, 7, and Nagata 1985, 117.

9. Iijima 1999, 35.

10. Asakura 1918, n.p.

11. Kokuritsu Kokkai Toshokan 1982, 12:40.

12. Katsushika Hokusai. Preface to *Illustrated Manual on Color.* 1st ed. Quoted in Iijima 1999, 266 and Nagata 1985, 117.

13. Ishizuka Hōkaishi. Addendum to *Courtesans' Lattice.* Quoted in Lane 1989, fig. 171, 298, and Iijima 1999, 37.

14. Images of the works mentioned here can be found in the following publications: Segawa Kikunojō III as the daughter of Masamune–Nikkei 2005, cat. 3. *Iwai Hanshirō IV as Kashiku*–Nikkei 2005, cat. 1.

15. Nikkei 2005, cat. 2.

16. Hillier 1980, 263; Lane 1989, pl. 11, 16.

17. Yasuda 1971, 181-91.

18. Ibid., 4.

19. Kikuchi 1972, 27.

20. Kobori 1939, p. 26-27.

21. Nikkei 2005, cat. 27.

22. Lane 1989, 300.

23. Naito 2002, 109.

24. Inoue 1929, n.p.

25. *Firing a Canon* is illustrated in Kubota 1995, 4.

26. Hillier 1980, 266; Lane 1989, 300.

27. The works mentioned here are illustrated as follows: *Saitan kyōka Edo Murasaki*–Hillier 1980, 266; Lane 1989, 300. *Spring in Every Quarter*–Hillier 1980, 266; Lane 1989, 300. *Dawn in Spring*–Nikkei 2005, cat. 120. *Willow-silk*–Hillier 1980, 32, 267; Nikkei 2005, cat. 122. *Elegance of Spring*–Hillier 1980, 28-29, 268; Lane 1989, 300; Nagata 1990, 3:nos. 71-72. *Men's New Year Ceremonial Dance*–Hillier 1980, 32-33, 267; Lane 1989, 300; Nikkei 2005, cat. 123. *Album of Springtime Diversions*–Lane 1989, 300.

28. Hillier 1980, 267; Nikkei 2005, cats. 51-61.

29. Hillier 1980, 267; Lane 1989, 300.

30. Hillier 1980, 21, 268; Lane 1989, pl. 90 and fig. 175; Nikkei 2005, cat. 131.

31. Hillier 1980, 269; Lane 1989, 301.

32. Ito 2003, 72-76.

33. The most extensive study to date in English is Sandler 1977.

34. Hillier 1980, 73, 270; Lane 1989, 301-02.

35. Hillier 1980, 73-76.

36. Nikkei 2005, cat. 198.

37. Four artists of the Utagawa school, plus Hokusai, Kiyonaga, and Shun'e, painted one figure each, and Santō Kyōden and his brother Kyōzan wrote the inscriptions. Calza 2003, III.50, 163, 445; Nikkei 2005, cat. 198.

38. Hillier 1980, 271; Nagata 1990, 5:no. 33; Nikkei 2005, cat. 185.

39. Hillier 1980, 273; Lane 1989, 303; Carpenter 2005, 299.

40. Katsushika Hokusai. *A Quick Lesson in Simplified Drawings.* Vol. 1. Edo: 1812. Vol. 2 Edo: 1814. Vol. 3 Edo: 1815. Quoted in Hillier 1980, 140-42, 184, 274; Nikkei 2005, cats. 186-87; Lane 1989, pls. 132-33, fig. 193; Carpenter 2005, 347.

41. Illustrations of the works mentioned here can be found in the following publications: *Modern Designs for Combs and Tobacco*–Hillier 1980, 181-84, 276; Lane 1989, pls. 168-71, 138, fig. 214, 307; Nikkei 2005, cat. 429. *Notebook of New Patterns for Textiles*–Hillier 1980, 185-87, 276; Lane 1989, pl. 173, 139; Carpenter 2005, 314.

42. *Unusual Views of Famous Bridges in Various Provinces* is illustrated in Nikkei 2005, cats. 314-16.

43. Images of these works can be found in the following publications: *Eight Views of Edo*–Nagata 1990, 4:nos.35-41, 43. *Snow, Moon, and Flowers in Landscape*–Ibid., 4:nos. 69-77. *Snow, Moon, and Flowers*–Ibid., 4:nos. 78-80. *Eight Views of the Ryūkyū Islands*–Ibid., 4:nos. 111, 115-19, 123, 125; Nikkei 2005, cats. 327-34.

44. Suzuki 1963, 62-64.

45. Ibid.

46. Ibid.

47. Katsushika Hokusai. Introduction to *One Hundred Views of Mount Fuji.* Quoted in Nagata 1985, 117; English translation in Smith 1988.

48. Katsushika Hokusai. Postscript to *New Designs for Craftsmen.* Quoted in Lane 1989, pls. 317-18, 248.

49. Hokusai 1848, postscript, quoted in Iijima 1999, 267-8.

THE REAL HOKUSAI: ARTIST "MAD ABOUT PAINTING"
KOBAYASHI TADASHI

Katsushika Hokusai was born in 1760, on the twenty-third day of the ninth month, in Warigesui, part of the Honjo district of the old city of Edo. Warigesui was on the eastern bank of the Sumida River and was divided into two sections, north and south, by a drainage canal that ran down its center and was the source of its name. Hokusai's house was probably in South Warigesui. This area, which is now known as Kamezawa in present-day Sumida ward, backs onto that great modern source of knowledge on the Edo period, the Edo-Tokyo Museum.

Hokusai was born into the Kawamura family and adopted by Nakajima Ise, a mirrormaker and polisher for the shogun. His mother's name is unknown, as is often the case with women of that era, but we do know that she was a descendant of the master swordsman Kobayashi Heihachirō, who fought for Lord Kira against the forty-seven masterless samurai of Akō, whose loyalty was made famous in the plays and narratives titled *Chūshingura*. Since they worked for the shogun, mirror smiths were listed in the samurai registry known as the *bukan*, and, like the official Kano painters in the art world, they were treated almost like men of samurai rank. For Hokusai, or Nakajima Tetsuzō as he was commonly called, this lineage was a tremendous source of pride. Though he lived his life as a humble *chōnin* (townspeople), he seems to have been very conscious of his samurai background and to have held himself in high regard because of it.

Hokusai died early in the morning on the eighteenth day of the fourth month of 1849 in a small rented row house on the grounds of the Henshōin temple in Asakusa Shōdenchō. He was ninety years old. Although this was close to double the life expectancy of the time, Hokusai pleaded on his deathbed to remain just a little while longer. His last words, recorded in the earliest biography of the artist, *Katsushika Hokusai den* by Iijima Kyoshin, reveal an extraordinary dedication to the pursuit of art. Breathing with great difficulty, Hokusai begged the gods for ten more years, or even five years, so that he might become a true artist.[1]

The period between the birth in Honjo of this single-minded pursuer of art, the "man mad about painting," as he called himself, and his death in Asakusa at the age of ninety coincided with the years just before the advent of the modern era, a time of relative peace and tranquility for Japan. The country had been closed to the outside world since the early seventeenth century, allowing a creative refinement and reinvention of traditional art forms. The arrival in Edo (now Tokyo) Bay of Commodore Matthew C. Perry (1794–1858) of the U.S. Navy and his four black warships, an event that made the Bakufu's closed-country policy untenable, did not occur until the sixth month of 1853, four years after Hokusai's death.

THE EDO-PERIOD PAINTING WORLD AND UKIYO-E

A military government under the all-powerful Tokugawa shoguns ruled during the Edo period. The Tokugawa moved the seat of government from Kyoto to the city of Edo on the Kanto plain, and from there they controlled the country through a political system known as *bakuhan taisei*. Lands directly under the control of the Bakufu were located throughout the country, and retainers directly supervised by the shogun were dispatched as deputies (*daikan*) to run them. In the majority of the other regions, large and small daimyo (of which there were around two hundred sixty by the end of the Edo period) were awarded domains (*han*) and given great autonomy in the management of domain affairs. The imperial court remained in Kyoto under the watchful eye of the Bakufu. Far from the centers of power, the emperor and his court functioned to preserve scholarship, court rituals and practices, poetry and the arts, and other aspects of traditional culture.

As the school of art patronized by the shogun and daimyo, the Kano school dominated the art world, especially painting. Their successful Japanese-style interpretations of Chinese painting, particularly of the Song (960–1279) and Yuan (1279–1368) dynasties, had made the school a favorite of the samurai class since the latter part of the Muromachi period (1392–1573). The Kano ceded none of their power during the Edo period. Public commissions from the shogun and daimyo were given almost exclusively to the official shogunate painters (*goyō-eshi*), a group comprising the *oku-eshi*, the highest ranking government painters, of which there were three (later four) branches, and the lower-ranking *omote-eshi*, of which there were some ten branches. The painting studios set up by the various branches of the Kano functioned as centers for art instruction from which students were sent to every domain to work as *goyō-eshi* (or *daimyō-eshi*). Through this extensive network of artists, Kano theory and style were disseminated throughout Japan. It was the Kano style that came to be regarded as orthodox, and it was the Kano school that defined "true painting."

While the Kano served the warrior class, another school of official painters, one with a longer history than that of the Kano, served the aristocracy. This was the Tosa school, self-proclaimed successor to the traditional Japanese style known as *yamato-e*. Leadership of the court atelier, a position dating from the Heian period (794–1185) and designated by the title *edokoro azukari*, had been bestowed upon the head of the Tosa family for many generations. In addition to the Kano and Tosa, nonofficial painters and artists unaffiliated with other schools were increasingly active in the Edo art world.

The domestic policies of the Tokugawa Bakufu for the newly unified country resulted in the preservation of peace and the rapid growth of productivity in agriculture, fishing, and mining. Improvements in ocean and river transportation and the development of a system of roadways meant an increased circulation of goods within the country. And it was not only the samurai and aristocracy who could afford luxury goods; members of the farmer and merchant classes had economic power as well.

The surprisingly high rate of growth in all parts of Japan during the early Edo period was reflected in a precipitous rise in population. According to recent demographic research, the total population of Japan almost tripled in one hundred twenty years. In 1600, the year of the Battle of Sekigahara, between 10 and 12 million people lived in Japan; by 1721, that number had increased to around 31 million (26,070,000 listed, plus another 5 million or so that had been omitted from the census).[2] Improvement in the lives of all people created a sudden rise in the demand for handicrafts. Pictures, high-quality crafts, and other goods were made in great numbers, not for specific patrons, but as commercial objects for general sale.

The city painters (machi-eshi), who earned their livelihood by selling their work, were noteworthy in the Edo art world. The unprecedented role they played contributed to the distinctive character of the Edo period. Among them were the painters of the Rinpa school, which originated in Kyoto under the auspices of wealthy merchant patrons and was later transplanted to Edo. Artists of ukiyo-e genre painting (fūzokuga), whom the newly rich merchants of Edo nurtured, were another important part of the art scene. In addition, one also finds painting beloved by the intellectuals — literati painting (bun-jinga) and the realistic works of the Maruyama-Shijō school. There was, in fact, a school to suit everyone, with styles established in response to the tastes of the commoner as well as that of the elite. Ukiyo-e artists were particularly aware of current popular trends, and, always conscious of what the Kano school was doing, strove for an appeal and an urban, contemporary machi-e flavor that set them apart from orthodox painters.

The samurai class favored traditional and unchanging painting styles; in contrast, ukiyo-e artists had to respond quickly to the shifting interests and aesthetics of a fickle public and always had to reflect the latest device or fad. While an elegant stability distinguished the work of official painters, ukiyo-e artists sought escape in popular forms of expression that prized change and transformation. Rather than conforming to principles of Confucian morality, ukiyo-e artists valued underlying human motives, and instead of inhibiting expression, emphasized exaggeration and excitement. Ukiyo-e, which was in tune with the times and represented a choice diametrically opposed to the

work of the Kano painters, was loathed by the Kano school — a situation that would have prohibited any interaction between artists of the two schools.[3] Active in the world of Edo ukiyo-e for seventy years, from his debut at the age of twenty to his death at the age of ninety, Hokusai epitomized the ukiyo-e artist.

HOKUSAI THE MAN

Iijima Kyoshin's *Katsushika Hokusai den* is an essential reference for information about Hokusai's appearance, character, likes and dislikes, beliefs, and convictions. As the author himself states in the introduction, the book was written merely forty years after Hokusai's death; thus, Iijima was able to include direct testimony from people and publishers who had known the artist while he was alive. This valuable collection of material brings us closer to a true picture of Hokusai.[4]

A woodblock print illustration titled *Portrait of Katsushika Hokusai* appears at the beginning of *Katsushika Hokusai den*.[5] Probably from the hand of one of Hokusai's students, it is an image expressive of great dignity and affection. While the portrait is certainly idealized, the fact that it was included at the suggestion of Hokusai's friends and relatives indicates that it contains some measure of likeness. A self-portrait completed when Hokusai was eighty-three years old depicts an unpretentious and good-natured old man (cat. 147). By looking at these two works together, we can perhaps get something of a true image of the artist. In both portraits, Hokusai is drawn with particularly large ears. The scholar of history Sekine Shisei (1825–93), who met Hokusai the year before his death, confirmed that he did indeed have big ears: "He was thin and his hair was white. … He looked like an ordinary person except for his ears, which were enormous." Later, he describes Hokusai as having "the energy of a young man … he should live to be over one hundred."[6]

Hokusai devoted all his time to art and was not particularly concerned with other matters. Not being fussy about where he lived and never able to settle down in one place, he changed his residences constantly, moving from row house to rented row house. By the end of his life, he had lived in a total of ninety-three different places. His possessions consisted only of an earthenware teapot and two or three teacups, and since he had neither plates nor bowls, neighbors brought meals to him or he had food delivered. He paid little attention to his personal appearance, and owning no more than one plain cotton robe, was certainly not worried about the latest fashion trends.

At the same time, as a top ukiyo-e artist with a huge following, he was paid double the amount of what other ukiyo-e artists usually received (for example, instead of receiving two *shu* for two pages of sketches for a picture album, he got twice that, or one *bu*; today, he would have been paid 20,000 [about 200 dollars] rather than 10,000 yen). Still, there are a number of letters extant in which he asks his publisher for an advance.[7] With a relatively large salary and a very simple lifestyle, why was the elderly Hokusai always so poor? He was burdened with two dissolute grandsons, but, as is frequently the case with geniuses, he may have possessed very little practical money sense.

The question of whether Hokusai was a sake drinker is one with which Iijima Kyoshin was extremely concerned. He devoted some ten pages to the issue at the beginning of volume two of *Katsushika Hokusai den*. His final conclusion was that Hokusai did not drink, but rather had a weakness for sweets, especially the bean-filled rice cakes called *daifukumochi*. A certain Mr. Tozaki wrote that "Old man [Hokusai] did not drink sake, but was fond of cakes. Every time I visited him, I was sure to bring seven or eight *daifuku-mochi* with me. When he saw them, he would smack his lips with great delight." Hokusai also loved *soba*: According to a story from the wife of Utagawa Toyokuni III (Kunisada), he would have two plates of noodles before going to bed.[8]

Hokusai believed in the bodhisattva Myōken, a Buddhist deity of the North Star, and the Big Dipper. His worship of these stars and their associated deities was probably the source for certain of his artistic names, such as Taito and Tokimasa, and the reason behind paintings such as *The Deity of the Big Dipper, Bunshōsei (Bunshōsei-zu [Hokutosei-zu]*; cat. 127). Myōken was revered in Nichiren Buddhism, and Hokusai was a devotee of that sect as well. His numerous works featuring Mount Fuji — the woodblock series *Thirty-six Views of Mount Fuji* (cats. 96–100) and the three-volume *One Hundred Views of Mount Fuji* (cat. 162) — indicate his deep response to Fuji *shinkō*, a belief in the sacred nature of the mountain. Thus, Hokusai did not adhere to a single sect or belief, and in this, as in the deep and pure faith he had for the Shinto and Buddhist gods, he was typical of the Edo commoner.

The following anecdote, an event that seems to have actually happened and one that I cannot help but like, illustrates Hokusai's intrinsic sense of self-respect and his indomitable spirit. Once, the young Hokusai, then using the name Katsukawa Shunrō, painted a signboard for a shop in Ryōgoku that sold *ezōshi* (illustrated storybooks) and ukiyo-e prints. Katsukawa Shunkō (1743–1812), a senior disciple of Shunrō's teacher, happened to pass by, and believing that the painting was so bad it would shame their teacher, tore it up and threw it away, right in front of Shunrō.[9] In all likelihood, the usual jealousy felt by artists studying under the same master who do not want to see someone junior to them publicly recognized prompted the incident. The occurrence of a number of similar episodes, however, finally led to Shunrō's departure from the Katsukawa school. The experience only strengthened his resolve. Devoting himself even more diligently to art, he vowed to become the best painter in the world and so wipe out the insult he had suffered. Those close to Hokusai believed that it was the sense of shame Shunkō had caused him that made his late work so much better.[10]

Hokusai was thirty-three years old when his ukiyo-e master Katsukawa Shunshō died in 1792. He had already distinguished himself in the ukiyo-e world through his actor prints and book illustrations. Two years later, in 1794, he stopped using the name Katsukawa Shunrō, a decision that likely coincided with his departure from the Katsukawa school. *Katsushika Hokusai den* places the break during Shunshō's lifetime, with the teacher himself expelling Hokusai, but it seems more likely that he was forced out as a result of poor treatment at the hands of Shunkō and others after Shunshō's death.[11] One can imagine such a thing happening even today, which lends the story a certain credibility.

Much of what we know about Hokusai as a person is based on the descriptions in *Katsushika Hokusai den*. It gives us an intimate picture of the artist — an image very different from that obtained through study of his works alone.

BELOVED BY SHOGUN AND EMPEROR ALIKE

Suiyo sōko by Saitō Gesshin (1804–78) includes a character sketch of Hokusai in his last years. Gesshin was a remarkable man, who, while acting as district head of Kanda Kijichō, also made a number of important contributions to the fields of Edo topography, history, and biography. This very interesting document, which Mori Senzō first introduced, helps flesh out the description of Hokusai given above:

> Katsushika Hokusai has used a number of names, including Raishin, Sōri, Shunrō, and Taito; now it is Iitsu that he goes by. This year, the first year of Kaei (1848), he turned eighty-nine, but his health is good, and he walks without difficulty. He wears glasses when he draws. Even now he does very fine, detailed work. He has moved dozens of times, always to another small rented house. His youngest daughter Ei [better known by the name Ōi] resembles her father — instead of washing the dishes after a meal, she just leaves them lying around without thinking twice about it. She was married to the ukiyo-e artist Nantaku [Minamizawa Tōmei], but divorced him and now lives with her father. She is about fifty years old. She paints and has done many designs for woodblock prints published under the name of Iitsu. … When they receive a raw fish as a present, they usually end up just giving it away to someone else, since cooking it is too much trouble. This account is based on stories told by Naruse Kichiemon.[12]

The statement that Hokusai's daughter was responsible for many of the works done under the name of Iitsu is important evidence of her role in the production of Hokusai's designs, but it also raises an issue beyond the scope of this essay.

Saitō Gesshin also compiled the *Expanded Thoughts on Ukiyo-e (Zōho ukiyo-e ruikō)*, a great collection of biographies of ukiyo-e artists. The final manuscript that he prepared for the printer, with each character carefully copied and blank spaces for the illustrations indicated by drawn lines, is now in the

Cambridge University library. The entry on Katsushika Iitsu contains a sentence worthy of special note. It states that Hokusai's reputation had reached even the ears of the shogun, and when the lord left Edo castle for falconry or other pastimes, he frequently asked Hokusai to come and do a painting in his presence (the impromptu work that resulted was called a *sekiga*).[13]

Katsushika Hokusai den recounts an anecdote about a very unusual *sekiga* gathering held for Ienari, the eleventh-generation Tokugawa shogun. Ienari, whose love of painting was well known, once summoned the famous literati painter Tani Bunchō (1763–1840) and Hokusai to Denpōin (the main temple of Sensōji), where he had stopped en route to a falconry hunt. Bunchō, probably because of his high status as retainer to the head of the Shirakawa clan, Matsudaira Sadanobu (1758–1829), went first. After Bunchō had finished, Hokusai walked slowly up to the shogun and stood before him. Calmly, with no sign of fear or apprehension, he took up his brush and proceeded with bird-and-flower paintings and landscapes. When these were done, he unrolled a long horizontal scroll made of single sheets pasted together. Dipping his brush in indigo-colored ink, he drew a long line. He then took a chicken he had brought with him out of its cage, pressed its feet into red ink, and released the bird onto the paper, where it proceeded to walk around, leaving vermilion-colored footprints. Hokusai bowed deeply, saying "Here, my lord, is the scenery of the celebrated Tatsutagawa river in autumn." Meanwhile, Bunchō was standing nearby, waiting in breathless suspense.[14] The story seems incredible, but since Bunchō himself was cited as the source, there must be some truth to it.

Among paintings of beautiful women, a genre in which Hokusai was particularly skilled, is the masterpiece entitled *Two Beauties (Ni bijin-zu)*. The mounting includes the narrow strips of fine material called *ichimonji*, which border the top and bottom of the painting. The gold brocade with which they are made incorporates the three-leaf crest of the Tokugawa family. Its presence here indicates that the work was created for the shogun, since no one else was permitted to use the design. Finely detailed and on silk, the painting is very different from *sekiga*, which were usually done on paper and in an abbreviated style.

The fact that Hokusai was not only recognized by the most powerful man of the time and summoned by him to do impromptu paintings, but that he also occasionally received special painting commissions from the shogun elevates him far above the status of the usual ukiyo-e artist. It is substantive evidence of the power Hokusai held as an artist.

Hokusai's fame spread beyond Edo to every part of Japan. In Nagoya, the publisher Eirakuya Tōshirō published copies of the *Hokusai manga;* in Osaka, Shunkōsai Hokushū (fl. ca. 1810–32) and other artists felt his influence, contributing to a rise in popularity of prints of Kyoto-Osaka actors. Most importantly, Hokusai's reputation reached the inner sanctum of the imperial court.

Hokusai's painting titled *Watermelon (Suika-zu)* presents tantalizing evidence for imperial patronage. In her excellent study *The Art of Describing in Tokugawa Japan: Painting and Literature (Edo kaiga to bungaku — byōsha to kotoba no Edo bunkashi),* Imahashi Riko makes it clear that someone high up in the imperial court commissioned the work, the subject itself being a veiled reference to the elegant theme of Tanabata. While Imahashi merely hints at who the patron could have been, the signature on the painting gives Hokusai's age as eighty, dating the work to 1839 and placing it within the reign of Emperor Ninkō (1800–46) and at the end of the life of Retired Emperor Kōkaku (1771–1840).[15] Naitō Masato's recent book, *Rediscovery of Ukiyo-e — Masterpieces of Art Admired by the Daimyō (Ukiyo-e saihakken — daimyōtachi ga medeta ippin zeppin)* emphasizes that it was not just commoners who loved ukiyo-e, but the aristocracy as well, and stresses the possibility that it was on the orders of Retired Emperor Kōkaku, with his deep love of scholarship and the arts, that the painting was done.[16]

CRITICAL ASSESSMENTS OF HOKUSAI DURING HIS LIFETIME

By the latter part of the eighteenth century, the population of *chōnin* in Edo was steady at a half million people.[17] When one adds to this the half million or so samurai and those connected to monasteries and shrines, it brings the total population to more than one million, huge for an urban center anywhere in the world at the time. *Chōnin* culture flourished. City dwellers enjoyed ukiyo-e and kabuki, illustrated popular novels, and humorous or satirical poetry — *haikai, kyōka, senryū,* and the like — as well as musical performances, tea ceremony, and ikebana (flower arrangement).

Edo was also a publishing center, and among the books printed is *Directory of Outstanding Persons (Kōeki shoka jinmei roku),* a directory of famous people active during the period.[18] The entries, listed in alphabetical order, give a brief introduction to each person, providing their address, specialization, the days on which they gave lessons, and other information. The sections on Hokusai in the *Kōeki shoka jinmei roku* of 1836, when Hokusai was seventy-seven years old, and of 1842, when he was eighty-three years old are excellent sources for contemporary evaluations of the artist. As the title preface "*Tōji genzai*" makes clear, the book includes only those persons alive at the time of its publication. People listed with the character for "picture" beside their name were treated purely as painters. In 1836, there were one hundred thirty-nine people so designated; in 1842, the number had risen to one hundred sixty-three. Many of these artists are unknown today, but even so, the number of ukiyo-e artists listed is quite small. In the earlier edition, for example, only four appear: Hokusai, his pupil Teisai Hokuba, Keisai Eisen, and Utagawa Kunisada. By 1842, the number had risen to ten: Hokusai and four of his students (Hokkei, Hokuga, Hokusai II, and Taito II), Kunisada, Kuninao, Kuniyoshi, and

Hiroshige from the Utagawa school, and Keisai Eisen, who was not affiliated with a particular school.[19] A detailed examination of the directory sheds light on issues such as the low status of ukiyo-e artists, Hokusai's relatively high rank among them, the preference for artists who specialized in painting over those who did not, and the irrelevance to the compilers of renowned artists in the print world.

Another useful reference is the *Brief History of Artists (Gajō yōryaku;* printed in Kyoto in 1831*)*, a directory that includes entries on contemporary artists. Even though Tani Bunchō, the artist who was present at the *sekiga* gathering described above, and his student Watanabe Kazan (1793–1841) are listed, ukiyo-e artists are given shabby treatment. There is an entry for the father of ukiyo-e, Hishikawa Moronobu (d. 1694), but his given name is written with the wrong characters, and only Nishikawa Sukenobu (1671–1750) and Tsukioka Settei (1710–86) merit mention among the artists of genre painting (*fūzokuga*) in the Kyoto-Osaka area. The existence of Edo ukiyo-e artists, including Hokusai, is completely ignored. This source makes clear the contempt with which ukiyo-e artists were regarded, an attitude completely different from that toward other artists, even fellow town painters (*machi-eshi*). And Hokusai was no exception.[20]

At the same time, Hokusai was well known by and enjoyed the esteem of contemporary members of the cultural elite who valued his work highly. They include the writers Kyokutei Bakin and Santō Kyōden (1761–1816), with whom Hokusai had a close relationship as the illustrator of their *yomihon* (historical novels), and the men who contributed prefaces to volumes of the *Hokusai manga*. The second, fifth, and ninth volumes, for example, carry a preface by Rokujuen Shujin (Ishikawa Masamochi, who also wrote *kyōka* under the name Yadoya no Meshimori), Shokusanjin (1749–1823, Ōta Nanpo; also known as Yomo no Akara) contributed the preface for volumes 3 and 6, Shikitei Sanba (1776–1822) the preface for volume 7, Ryūtei Tanehiko (1783–1842) for volume 11, and Shakuyakutei Nagane for volume 12. All these men were well known in the fields of poetry and literature, and they all had a deep attachment to ukiyo-e. Hokusai also relished *kyōka*, and he even wrote novels (*gesaku*) in his youth. He was certainly a highly cultured man of literary talent.[21]

Ishikawa Masamochi extolled the skill of Hokusai's painting, compared him to the beautiful flowers of Katsushika, and praised the power of his brush.[22] Ōta Nanpo, the leader of the Edo literary world, expressed great admiration for the brilliance of Hokusai's sketches: "He must put into visual form all he sees and all that is in his mind, and there is no detail that he does not include." He also characterized Hokusai's work as animated with grace and refinement and highly praised his subtlety in portraying true form through the strength of his brush.[23]

The seventh volume of the *Hokusai manga* contains views of famous places in Japan. Shikitei Sanba wrote in his preface that just looking at Hokusai's pictures made him feel as if he were enjoying himself in the actual spot.[24] Ryūtei Tanehiko praised the "remarkable skill of this old veteran," who "drinks no sake, nor is fond of tea, but who for fifty years has been devoted only to his art, which becomes better and better."[25] According to the preface written by Shakuyakutei Nagane for volume 12, which is filled with caricatures, Hokusai's scandalous behavior only increased with age and his brushstrokes became more vigorous; thus he stood shoulder to shoulder with artists of old like Toba Sōjō (1053–1140) and Hanabusa Itchō (1652–1724).[26]

UNFAVORABLE CRITICISM FROM FELLOW UKIYO-E ARTISTS

How was Hokusai viewed by ukiyo-e artists of the time? Of course, the group of students who gathered around him treated him with marked respect, and painters of other schools acknowledged his tremendous skill. And it is well known that Kuniyoshi of the Utagawa school and his student Kawanabe Kyōsai (1831–89), among others, held Hokusai in high regard and imitated his style. Scathing criticisms also survive, including the comment below from Kitao Masayoshi (1764–1824).

Masayoshi was only four years Hokusai's junior and so almost the same age. He later worked for the Tsuyama *han*, where he was promoted to *daimyo-eshi*, and changed his name to Kuwagata Keisai. In the *Chronology of Edo (Bukō nenpyō)*, a chronology of Edo city by the aforementioned Saitō Gesshin, is a section entitled *Record of the Kansei Era (Kansei nenkan no kiji)* giving an account of the Kansei era (1789-1801). Kitamura Nobuyo added the following describing Keisai's assessment of Hokusai:

> Kitao Masayoshi says that "Hokusai tends to always copy others. There is nothing he began himself." After Keisai published his *Ryakugashiki* [paintings done in an abbreviated style], the *Hokusai manga* appeared, and when Tsuguzane [i.e., Keisai] devised a composition depicting the whole of Edo as if seen from above, Hokusai came out with his *nishiki-e* series of similar views of the Tōkaidō road.[27]

It is only natural that Keisai was not amused when Hokusai used his idea to create his own *Paintings in Abbreviated Style (Ryakuga-shiki;* 1795) or to compose an overview of Edo (1810; later also published in woodblock form); or that Hokusai's *nishiki-e* series employing a bird's-eye view, such as the *Famous Places on the Tōkaidō at a Glance (Tōkaidō meisho ichiran;* 1818) and *Famous Places on the Kiso Road in One View (Kisoji meisho ichiran;* 1819), proved to be more popular than Keisai's own works.[28] That Hokusai used the scene of carpenters from Keisai's painting *A Modern Handscroll of Craftsmen (Kinsei shokunin zukushi ekotoba)* for his work *In the Mountains of Tōtōmi Province (Tōtōmi sanchū;* cat. 99) from the series *Thirty-six Views of Mount Fuji* has long been understood.[29] Recently, however, research by Uchida Kinzō has made it clear that an additional design from the series, *[Reflection in the] Surface of the Water, Misaka, Kai Province (Kōshū Misaka no suimen)*, borrows from another painting by Keisai, the *Sai Bank at Hakone in Sagami Province (Sōshū Hakone Sainokawara)* from his handscroll of famous places (*Meisho-zu*).[30]

There are certainly many examples of Hokusai's borrowing a design that had already been published or a technique still in the experimental stage and applying it successfully to his own work. Even his use of Prussian (Berlin) blue in *Thirty-six Views of Mount Fuji* followed Keisai Eisen's earlier use of the pigment on fan-shaped prints.

From the point of view of those whom he was copying, Hokusai's borrowings were regarded as a despicable practice, bordering on fraud. For those of us who are partial to Hokusai, however, it seems that it was precisely his sensitivity to current tastes and the ability to judge the best time and method of publication that allowed him to maintain his long, active life as an ukiyo-e artist. Hokusai blithely ignored the envious words of his contemporaries and continued into old age as a hero of the times. Indeed, the great Katsushika Hokusai was an ukiyo-e artist without equal, a man who rode the changing times as if surfing a huge wave, or to use another image, who, like a magnificent kabuki actor, strode majestically alone down the center of the brightly lit *hanamichi*.

Translated by Carol Morland

NOTES

1. Iijima 1999, 169.
2. Hayami 2001, 66-70.
3. Hashimoto 1889, 15-19.
4. Iijima 1999, 25-26.
5. Ibid., 23.
6. Ibid., 199.
7. Ibid., 151.
8. Ibid., 48.
9. Ibid., 40.
10. Ibid., 41.
11. Ibid., 40.
12. Saitō 1862, n.p.
13. Saitō 1844, n.p.; Yura 1979, 139.
14. Iijima 1999, 77.
15. Imahashi 1999, 326-27.
16. Naitō 2005, 26-29.
17. Takeuchi 2002, 140.
18. *Kōeki shoka jinmei roku* 1842, 2:n.p.
19. Known life dates for the various artists listed here are as follows: Keisai Eisen (d. 1848), Utagawa Kunisada (1786-1864), Hokkei (1780-1850), Kuninao (1793-1854), Kuniyoshi (1797-1861), and Hiroshige (1797-1858).
20. Shirai 1831, n.p.
21. Iijima 1999, 57.
22. Ishikawa Masamochi. Preface to *Hokusai manga.* Vol 2. Edo: 1815. Idem. Preface to *Hokusai manga.* Vol. 5. Edo: 1816. Idem. Preface to *Hokusai manga.* Vol. 9. Edo: 1862.
23. Ōta Nanpo. Preface to *Hokusai manga.* Vol. 3. Edo: 1815. Idem. Preface to *Hokusai manga.* Vol. 6. Edo: 1817.
24. Shikitei Sanba. Preface to *Hokusai manga.* Vol. 7. Edo: 1817.
25. Ryūtei Tanehiko. Preface to *Hokusai manga.* Vol. 11. Edo: 1834.
26. Shakuyakutei Nagane. Preface to *Hokusai manga.* Vol. 12. Edo: 1834.
27. Saitō 1850, 7:n.p.
28. Iijima 1999, 72.
29. Uchida 1993, 94-95.
30. Ibid.

THE ARTIST ASCENDANT: THE RECEPTION OF HOKUSAI IN THE WEST AND CHARLES LANG FREER'S COLLECTION

ANN YONEMURA

In the Year of the Dragon, 1760, the artist known to the world as Hokusai was born in Edo, beginning his life in obscurity as a commoner in the hierarchical society under the shogun's rule. Hokusai's good fortune, as a craftsman with artistic aspirations that began in early childhood, according to his own later account, was to find a way to hone his artistic skills and establish his reputation among the artists of the *ukiyo* (floating world), where he first realized a market for his prints and illustrated books.

Hokusai's lifelong pursuit of creating pictures spanned a career of more than seventy years. His mastery of subject, style, color, draftsmanship, and design resulted in a prodigious artistic production estimated at tens of thousands of works in various media, including his celebrated series of commercial prints such as the *Thirty-six Views of Mount Fuji*, and some two hundred seventy illustrated books. Less well known, but important as a measure of the recognition accorded by Japanese patrons to Hokusai's artistic talent, are many private commissions of *surimono* prints and paintings. Despite his aspirations to perfect his art by living to the age of one hundred or more, Hokusai died in Edo in 1849, still wishing for a few more years to continue his creative life.

What Hokusai did not know was that profound changes were imminent. His work would travel farther in space and time than he could have imagined, and would find new acclaim in the distant nations of Europe that had produced the pictures he had studied in his quest to perfect his own work. In 1853, less than five years after Hokusai's death, the American commodore Matthew C. Perry (1794–1858) arrived in Japan to negotiate commercial treaties with the shogunate that would initiate formal relations between the two nations. In 1859, only ten years after Hokusai's last words, the port of Yokohama opened to trade with the United States and four European nations, including France, the first foreign country to embrace Hokusai's art. Japan ended its isolation and began its emergence and transformation into a modern, technologically advanced nation and world power. By the end of the century, in his *Étude sur Hoksaï* published in 1896, the French scholar Michel Revon remarked on Europe's "astonishment at Japan's military victory [in the Sino-Japanese War of 1894–95]" and also its admiration of the "moral treasure accumulated during twenty centuries of history."[1]

Hokusai's reputation in the West was initially established by his great commercial print series of the 1830s, especially the *Thirty-six Views of Mount Fuji*, his illustrated books such as the fifteen-volume *Hokusai manga*, and *One Hundred Views of Mount Fuji*. The myriad subjects and imaginative renderings among the four thousand illustrations in the *Manga*, which were sequentially published from 1814, created a commercial market for reprints through the late 1870s, when foreign residents of Japan were collecting large numbers of Japanese prints and paintings.

Japanese prints and printed books were readily transported abroad, and were sold at affordable prices to collectors and artists. These popular images first reached Europe at a time when artists and critics were sympathetic to Japanese subjects and aesthetic qualities, especially in Paris, a thriving cultural center. During the period between 1856 — when Félix Bracquemond (1883–1914) discovered the first *Hokusai manga* in the shop of the printer Delâtre — and 1867, the year of the Exposition Universelle, Japanese prints and printed books became widely available in Paris. The exportation of Edo popular art accelerated in Europe and America through the end of the century, when Japanese and foreign dealers sold thousands of prints and books that changed hands among collectors and were deposited in museums. The impact of these works on European art and design affected many modern artistic developments, especially those opposed to academic art — most prominently, Japonisme, Impressionism, and Art Nouveau. American collectors and artists also embraced Japanese art. In 1883, Louis Gonse (1846–1921) devoted a chapter of his *L'Art Japonais* to Hokusai, beginning with effusive praise: "one of the greatest painters of his nation; from our European point of view he is the greatest and the most ingenious." He marvels at Hokusai's "originality and humor, productivity, energy and elegance of invention, supreme style in design, the memory and education of [his] eye, [and] prodigious dexterity of his hand." He goes on to extol Hokusai's "depth of feeling and his comic power. He is at once the Rembrandt, the Callot, and the Daumier of Japan."[2]

A confluence of philosophical, societal, and artistic movements already developing when Hokusai's work came to the attention of Western audiences propelled his ascent to a pinnacle of admiration during the first half-century following his death. It was not difficult to find in Hokusai's biography, as it was related through anecdotes, articles, and books, details that reinforced the popular concept of the artist as a creative, independent, and eccentric genius. Hokusai's reputation for unorthodox behavior, even in Japan during his lifetime, fits this concept well. He changed residences constantly, and changed his names and artistic directions frequently. He was untidy and reputedly disorganized, yet he produced and delivered thousands of pages of finished designs to publishers.

In a book published in Edo in 1845, *Extraordinary Persons of Japan: Abbreviated Biographies of those Famous for Their Behavior (Nihon kijin den: Fūzoku kōmei ryaku den),* Hokusai is included among two hundred people known as extraordinary or eccentric. Many aspects of his artistic achievement—his extreme productivity, exceptional versatility, and constant desire to see and render objects from new perspectives—reinforced his unique qualities in the eyes of Japanese observers.[3] This was true as well as for the Europeans who encountered Hokusai's pictures, especially those artists who sought to break free of the orthodoxy of established art academies, as Hokusai had done. He became a model for the ideal of an unhampered pursuit of creativity that transcended prescribed subjects and techniques. Another aspect of Hokusai's art that was received with interest abroad is his sympathetic and occasionally humorous treatment of human and animal subjects. Balancing the image of Hokusai the eccentric and creative genius was the nineteenth-century archetype of a sincere and patient craftsman. To European observers, he embodied an appealing ideal of great and serious talent flourishing in modest circumstances.

Hokusai's subjects, especially his landscapes and natural images, appealed to European and American artists and collectors who sought in the beauty and harmony of nature an antidote to the dreary industrial development that was overtaking the cities. His landscapes and renderings of the natural world—which range from startlingly powerful original designs like "The Great Wave" (cat. 97), and the stark abstractions of his "Waterfalls" series, to minutely detailed studies of insects, plants, and sea life—reveal an observant, bold, and patient spirit. As more of Hokusai's print designs and picture books *(ehon)* came to the West, their technical virtuosity, color, and quality were extolled as examples in themselves of the superiority of Japanese art and craft techniques. The *Manga* and technical manuals on painting and drawing provided a rich, encyclopedic source for visual models and methodology not only for painters, but also for craft designers and architects such as Edward William Godwin (1833–86), a leading figure of the Aesthetic Movement.[4]

In France, interest in Hokusai and in Japanese prints and illustrated books remained high, due in part to the activities of two influential art dealers, Siegfried Bing (1838–1905) and Hayashi Tadamasa (1853–1906). Bing promoted interest in Japanese prints through a journal titled *Le Japon artistique,*

sponsored exhibitions of Japanese prints, and supplied prints to artists such as Edgar Degas (1834–1917), Vincent van Gogh (1853–1890), and Henri de Toulouse-Lautrec (1864–1901). Beginning in the late 1880s, through associations with Bing, and later, Hayashi, the French jeweler Henri Vever (1854–1943) formed a collection of more than eight thousand ukiyo-e prints that was purchased by the Japanese collector Matsukata Kōjirō (1868–1950); the collection is now in the Tokyo National Museum. Hayashi was an interpreter for the Paris International Exposition Universelle in 1878 and stayed in France to make his fortune as a dealer of Japanese prints, selling some one hundred sixty thousand prints and ten thousand illustrated books in the period from 1889 to 1900.[5]

Publication of Edmond de Goncourt's *Hokousaï* in 1896 provided an extensive and informative account of Hokusai's life and work, a list of all Hokusai's paintings that Goncourt (1822–96) could locate at the time, and an accounting of major collections of *surimono* and prints.[6] Goncourt's work became a standard reference for the study of Hokusai and a rich source of biographical information. European interest in Hokusai was at a peak, culminating in 1901 in a landmark exhibition in Vienna of six hundred twenty-nine of his paintings, drawings, prints, and books.[7] The American scholar Ernest F. Fenollosa (1853–1908) mounted one of the few challenges to Hokusai's rising reputation in the West. A graduate of Harvard University who had studied philosophy and theology, Fenollosa taught philosophy and other subjects at Tokyo University between 1878 and 1886. He made a serious study of contemporary and premodern Japanese art during these years, and he later served as an advisor to the Japanese government, acquiring through his activities extensive knowledge of Japanese cultural properties. In his review in 1885 of Louis Gonse's chapter on Japanese painting in *L'Art Japonais,* Fenollosa expressed his strong disagreement with the supreme rank that Gonse and other French authors such as Théodore Duret (1838–1927) accorded Hokusai. Instead, while admitting the "originality and vigor" of his designs, the technical skill of his books, and the range of his subject matter, Fenollosa argued that Hokusai's work, especially his paintings, did not deserve top rank in relation to the work of other Japanese painters.[8]

Nevertheless, in 1893, it was Fenollosa, appointed to head the oriental department of the Museum of Fine Arts, Boston, who organized *Hokusai, and His School,* the first Japanese art exhibition in an American museum to be accompanied by a published catalogue.[9] The one hundred seventy-two screens, panels, albums, and drawings by Hokusai and his pupils in this historic and groundbreaking exhibition came from the extensive Japanese art collection of William Sturgis Bigelow (1850–1926),[10] the collection of Japanese paintings that Fenollosa had assembled and sold to Charles Goddard Weld (1857–1911), and other private collectors.[11]

Fenollosa's catalogue makes clear that in the eight years following his negative assessment of Hokusai as a painter, he had refined his views, perhaps in part through studying better quality examples of Hokusai's work, especially the paintings in Bigelow's collection. Fenollosa asserts that after 1835, Hokusai developed a unique scheme of tints, including a warm, subdued red, greenish blue, warm green, and yellow. "This coloring is Hokusai's own creation, the most unlike anything else in Japanese art, the nearest to the rich effects of European oil work."[12] He observes that, in contrast to many other ukiyo-e artists, Hokusai balanced his work between printed designs and paintings:

> The importance of a primary study of Hokusai's paintings is two-fold: first, for their own intrinsic qualities; second for the light they throw upon his prints. Their larger size exhibits the true scope of his draughtsmanship [sic]; and in color, especially, the prints give but a small idea of the master's depth. They become a new thing for us when we can view their peculiarities in the light of the pictorial technicalities which they aim to render. The several series of original drawings for woodcutting are particularly instructive. In fact, the true history of the course of changes in Hokusai's style must be founded primarily upon a study of his paintings rather than of his prints.[13]

Fenollosa's research of Hokusai's paintings continued, and he worked closely with the art dealer Kobayashi Bunshichi (1864–1923), who specialized in ukiyo-e paintings. In 1900, Fenollosa organized the first exhibition of paintings by Hokusai and his pupils to be held in Japan. The exhibition was displayed at the Japan Fine Art Association in Ueno Park for two weeks, and in the following year, Kobayashi published the exhibition catalogue. Fenollosa's book includes some photographic reproductions of the paintings and an essay that discusses the merits of certain research methodologies, such as the dating of printed books and their use as evidence for brushwork styles.

Fenollosa also noted in his preface that despite Hokusai's fame in Europe, this exhibition would be the first of his work in Japan. He suggests that the remnants of social class divisions remaining from the "Tokugawa age" were responsible for Hokusai's lack of recognition in his homeland. "In vain one urged that his sympathy with the common people has left us a visible record of a national popular life, more minute and vivid than any the world had known before the era of photography. … Some government officials have professed to consider this very exhibition demoralizing; and a few gentlemen who have collected on the sly, are said to be ashamed to allow their names to be published as contributors." One who did allow his name to be published was "K. Homma," whose collection of Hokusai paintings was sold to the American collector Charles Lang Freer in 1904. Fenollosa remarks with pleasure that the "general interest expressed by the public journals and displayed in popular attendance is making of this temporary exhibition something of a national event."[14]

Fenollosa regarded the Tokyo exhibition, which displayed three hundred works, including sixty unsigned brush drawings, as an opportunity to demonstrate, with fewer lacunae, the changes in Hokusai's styles throughout his career. He believed that he had laid the foundation for future research of Hokusai's paintings. Fenollosa died suddenly in 1908, with many scholarly writings on Japanese and Chinese painting in process but incomplete. For another half-century after Fenollosa's death, research of Hokusai concentrated primarily on his prints and printed books. But Fenollosa's role as an advisor to Charles Lang Freer eventually placed an invaluable resource for the study of Hokusai's paintings and drawings in the hands of an American collector with philanthropic aspirations to share his collection with the world.

CHARLES LANG FREER AND HIS COLLECTION OF PAINTINGS AND DRAWINGS BY HOKUSAI

Charles Lang Freer (1854–1919) began collecting Japanese art in the late 1880s. He lived in Detroit, where he was vice president of the Peninsular Car Works, which manufactured railroad cars. In the collection Freer gave to the Freer Gallery of Art, his earliest acquisition of Japanese art, purchased in 1887, is a folding fan with a simple painting of the head of a crane then attributed to the artist Ogata Kōrin (1658–1716). Before turning his interests toward Japanese art and later to a broader range of Asian art, Freer had been a collector of European prints, including the etchings of the American painter James McNeill Whistler (1834–1903). Whistler had been one of the first Western artists to recognize in Japanese prints, paintings, and objects ideas that would transform his own work. His paintings from the 1860s show a strong Japanese influence, and the painter, whom Freer met on a visit to London in 1890, encouraged Freer's nascent interest in Japan.

Freer made his first trip to Asia in 1894–95, when he traveled eastward through India, Singapore, Hong Kong, and Shanghai before reaching Nagasaki. Twelve years later, in 1907, he made his second visit to Japan. During the years between these two trips, Freer purchased most of the Japanese art in the initial collection of the Freer Gallery of Art, including his paintings and drawings by Hokusai, all of which were purchased in the nine-year period between 1898 and 1907, at the peak of Hokusai's fame in the West.

Freer probably became acquainted with Hokusai's work through the Japanese prints he collected in the period from 1894 to 1904.[15] Purchases of Japanese ceramics and paintings suggested new directions for his collection. In 1898, Freer purchased his first Hokusai paintings from the attorney E. S. Hull, who was acting as an agent for Ernest Fenollosa during Fenollosa's divorce and remarriage, when he was forced to sell some of his Japanese art collection. Included in the mixed lots of hanging scrolls, pottery, panels, and screens were several paintings signed "Sōri," which were attributed to Hokusai at the time but are now understood by scholars to have been painted by Hishikawa Sōri (fl. late eighteenth century–early nineteenth century), Hokusai's pupil to whom he gave his art name after he abandoned it in 1798. This group of Hokusai paintings from Fenollosa's collection, nineteen of which are still in the Freer Gallery of Art, also include *Woman Holding a Tobacco Pipe* (cat. 64), *Flowering Pumpkin Vine and Horsefly* (cat. 85), *Egret on a Bridge Post* (cat. 29), and nine fan paintings (see cat. 15). One other painting mentioned in Freer's correspondence regarding this transaction, a "Hokusai Kakemono, Cock and Drum," apparently was not retained by Freer when he culled his collection to leave only what he regarded as his best paintings to the Smithsonian Institution.

Boy Viewing Mount Fuji (cat. 119), one of the most famous paintings in the Freer Gallery of Art, was also in Freer's first purchase of Hokusai's paintings. Several generations of scholars have held widely divergent opinions concerning the authorship of this engaging work, but today, with recent advances in the study of Hokusai's signatures, seals, and a larger corpus of paintings than was known in Freer's time, its authenticity has once again become more widely accepted. Considering the aesthetic qualities of this painting and the others by Hokusai in Freer's first purchase of the artist's painted works, one can understand why Hokusai's paintings appealed to him so strongly.

Freer spent hours viewing and studying his paintings one at a time at his Detroit home, occasionally in the company of a friend or a small group. In Japanese painting, he had already developed a taste for works by artists of the Rinpa school, whom contemporary writers on Japanese art also extolled. His first group of Hokusai paintings included nature and figure subjects. The compositions were simple, the color schemes original, clear, and at times subtle, and the brush manner varied from the simple, bold strokes of the fencepost on which the egret sits to the sinuous contours of the woman's kimono and the fine, meticulous rendering of the fly in the pumpkin vine painting. Freer was especially fond of the beauties of nature, and it is likely that these paintings by Hokusai reminded him not only of pleasant memories of his recent travels in Japan, but also of the beauty and serenity of mountains and gardens.

In 1900, Freer purchased *Thunder God* (cat. 132), a large and dynamic painting with an inscription giving Hokusai's age as eighty-eight, from Fenollosa's agent, E. S. Hull for the substantial sum of five hundred dollars. Freer requested that Hull convey to him Professor Fenollosa's opinion of this painting. Hull reported that Fenollosa had pronounced it "a remarkably fine painting by Hokusai, the finest painting of the 'Thunder God' I have ever seen in Japanese art."[16] At the time Freer's opinion favored "a much finer painting of the same subject by Sōtatsu" that was then in his collection. Freer suggested that he might show his Sōtatsu to Fenollosa. "The Hokusai is really fine, but I think when I show him the one by Sōtatsu, he will take his hat off to the latter."[17]

Two years later, in 1902, Freer engaged the art dealer Siegfried Bing to bid for him on several Japanese paintings that Hayashi Tadamasa arranged for sale in Paris. The results were mixed, but Freer succeeded in purchasing an exceptional long handscroll of miscellaneous subjects (cat. 118). The individual paintings in the handscroll cover a wide range of subjects, including landscapes, several superb still-life compositions reminiscent of Hokusai's *surimono* designs, and figure subjects. An image of a man and boy viewing a waterfall closely resembles one of Hokusai's last works, a painting of the Chinese poet Li Bo (d. 762) viewing a waterfall in the company of a small child.[18]

In the same year, Freer acquired a unique pair of six-panel folding screens depicting rural scenery and Mount Fuji. He purchased the screens from Fenollosa and his former wife in separate transactions for a total price of three thousand two hundred fifty dollars. The screens were nearly separated permanently, as Mrs. Fenollosa had already begun discussions with another potential purchaser, but Freer politely made his offer "provided it pleases me as well as I am led to belive [*sic*] it will."[19] Even today, when interest in Hokusai's paintings has grown and many previously unknown works have come to light, the screens from Fenollosa's collection are the only pair of full-size screens by Hokusai with large-scale landscapes conceived as continuous compositions. They are highly important not only for understanding Hokusai's ability to work in an unusually large format, but also as documents of what must have been a high-level commission. Recent research confirms Fenollosa's opinion that these screens, which are embellished with gold and painted with great attention to color and tonality, may have been commissioned during the same time that Hokusai's print series, *Thirty-six Views of Mount Fuji* was published.[20] In his catalogue for the exhibition in 1893 at the Museum of Fine Arts, Boston, Fenollosa noted the similarities between the prints and the screen paintings, suggesting that the date of the screens should be around 1835. He wrote of the unusual effect of the deep-yellow, stippled color tones in the trees, "supporting the cloudy background of spotted gold, [which] gives tone to the warm soft orange of the sky and to the cool blue gray spaces of the marsh and the distance."[21]

Freer continued to seek Fenollosa's advice when he considered important additions to his collection of Japanese and Chinese paintings. A famous pair of hanging scrolls depicting women preparing for the New Year (cat. 36) was purchased through Siegfried Bing in the Hayashi sale in 1903, which was also the source of one of the masterpieces of Freer's ukiyo-e painting collection, *Moonlight Revelry at Dozō Sagami* by Kitagawa Utamaro (d. 1806).

Freer's most important acquisitions of paintings and drawings by Hokusai were offered to him in the years 1903 and 1904 by Kobayashi Bunshichi (1864–1923), the leading dealer of ukiyo-e in Tokyo and a close associate of Fenollosa. From Kobayashi in 1903, Freer purchased a rare painting from Hokusai's "Sōri" period, a portrait of a courtesan in full color (cat. 17). Nagata Seiji, a prominent scholar of Hokusai's paintings and prints, has pointed out its similarities to a pair of unsigned hanging scrolls titled *Women in Various*

Walks of Life (cat. 2).[22] From Kobayashi, Freer purchased another early work signed "Sōri," which depicts a young man wearing feminine attire and carrying a sedge hat (cat. 16). Originally recorded in Freer's list of *kakemono* as a work by Hokusai, this painting was later reattributed in museum records to "Sōri III" based on the opinion of the Freer gallery's first director, John Ellerton Lodge (1876–1942), who expressed similar doubts about many of Freer's Hokusai paintings. Today, as in Freer's time, scholars recognize it as a rare example of Hokusai's early portrayals of elegant young men.

In early August 1904, Freer wrote to Fenollosa:

> Advice has come from Kobayashi, telling me that he is sending a large shipment of things, I think, something like thirty specimens of Hokusai's work, including the collection owned by Mr. Homer [corrected by hand to read Homma]. He states that Mr. Homer [Homma] is to accompany Kobayashi here, and that after his arrival, he intends to make an exhibition of his collection, and give the proceeds to the [Russo-Japanese] war relief fund (!!). I wonder if it is wrong to entertain suspicions concerning the proposed gift? The shipment includes the very fine Hokusai screens owned by Homer [*sic*]. Mention is also made of specimens of the work of Motonobu, Korin and three or four of the leading masters of Ukiyoye [*sic*]. A memorandum giving the prices of a few of the Homer things is startling. One pair of Hokusai screens is marked six thousand dollars, and a few other items have correspondingly ridiculous prices. However, when the cases are received, I shall look them through carefully, but, at the prices named, I shall certainly decline to buy a single specimen."[23]

At the end of the same month, Freer wrote to his friend Charles J. Morse (1852–1911),[24] a fellow Japanese art collector, regarding his interest in the Hokusai paintings that had just arrived in two shipments from Kobayashi:

> The bulk of the two shipments consists of examples of Hokusai's painting. There are screens, kakemono and panels, and the majority of them are extremely interesting. I am inclined to think that the lot as a whole ranks fully equal to those in the Boston Museum or the group in my own collection. The pair of six-fold screens called "The Six Tamagawas" are really wonderful. … Another pair of six-fold screens represent the twelve months of the year, and are veritable masterpieces."[25]

In a letter to Morse a month later, Freer began with some details regarding his proposed sale of his Japanese print collection to Morse's friend David Tod Ford, but then continues with a detailed description of a visit at his home with Kobayashi, Homma, and the Japanese art dealer Matsuki Bunkyō (1867–1940). He enjoyed describing the "beautiful jealousy existing between Kobayashi and Matsuki."[26] Freer was an important client for both dealers, who understood his interests and offered many of the most important Japanese paintings in his col-

lection.[27] At the time, Freer was actively building his collection of Japanese paintings and he had begun collecting Chinese paintings, for which the Japanese dealers were also an important source. In the same letter, Freer described reviewing an estimated seventy-five paintings presented by Matsuki:

> Of which twenty seemed to me worthy of consideration. The twenty I finally weeded down to seven, and those seven I have offered to buy subject to Fenollosa's examination and certification.

> I bought from Kobayashi and Homma all the Hokusai's of first-class quality which you saw while you were here, excepting the pair of Tamagawa Screens. I passed the latter, because of the price asked, $10,000. Before they left Detroit, they cut the price to $7,500. Yesterday, they telegraphed from St. Louis, where they now are, cutting their price to $5,000. I am standing pat on the offer I made them while here—$3,600.00 for the pair of screens. What the result will be, I know not. In addition to a lot of rubbish, Kobayashi brought personally with him forty-nine very interesting original drawings by Hokusai, all of which I bought. He also brought five tall landscape prints ["by Hokusai" added by hand], similar to the four I had of like nature. These also, I bought."[28]

On the same day, Freer wrote to Ushikubo Daijirō, an agent for Yamanaka and Company, which had offices in New York, to thank him for the caution he had conveyed regarding forgeries of early paintings. Freer noted that he would consult Professor Fenollosa, but he had also by this time developed confidence in his own judgment of Japanese paintings. In a handwritten postscript, Freer wrote, "The paintings by Hokusai bought from Homma are all genuine and splendid in every way."[29]

The purchase of twenty paintings by Hokusai from Kobayashi and Homma in 1904 provided many of the most important works in Freer's collection. Most of the folding screens in the collection were acquired in that transaction. A pair of two-panel landscapes of Mount Fuji and Enoshima (cat. 81), a two-panel screen depicting a Shinto ceremony (cat. 28), a small folding screen mounted with several fan paintings of nature subjects and landscape (cat. 123), and a pair of six-panel screens mounted with twelve unsigned paintings titled *Birds, Animals, and Plants Representing the Twelve Months* (cat. 86) were also included in the purchase. The most elegant of the screens, which Freer admired but initially rejected because of the high asking price, was the work titled *Six Tama Rivers* (cat. 89), of which one screen is mounted with six landscapes and the other with six figure subjects, including portraits of poets.

The hanging scrolls in the group also include important works. Among these are two paintings of a fisherman and woodcutter, which are considered to be masterpieces from the last year of Hokusai's life (cat. 142). The peaceful introspection of the figures and the contrasting landscapes of open water and a towering mountain peak create a serene and tranquil mood that contrasts with the terrifying energy of the *Thunder God* (cat. 132), painted less than two years earlier. The group of paintings from Homma also includes a scene from the early eleventh-century classic of court literature, *The Tale of Genji* (cat. 63), an image of a woman holding a letter behind her back (see p. 32, F1904.185), a painting of a traveler beside a tall tree (cat. 138), and two paintings of ascending and descending dragons that Freer particularly admired.

"K. Homma," the Japanese art collector who sold Freer some of his most important Hokusai paintings, was Honma Kōsō (1841–1909). Honma was a member of a prominent family of major landholders and officials of Sakata in Dewa (modern Yamagata Prefecture). He was a distant relative of Hokusai's pupil Honma Hokuyō (1822–68), who studied art under Hokusai's instruction in about 1843 when Hokusai was in his eighties. Hokuyō's close relationship to Hokusai in the artist's later years is documented by a small present that Hokusai gave him before Hokuyō's journey to Nagasaki in 1848 (cat. 141). Hokuyō's special place in Hokusai's inner circle at the end of his life may have been a factor in the exceptional interest Honma Kōsō took in Hokusai's paintings.[30] As was customary in his family, Honma Kōsō was broadly educated in martial arts such as *kendō*, in traditional arts, and in European studies (Rangaku). Honma traveled to Europe in 1873–75 under the auspices of the Buddhist temple Higashi Honganji. After moving to Tokyo following an inheritance dispute in which he won a large settlement, he studied foreign languages and became a successful collector who sold some Japanese works to foreign clients.[31]

Also in 1904, Freer purchased ninety-three drawings from Kobayashi, including some in full color. They vary in quality and authorship, but the group contains many important and credible examples of Hokusai's work. As a whole they form an important body of material for studying Hokusai's draftsmanship and working methods. Three small sketches cut out and pasted on a sheet of paper were also part of the purchase. The work is now considered a preparatory compositional model for a small full-color painting titled *The Courtesan Eguchi as the Bodhisattva Fugen and the Monk Saigyō* (cat. 37), which was apparently unknown when Freer purchased the drawing.

Following the sale of Honma's paintings to Freer, Kobayashi wrote that there were no more important Hokusai paintings in Japan, and that he would have no further examples of Hokusai paintings to offer for sale. Nonetheless Freer purchased a few additional Hokusai paintings in 1905 and 1906, including a copy of a work attributed to Hokusai depicting Kōbō Daishi and a demon in the Nishi Arai Daishi temple in Tokyo.[32] Two good landscapes were purchased from Kobayashi in 1905 (cat. 131 and F1905.228). Freer's purchases of Hokusai paintings in 1906 were disappointing, and nearly all have been attributed to other artists. The only significant Hokusai paintings acquired by Freer after the purchase of paintings from Honma were a set of six hanging scrolls of the Six Immortals of Poetry offered to him by Yamanaka Sadajirō in 1907. The six poets are striking for their scale, which is suitable for a full-size six-panel screen, and also for their unusual coloration and the solemnity and monumentality of the figures.

Among the drawings by Hokusai in Freer's collection, the most important are thirty-four works *(hanshita-e)* for the unfinished print series, *One Hundred Poets, One Verse Each, as Explained by the Nurse*. Hokusai began designing this ambitious series at the peak of his fame as a designer of ukiyo-e prints. The twenty-seven published prints of this set reveal varied compositions and coloration unlike any other prints published in the mid-1830s (cats. 150–61). The quality and variety of design, color, and subjects would have made this group a masterpiece among Hokusai's print series had it been completed, but publication was stopped and never resumed. Economic duress caused by the Tenpō famine of 1834–36 cannot have favored publication and sale of print designs that demanded expert block cutting and printing. Moreover, although the "One Hundred Poets" anthology was widely known, popular taste in ukiyo-e prints may have preferred the designs of other artists, such as Hiroshige (1797–1858), who continued to prevail in landscape prints for the remainder of his life, and Kuniyoshi (1797–1861), whose dramatic warrior designs were popular in the 1830s and 1840s.

Freer, whose appreciation for finely detailed monochromatic designs had developed in the 1880s and 1890s through his collection of etchings by Whistler and other artists, purchased thirty-three of Hokusai's final drawings for the "One Hundred Poets" series from the English collector and art dealer Michael Tomkinson (1841–1921), who had acquired them from a collection formed by Dr. Ernest Hart (1835–98). Hart had acquired the works in about 1885.[33] Freer also purchased zinc plate printing blocks and proof prints of eighty-six designs from Hokusai's series reproduced in miniature by a printing technique known as gillotage.[34] An additional drawing was purchased from Yamanaka in 1903, and Harold P. Stern (1922–77) acquired seven more drawings for the Freer gallery in 1955 and 1968. The forty-one drawings are the largest single collection of the sixty-one drawings known to have survived (see cats. 150–154). Beautiful for their imaginative and evocative treatment of subjects as well as brushwork, these works also reveal Hokusai's meticulous attention to every compositional detail. Many of the designs contain carefully inserted paper patches where the artist wished to make a change, and thus also serve as valuable evidence for Hokusai's painstaking preparation for each keyblock design. Despite the fame and importance of the drawings in Europe since 1885, when fifty-seven of them were viewed at a gathering of Japanese art enthusiasts, including Edmond de Goncourt, Siegfried Bing, and Hayashi Tadamasa, the first comprehensive scholarly study of Hokusai's "One Hundred Poets" series, by the American scholar and collector Peter Morse, was published in 1989, more than a century later.

Charles Lang Freer's collection of Hokusai paintings and drawings was brought together at a peak of enthusiasm for Hokusai's artistic achievement in the West. Before Hokusai became a focus of his growing collection of Japanese paintings, Freer had become one of the first American collectors to appreciate ukiyo-e painting as well as prints. Hokusai was by no means Freer's only focus as he collected the artist's paintings and drawings between 1898 and 1907. At the same time, Freer continued to purchase, often from the same art dealers and in the same transactions, paintings by artists of the Rinpa school, calligraphy by Kōetsu, Muromachi-period ink paintings, works by artists he termed "old masters" of Japan, and a substantial number of important ukiyo-e paintings. He also continued to develop his collection of American paintings by artists whose work he considered to create an aesthetic harmony with the glazed ceramics and Asian paintings in his collection. Throughout this period, as his understanding and appreciation of Japanese and Chinese painting grew, he shared his interests through correspondence and private viewings in his home with a small circle of friends who included artists such as the American painter Dwight William Tryon (1849–1925) and art collectors.

Freer generously cooperated with college museums to arrange small exhibitions of Japanese paintings for the Hillyer Gallery at Smith College in 1897 and 1901 and for Williams College in 1905. In addition, Freer lent one hundred Japanese prints to the Detroit Museum of Arts (now the Detroit Institute of Arts) when Fenollosa was scheduled to present a series of lectures there in 1901. Larger exhibitions with works from Freer's Asian art collection were organized for the opening of Alumni Memorial Hall at the University of Michigan in 1910, the Smithsonian Institution in 1912, the Knoedler Galleries in New York in 1914, the Metropolitan Museum of Art in 1916, and the Art Institute of Chicago in 1917.[35]

In 1906, with the full support of President Theodore Roosevelt (1858–1919), Freer's proposal to give his art collection and a building to house it in perpetuity to the United States was approved, and he began to plan for the building and gift. The American architect Charles Adams Platt (1861–1933) designed a building that suited Freer's preference for an open central courtyard and harmonious façade. Freer retained, edited, and added to his collections until his death in 1919, and the building, which had begun construction in 1916, opened in 1923 on a site adjacent to the original Smithsonian Building, known as the "Castle."

The ninety-two paintings and one hundred twenty-four drawings by Hokusai were the largest representation of work by any artist other than Whistler in Freer's gift to the nation. Collected from sources in Japan, the United States, and Europe, Freer's Hokusai paintings, despite reduction in numbers through subsequent research that has judged some works unattributable to the master, represent Hokusai's work from the 1790s to the end of his life, a period of more than fifty years. The drawings for the unfinished "One Hundred Poets"

Charles L. Freer comparing Whistler's *Venus Rising from the Sea* to an Islamic glazed pot, 1909. Platinum print. (Photographer: Alvin Langdon Coburn. Charles Lang Freer Papers, Freer Gallery of Art and Arthur M. Sackler Gallery Archives, Smithsonian Institution, Washington, D.C.)

series provide invaluable evidence not only for Hokusai's ideas at the peak of his career as a designer of landscape prints, but also for his artistic methodology. Only two important paintings, a promenading courtesan representing the flamboyant style of Hokusai's "Taito" period that was purchased in 1954 (cat. 68), and a painting of peasants preparing *mochi* (rice cakes; cat. 78), which was a gift from Lawrence and Sonia Klein to the museum in 1992, have been added to the collection since Freer's gift.

Despite the importance of its collection, the Freer Gallery of Art's first exhibition devoted to its paintings and drawings by Hokusai was organized in 1960 by Harold P. Stern, the museum's first curator of Japanese art, who was a specialist of ukiyo-e prints and paintings. Stern was an influential advocate for the serious study of ukiyo-e paintings, which he supported through his own lectures and writing, as well as by encouraging scholarly studies throughout the world. In 1973, in celebration of the fiftieth anniversary of the Freer Gallery of Art, Stern organized the exhibition *Ukiyo-e Paintings*, wrote a catalogue of selected paintings, and hosted an important international symposium on a subject that was just gaining attention. All this followed nearly three quarters of a century after Fenollosa's exhibition in Tokyo in 1900 of Hokusai's paintings.

Whereas prints were the primary focus of Hokusai studies prior to 1950, recent publications and exhibitions have turned increasingly to other aspects of Hokusai's work—his printed books, drawings, and most recently, his paintings. Previously unknown art by Hokusai's hand and materials shedding light on the production of his work are being rediscovered, and the corpus of pieces in longstanding collections such as that of the Freer are being reevaluated in view of systematic studies by an international group of dedicated scholars.

The present exhibition, organized through an unprecedented collaboration with the Nihon Keizai Shimbun, Inc., and the Tokyo National Museum, celebrates the one hundredth anniversary of Freer's gift of his collection and museum to the United States. His collection of Hokusai paintings, which he believed represented some of the artist's finest work, are shown for the first time with prints, paintings, drawings, and printed books borrowed from other collections. By the measure of the vast amount of research, publication, exhibition, and specialized scholarly study of Hokusai within the past two decades, the artist seems once more to be ascendant, still eliciting interest on many levels, and, for some scholars, a lifetime passion similar to Hokusai's own dedication to his art. It has now been nearly two hundred fifty years since Hokusai's birth in Edo and more than a century and a half since his last wish to go on painting for a few more years, yet Hokusai's art and the remarkable spirit we sense within it continue to draw us closer and hold us in their thrall.

NOTES

1. English translation by the author. Revon 1896, i.

2. English translation by the author. Gonse 1883, 2:269-70.

3. Rosenfield 1994, 17.

4. Lambourne 1991, 32.

5. Meech 1988, 18-19.

6. Goncourt's book has been published in English translation with extensive commentary by Matthi Forrer (1988).

7. *Werke Hokusais Ausgestellt im Kuferstich Kabinet Österreichs Museum für Kunst und Industrie,* Wien, 1901.

8. Fenollosa 1885, 46.

9. Fenollosa 1893.

10. Meech 2005, 35. Part 2 of this article contains useful brief biographies of American collectors of Japanese prints from the 1860s to the 1950s.

11. Weld bequeathed the collection to the Museum of Fine Arts, Boston, and it is now known as the Fenollosa-Weld Collection.

12. Fenollosa 1893, xvii.

13. Ibid., xviii.

14. Fenollosa 1901, 1.

15. Freer sold his collection of three hundred twenty-five prints at original cost ($7,000) to his friend Charles James Morse (1852-1911) of Evanston, Illinois, and Morse's friend David Tod Ford, Sr., of Pasadena, California.

16. E. S. Hull to Charles Lang Freer, July 12, 1900 (Freer Papers).

17. Charles Lang Freer to E. S. Hull, Jr., June 30, 1900 (Freer Papers).

18. *Li Bo Viewing a Waterfall* is in the Museum of Fine Arts, Boston. Nagata 2000, cat. 139 (color), 134, 299.

19. Charles Lang Freer to Mrs. Lisa G. Fenollosa, February 21, 1902 (Freer Papers).

20. See in this volume Naitō, cat. 88, p. 78.

21. Fenollosa 1893, no. 145, 27-28.

22. Nagata 2000, 258.

23. Charles Lang Freer to Professor Ernest Fenollosa, August 8, 1904 (Freer Papers).

24. For an informative biography of Charles James Morse, see Meech 2005, 46-47. Morse and David Tod Ford of Pasadena purchased Freer's Japanese print collection in 1905. Meech also gives a brief account of Freer's collection of Japanese prints, three hundred twenty-five in all, collected between 1894 and 1904. Some of the prints in the Ford collection were eventually sold to Edwin Grabhorn (1889-1968). Ibid., 39.

25. Charles Lang Freer to Charles J. Morse, Esq., August 26, 1904 (Freer Papers).

26. Charles Lang Freer to Charles J. Morse, Esq., September 26, 1904 (Freer Papers).

27. Shimizu 1983, 136-49.

28. Ibid., 35.

29. Charles Lang Freer to D. J. R. Ushikubo, September 26, 1904 (Freer Papers).

30. Nikkei 2005, cat. 493, entry by Nagata Seiji. Hokuyō had a strong interest in Europe, and studied English under Guido Verbeck (1830-98), a missionary and teacher in Nagasaki. In 1862 he traveled extensively to London, Russia, the United States, and China, hoping to learn how to establish a modern company in Japan. He became an English instructor after returning to Japan. Nagata 1990, 5:151.

31. Biographical information on Honma Kosō was provided by historian Tamura Kanzō of Sakata in telephone conversations with Takako Sarai, February 1-2, 2006. Additional information was provided by the Honma Bijutsukan in Sakata.

32. Three versions of this painting exist, including one in the Edoardo Chiossone Museum of Oriental Art, Genoa. All three are illustrated in Carpenter 2005, 146. These paintings are discussed in Calza 2005, 145.

33. Morse 1989, 19. Morse's study provides a detailed scholarly account of the history of the surviving prints and drawings from this series as well as full-color reproduction of all prints and drawings.

34. Gillotage was a printing technique developed in France by Firmin Gillot (1820-72). Zinc plates cut in relief enabled commercial printers to run text and illustrations through a press in a single pass. The European plates and blocks that Freer purchased provide evidence for four designs for Hokusai's One Hundred Poets series that have not survived as drawings or as prints. Ibid., 17-18. According to Morse, although the blocks Freer purchased were attributed to Firmin Gillot's son, Charles Gillot (1854-1903), they are standard photomechanical plates.

35. Thomas Lawton describes these exhibitions in Lawton and Merrill 1993, 207-32.

HOKUSAI'S CHOICE OF SUBJECT MATTER: PAINTINGS IN THE FREER GALLERY OF ART

ASANO SHŪGŌ

Hokusai was a true giant in the world of ukiyo-e, an artist who treated the widest range of subjects in a style uniquely his own. When his work is examined closely, one finds that he tended to follow his own preferences in the subjects he depicted, and that the themes he chose as well as the technical methods and formats he employed varied depending on the period in which he was working. The following text will discuss the themes Hokusai selected, the technique and formats he used, and a study of his paintings in the collection of the Freer Gallery of Art.

SUBJECTS, TECHNIQUES, AND FORMATS

Hokusai used a variety of subjects in his work, including genre pictures (*fūzokuga*), pictures of beauties (*bijinga*), prints portraying kabuki actors (*yakusha-e*), warrior pictures (*musha-e*), landscapes (*fūkeiga*), bird-and-flower pictures (*kachōga*), and still lifes (*seibutsuga*). He also used a variety of techniques and formats such as single-sheet prints (*ichimai-e*), privately commissioned or issued prints (*surimono*), woodblock printed books, and paintings.

The depiction of customs and manners was a primary subject in ukiyo-e, and Hokusai produced a considerable number of works in this genre. Different effects were achieved, however, depending on the format and techniques. Roughly speaking, single-sheet prints are identified as a popular artform, *surimono* as tasteful expressions with connections to particular interests, woodblock printed books as syntheses of image and text, and paintings as single, unique objects. These characterizations generally hold true for Hokusai's work.[1] Surprisingly few single-sheet genre prints by Hokusai exist. *Eight Views of Traveling Lovers from* Jōruri *Plays*, which was published from about 1800 to 1804, is one of the only examples.[2] Hokusai did not produce any single-sheet print series that can be definitively termed genre pictures. There are numerous extant examples of genre pictures in other formats however; Hokusai concentrated on genre until about 1813, and he produced few genre paintings thereafter. The works done later in his career, such as the painting *Rice Planting (Taue zu)*, tend to emphasize a sense of illusion and strangeness.[3] From the Kansei (1789–1801) to the Bunka (1804–18) era , Hokusai designed *surimono* depicting a variety of scenes of contemporary life. In the large-scale formats of *ōbōsho zenshiban* (uncut sheets of thick, high-quality paper) and *nagaban*, their appeal is abundantly evident. Among the illustrated albums incorporating *kyōka* verse, *The Bird of the Capital (Miyakodori)*, *Illustrated Book of* Kyōka: *Range upon Range of Mountains (Ehon kyōka yama mata yama;* cats. 61 and 62), and *Panoramic Views along the Banks of Sumida River (Ehon Sumidagawa ryōgan ichiran)* are representative of the work done at this time.[4] Paintings from this time period include *Pilgrims Worshiping the Great Buddha (Daibutsu mōde zu)*, *Returning from a Foliage-Viewing Excursion (Kōraku-gaeri zu)*, and *Gathering Shellfish at Ebb Tide (Shiohigari zu;* cat. 40).[5]

Bijin (meaning here both beautiful women and handsome men) are a major theme in Japanese painting. Hokusai painted many such works, from a streetwalker (cat. 18) and the immortal Yuzhi playing a one-stringed zither (cat. 19) of the Kansei era, to *The Third Princess from* The Tale of Genji *(Nyosannomiya zu)*,[6] and young men (cats. 121 and 122) done late in his career. He must have received many commissions for portrayals of beauties, but whether he enjoyed painting this subject is another question. *Bijinga* are extremely rare in his single-sheet prints and *surimono*, and not one illustrated book *(ehon)* on this theme is extant. A Hokusai *surimono* that does come immediately to mind is *An Array of Beautiful Women for the Year of the Sheep (Tsuchinoto hitsuji bijin awase no uchi [kokonotsugiriban])*, which consists of portrayals of beauties in head-and-shoulder views.[7] Dating to the spring of 1799 (Kansei 11), the prints may constitute the first such series in this format, and Hokusai must have been enthralled by the novelty of the project. The same close-up portrayal characterizes the treatment of the subjects in *Fashionable Seven Habits (Fūryū nakute nanakuse;* cats. 51 and 52). The two existing prints from the series are outstanding, and it is unclear why publication would have stopped before the set was completed.

Actor prints were the main subject depicted in single-sheet prints during the "Shunrō" period, the earliest in Hokusai's career. In the later periods, however, almost no prints on this theme were produced. It may be that Hokusai left the Katsukawa school on bad terms, but since he did not resume designing actor prints in the "Sōri" period, it appears that he decided against creating any more representations of the subject. Almost all the actor prints he produced from 1779 (An'ei 8) to 1793–94 (Kansei 5 or 6) include the name and role of the actor. This is important, as prints by his teacher Katsukawa Shunshō and fellow pupils Shunkō and Shun'ei carry no such designation, nor do the prints of Katsukawa Shunjō or Shunsen. Most of Hokusai's works in this genre are subdued in color, their limited palette recalling pictures printed with safflower red *(benizuri-e)*. This suggests that the actor prints he was producing were inexpensive. At the time, actor prints in the narrow *hosoban* format were designated "superior" (*jō*) or "ordinary" (*nami*), the highest-quality prints being the province of Shunshō and Shunkō, and the cheaper prints being assigned to Hokusai. Shunshō may also have passed on the designing of "ordinary" prints to Hokusai when artists like Torii Kiyotsune (fl. 1757–79) and Torii Kiyonaga (1752–1815) stopped producing them. The unpleasant memory of this treatment may have been the real reason Hokusai did so few actor prints after the "Shunrō" period. Though rare, later actor prints by Hokusai do exist: two single-sheet prints in *ōban* size dated to 1807 (Bunka 4) and a set of five *surimono* in small, square *shikishiban* format from 1824 (Bunsei 7) are representative examples.[8] Both works must have been specially commissioned. The latter bears an inscription in which Hokusai, humbling himself, writes: "From the brush of Katsushika, the old man Iitsu, Early spring, Year of that imitator of humankind, the Monkey." There are no secure actor paintings by Hokusai, and no designs of this subject appear in illustrated books after the "Shunrō" period.

Hokusai's warrior pictures appear primarily in woodblock printed books. The subject is also represented in paintings, single-sheet prints, and *surimono*, but they are equal in neither quantity nor quality to the book illustrations. *Tametomo and the Inhabitants of Onoshima Island* (cat. 66), however, and those paintings done in the "Manji" period are noteworthy. Warrior prints in single-sheet format include a set of five *ōban* from about 1833, in which the entire picture surface is filled with scenes of fighting, all rendered in Hokusai's individual style. Two *surimono* series expressive of a refined taste are *Matching Warriors of Japan and China for the Soramitsuya Group* (*Soramitsuya-ren wakan buyū awase sanban no uchi*) and *Five Sibling Pictures of China and Japan for the Zakurogaki Group* (*Zakurogaki-ren goban no uchi, wakan e-kyōdai*).[9]

Landscape is a major subject in Hokusai's woodblock printed books and single-sheet prints. In *kyōka* albums dating from about 1799 to 1805, one finds figures in landscape, but the later *Hokusai manga* (cat. 73) contains designs in which landscape itself is the subject. The three-volume *One Hundred Views of Mount Fuji* (cat. 162) is a comprehensive series of landscape prints. Excellent landscapes are found in *yomihon* as well. *Thirty-six Views of Mount Fuji* (cats. 96–100) comprises single-sheet prints representative of about 1830 to 1834. It was during the first part of this era that Hokusai and Hiroshige were battling for supremacy in the landscape genre. An interesting difference between the two is that while Hiroshige enclosed his designs in a frame, as with his *Fifty-three Stations along the Tōkaidō* series, Hokusai used no such device.[10] Was he too proud to follow Hiroshige in this technique? Or did he think the frame added nothing and only interfered with the design? The paintings *Mount Fuji and Enoshima* (cat. 81), *Country Scenes* (cat. 88), and *Breaking Waves* (cat. 131) from the collection of the Freer Gallery of Art deserve special mention here;

each was completed late in Hokusai's career. *Dragon Flying over Mount Fuji* (*Fuji goshi ryū zu*), which was painted the year he died, is also an important work.[11] In *surimono*, prints from the series *Horses of Every Fashion* (cats. 93 and 94) are outstanding examples of the landscape theme.

The bird-and-flower subject is also found in Hokusai's paintings and prints. He seemed to have particularly liked the subject, and the birds he depicted include the cuckoo and the cormorant. A ten-sheet set of *ōban*-size, full-color, single-sheet prints from about 1831 to 1832 is considered a comprehensive collection of Hokusai's flower-and-bird prints.

Still life, the last of Hokusai's chosen subjects category, are found mainly in his *surimono* designs. This was a difficult subject to sell in single-sheet prints, and so it was natural for Hokusai to turn to the more exclusive format. The subtle beauty and charm of *surimono* are given full expression in two major series: *Genroku Poetry Shell Match* (cat. 92) and *Horses of Every Fashion*. Still life is also depicted in Hokusai's paintings, and among the masterpieces *Five Fans* (*Senmen chirashi zu*; cat. 144) in the Tokyo National Museum and *The Lute and White Snake of Benten* (Sarasvati; cat. 139) in the Freer Gallery of Art deserve special mention.

PAINTINGS BY HOKUSAI IN THE FREER GALLERY OF ART

The Freer Gallery of Art and the Arthur M. Sackler Gallery together form the national museum of Asian art for the United States. The Freer gallery, which opened to the public in 1923, was a gift to the nation from businessman Charles Lang Freer. The extensive collection of high-quality Hokusai paintings in the Freer gallery is well known. However, because the stipulations of Freer's will prohibit the works from traveling, they were not included in the Hokusai exhibition that was held last year in Tokyo. Thus, one group of works from that exhibition will be displayed with the famous paintings from the Freer in this exhibition.

The Freer Gallery of Art houses the premier collection of Hokusai paintings in terms of both quantity and quality. In 2004, Timothy Clark, Naitō Masato, and I were able to examine the entire collection of Hokusai works in preparation for this exhibition. The results of that research, along with additional commentary, are discussed below. Those paintings included in this exhibition are detailed in the catalogue section of this book; therefore, discussions of those works have generally been omitted here.

Only a selection of the examined works is mentioned in this section. Naturally, paintings by other artists, such as Hishikawa Sōri and Hokusai II, are not included, nor are those bearing a Hokusai signature and seal but that the researchers agree are not authentic. However, if the seal on a particular work is good and the case was made for attribution to Hokusai, then that work is included here. The collection includes many charming sketches, but their number was so large and they posed so many questions, that they are excluded from this discussion.

The works are grouped according to seal, with those having no seal or signature listed last. In addition to my opinions expressed here,[12] Nagata Seiji has written comprehensively on the subject,[13] and his books and articles are a valuable source for further information.

Pair of square seals: Hokusai (intaglio) / Sōri (relief)

These seals from Hokusai's early period are found on one work in the collection of the Freer Gallery of Art: a fan painting from an album of ten leaves. Only one other example of a work with these seals is known.

Blossoming Plum Branches
ca. 1795–98
Signature: Sōri ga
Inscription by Kōdai Hōkei
folding fan mounted on panel; ink and color on paper
17.4 x 46.2 (upper border) / 21.3 (lower border) cm
F1898.135b
cat. 15

Square intaglio seal: Kanchi

This seal is found on the following two paintings. Both works are standard examples from Hokusai's "Sōri" period.

Young Man
ca. 1795–98
Signature: Sōri ga
hanging scroll; ink and color on paper
50.9 x 21.0 cm
F1903.130
cat. 16

Courtesan
ca. 1796–98
Signature: Hokusai Sōri giga
hanging scroll; ink and color on paper
70.9 x 24.0 cm
F1903.129
cat. 17

Pair of square seals: Toki (intaglio) / Masa (intaglio)

The following fan painting, one of four mounted on a two-panel screen, bears this seal.

Scholar in a House
ca. 1801–03
Signature: Gakyōjin Hokusai ga
one of four fans mounted on a two-panel folding screen; ink and color on paper
14.3 x 46.5 (upper border) / 22.5 (lower border) cm
F1904.178
cat. 123

Pair of square relief seals: Toki / Masa

This small seal found on fan paintings appears on the following three works:

Flying Cuckoo
ca. 1809
Signature: Tōyō Hokusai
Inscription by: Kawatsura
folding fan mounted on panel; ink and color on paper
17.8 x 50.4 (upper border) / 22.8 (lower border) cm
F1904.187
cat. 44

The following painting depicts a monk burning a branch of flowering plum; beside him is a hatchet:

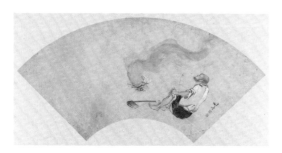

An Old Woodcutter Sitting by a Fire of Blossoming Plum Branches
ca. 1806–10
Signature: Hokusai
fan painting from an album of ten leaves; ink and color on paper
18.1 x 46.2 (upper border) / 19.8 (lower border) cm
F1898.135g

Frog on Lotus Leaf
ca. 1814–15
Signature: Hokusai aratame Taito hitsu
one of four fans mounted on a two-panel folding screen; ink and color on paper
17.5 x 48.4 (upper border) / 20.9 (lower border) cm
F1904.178
cat. 123

In the inscription for *Flying Cuckoo*, the work is dated 1809 (Bunka 6). According to the signature for *Frog on Lotus Leaf*, the work is dated 1814–15 (Bunka 11 or 12), which is especially important for setting the time period during which this seal was used. The woodcutter may be the same figure found in a print in the first volume of *Hokusai manga* that depicts a monk chopping off a branch of a plum tree with a hatchet. An interesting comparison of that work can be made with a fan painting in the Museum of Fine Arts, Boston, entitled *Tanxia Burning a Buddhist Image (Tanka shōbutsu zu)*.[14]

Square relief seal: Gakyōjin
(Man mad about pictures)
The following painting is the only work in the Freer Gallery of Art with this seal:

Shinto Priest, Three Women, and a Child
ca. 1799–1801
Signature: Tōyō Hokusai ga
two-panel folding screen; ink, gold, and color on paper
162.5 x 166.5 cm
F1904.177
cat. 28

Rectangular relief seal: Kimō dasoku
(Hair of turtle, leg of snake)
The following four paintings with the "Kimō dasoku" seal are representative of the Kyōwa (1801–04) and Bunka (1804–18) eras:

Landscape
ca. 1801–02
Signature: Gakyōjin Hokusai ga
hanging scroll; ink and color on paper
28.0 x 59.2 cm
F1904.174
cat. 30

Egret on a Bridge Post
ca. 1801–02
Signature: Gakyōjin Hokusai ga
hanging scroll; ink and color on paper
85.9 x 25.0 cm
F1898.95
cat. 29

Profile View of a Standing Geisha
ca. 1806–08
Signature: Hokusai ga
hanging scroll; ink and color on paper
51.9 x 18.1 cm
F1902.41
cat. 34

The signature and seal only appear on the portrait of Ōtomo no Kuronushi of the following work:

Six Immortals of Poetry
ca. 1806–08
Signature: Katsushika Hokusai
set of six hanging scrolls; ink and color on paper
131.1–132.4 x 53.1–55.5 cm
F1907.368, F1907.369, F1907.370, F1907.371, F1907.372, and F1907.373
cat. 43

The depictions of the landscape and the egret are works from the Kyōwa era, when Hokusai began to use this seal. It is thought that the courtesan scroll was completed during the early Bunka period, and that the *Six Immortals of Poetry* were executed in the mid-Bunka period.

Square intaglio seal: Raishin
The well-known painting of a beauty holding a fan and turning her head is the only work in the Freer collection with this seal:

Woman Holding a Fan
ca. 1810–11
Signature: Katsushika Hokusai hitsu
hanging scroll; ink and color on silk
82.4 x 30.5 cm
F1904.183
cat. 48

Square relief seal: Fumoto no sato
Both of the following paintings are considered a standard against which other works with this seal are compared:

"Early Ferns," Chapter 48 of The Tale of Genji
ca. 1810–14
Signature: Hokusai Taito hitsu
hanging scroll mounted on panel; ink and color on silk
103.1 x 40.5 cm
F1904.184
cat. 63

Woman Holding a Tobacco Pipe
ca. 1814–15
Signature: Hokusai aratame Taito hitsu
Inscription by Ōta Nanpo
hanging scroll; ink and color on silk
71.9 x 26.9 cm
F1898.107
cat. 64

Square relief seal: Yoshinoyama
Multiple versions of the "Yoshinoyama" seal are known. They include those used on painting fee receipts as well as on paintings. The version that appears on a number of standard works (Nagata designates this "Seal A") is found on only one painting in the collection of the Freer gallery. It is the celebrated scroll listed below and is representative of the *bijinga* Hokusai painted during his "Taito" period:

Portrait of a Courtesan Walking
ca. 1815–19
Signature: Saki no Hokusai Taito hitsu
hanging scroll; ink and color on silk
110.4 x 41.7 cm
F1954.119
cat. 68

The "Yoshinoyama" seal can also be deciphered on the following pair of folding screens:

Cherry Blossom Viewing
date uncertain, ca. 1820s–30s
Signature: Shōsei ōju saki no Hokusai Iitsu hitsu
pair of six-panel screens; color on paper
each panel: 81.3 x 216.6 cm
F1903.143 and F1903.144

The seal on this work is the same type, but the "yo" in "Yoshinoyama" is inverted. Nothing much is known about the "Shōsei" in the signature. These are impressive screens, but further study is needed before they can be confidently attributed to Hokusai.

Square intaglio seal: Musashi shimofusa

This seal requires more study, including the way it should be read. It appears on the following painting:

Woman Looking Back
ca. 1810–18 (?)
Signature: Katsushika Taito hitsu
hanging scroll; color on silk
88.0 x 32.2 cm
F1904.185

Opinion is divided on whether this painting is authentic, but the scholars agree that it attains a level high enough for inclusion here. Personally, I believe it is somewhat stiff.

Rectangular relief seal

This seal is called "Hitori ningyō" or "Tsuetsuki rōjin." It appears in woodblock printed books and on documents as well, leaving no doubt that it is one of Hokusai's seals. It is found on the following three paintings:

Fan with Bird and Maples
ca. 1822–23
Signature: Fusenkyo Iitsu hitsu
fan painting from an album of ten leaves; ink and color on paper
16.5 x 45.9 (upper border) / 20.7 (lower border) cm
F1898.135i

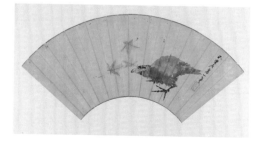

Crustaceans
ca. 1825–30
Signature: Hokusai aratame Iitsu hitsu
hanging scroll mounted on panel; ink and color on silk
47.7 x 60.1 cm
F1902.254
cat. 83

Landscape
ca. 1825–30
Signature: Hokusai Iitsu hitsu
one of four fans mounted on a two-panel folding screen; ink and color on paper
17.2 x 49.5 (upper border) / 22.2 (lower border) cm
F1904.178
cat. 123

The signature on *Fan with Bird and Maples* is close to that on *Pounding Rice for Mochi* (cat. 78; a work that bears the earliest version of the "Katsushika" seal), which means that the two paintings were probably done around the same time. *Crustaceans* is a typical work with this seal.

Square intaglio seal known as Katsushika seal 1

This seal, which reads "Katsushika,"[15] appears most often on Hokusai's late paintings. There are also forged versions of this seal. Hokusai is believed to have used a number of these seals, the earliest of which is designated "Katsushika 1." The "Katsushika" reading is becoming the established interpretation of this seal, but here we will refer to it as "seal 1." From early on, "seal 1" has been considered Hokusai's standard seal. Those paintings in the Freer gallery with the seal are listed below:

Pounding Rice for Mochi
ca. 1822
Signature: Fusenkyo Iitsu hitsu
Inscription by Hinamaro
hanging scroll; ink and color on silk
54.3 x 85.0 cm
F1992.24
cat. 78

Mount Fuji and Enoshima
ca. 1825–31
Signature: Katsushika saki no Hokusai Iitsu ga
pair of two-panel folding screens; ink and color on paper
each screen: 163.2 x 157.2 cm
F1904.175 and F1904.176
cat. 81

A Seated Man Looking at Potted Peonies
ca. 1825–31
Signature: Hokusai aratame Katsushika Iitsu hitsu
hanging scroll; color on paper
127.3 x 54.5 cm
F1903.216

Landscape
ca. 1825–31
Signature: Hokusai aratame Iitsu hitsu
ink and light color on silk
31.1 x 53.1 cm
F1905.228

Country Scenes
ca. 1830–32
Signature: right screen, Saki no Hokusai Iitsu hitsu; left screen, Hokusai aratame Iitsu hitsu
pair of six-panel folding screens; ink, gold, and color on paper
each screen: 150.7 x 350.8 cm
F1902.48 and F1902.49
cat. 88

Flowering Pumpkin Vine and Horsefly
ca. 1825–33
Signature: Saki no Hokusai Iitsu hitsu
hanging scroll mounted on panel; ink and color on silk
34.3 x 53.8 cm
F1898.111
cat. 85

The "Fusenkyo Iitsu hitsu" signature on *Pounding Rice for Mochi* (cat. 78) is consistent with the one on a series of thirty *surimono* published in Bunsei 5 and titled *Horses of Every Fashion* (cats. 93 and 94); the characters in "Fusenkyo" are particularly similar. Thus, it is presumed that *Pounding Rice for Mochi* was painted around the same time. *Seated Man Looking at Peonies* requires more study. Looking carefully, it is clear that about two-fifths of the upper section of the work is composed of separate pieces of paper. The area above the peony is cut out along the lines of the leaves, and paper was applied to fill in the space. The ink wash in the background shows creasing, making it likely that the painting was done as a *sekiga*. However, the work itself, the signature, and the seal pose no problem. *Landscape* is unusual in that it is an ink landscape. Although the painting is small, one can easily perceive the distinctive characteristics of Hokusai's style in the depiction of light and dark shading in the cliff, rocks, and trees; in the way the houses are lined up along the shoreline; and in the technique of making the boats smaller as they move into the distance. The large-scale pair of screens *Country Scenes* is likely related to the publication of *Thirty-six Views of Mount Fuji*, dating the Freer painting to about 1830–32.

F1902.222

Katsushika seal 2

As a result of the investigation undertaken at the Freer, we concluded that there are at least three versions of the Katsushika seal (thus, there is also a "seal 3"). Nagata Seiji has published similar results in recent years.[16] *Six Tama Rivers* is considered a prime example of a work with "seal 2." Three other paintings listed below bear the same seal:

Six Tama Rivers
1833
Signature: Tamagawa rokkei toki ni toshi nanajūyon saki no Hokusai Iitsu hitsu
pair of six-panel folding screens; ink and color on paper
each panel: 132.0 x 47.8 cm
F1904.204 and F1904.205
cat. 89

Poet Semimaru with His Lute in a Bag
1839
Signature: Gakyō rōjin Manji hitsu, yowai hachijū
hanging scroll mounted on panel; ink and color on paper
91.4 x 18.4 cm
F1902.27
cat. 120

A Boy Fishing from the Limb of a Tree
1839
Signature: Gakyō rōjin Manji hitsu, yowai hachijū
hanging scroll; color on silk
77.0 x 29.8 cm
F1902.222

A Herd-boy Seated on a Tree Trunk, Playing a Flute
1839
Signature: Gakyō rōjin Manji hitsu hachijū rei
hanging scroll; color on paper
90.0 x 28.2 cm
F1902.40

The inscription on *Six Tama Rivers* gives Hokusai's age as seventy-four, which corresponds to 1833 (Tenpō 4). The subject is unusual for Hokusai, and it is difficult to know what his intentions were. It is an excellent work, however, one that acts as a kind of comprehensive survey of Hokusai's output during the period. The signature is meticulously brushed in regular script *(kaisho)*, and the seal was carefully applied, creating a very clear impression. *Poet Semimaru* and *Boy Fishing*, which were inscribed when Hokusai was eighty years old, are dated to 1839 (Tenpō 10). Some scholars, including me, do not believe the scroll of the herd boy is a Hokusai work: It is a painting that requires further study. The work is included here because its seal appears to be Katsushika "seal 2." Nagata has pointed out that "seal 2" is found most often on works done when the artist was eighty years old.[17] Since Hokusai only began including his age in his inscriptions when he was eighty years old, Katsushika seals appearing on works done in his late seventies are also likely to be "seal 2." The reason Hokusai stopped using "seal 1" is not clear, but it is difficult to believe that it was because he handed the seal over to his students. Perhaps it was somehow damaged, and unable to bear the thought of not using his beloved seal, he made another. The appearance of "seal 2" on *Six Tama Rivers* suggests that the seal was in use at least by 1833 (Tenpō 4): Logically, one can conclude that Hokusai must have stopped using "seal 1" sometime before that year.

Katsushika seal 3

It is thought that Hokusai began using the third Katsushika seal (called here "seal 3") when he was eighty years old (Tenpō 10), and thus one can reasonably assume that "seal 2" was in use until then. It is unclear why he began to use the third seal. "Seal 3" is recognized as an authentic one that Hokusai used for many years, pressing it onto high-quality works, letters, and other documents. Among the paintings in the Freer gallery, *Handscroll with Miscellaneous Subjects* provides the best seal impression. There are eight other works in the museum bearing the seal, bringing the total number of Freer paintings with "seal 3" to nine. They are listed below:

Handscroll with Miscellaneous Subjects
1839
Signature: Tenpō jū tsuchinoto i no fuyu, Gakyō rōjin Manji hitsu, yowai hachijū
handscroll; ink and color on paper
26.7 x 1365.0 cm
F1902.42
cat. 118

Boy Viewing Mount Fuji
1839
Signature: Gakyō rōjin Manji hitsu, yowai hachijū
hanging scroll; ink and color on silk
36.2 x 51.2 cm
F1898.110
cat. 119

Boat and Rock
1841
Signature: Hachijūni rō Manji hitsu
one of four fans mounted on a two-panel folding screen; ink and color on paper
14.3 x 49.3 (upper border) / 25.7 (lower border) cm
F1904.178
cat. 123

River Landscape: Ferryboat and Mount Fuji
1842
Signature: Gakyō rōjin Manji hitsu, yowai hachijū-san sai
hanging scroll mounted on panel; ink and color on silk
84.8 x 42.2 cm
F1903.109
cat. 124

Zhong Kui (Shōki) Killing a Demon

1842

Signature: Gakyō rōjin Manji hitsu, yowai hachijū-san sai

hanging scroll mounted on panel; ink and color on silk

85.2 x 42.2 cm

F1902.221

Rats and Rice Bales

1843

Signature: Hachijū-yon rō Manji hitsu

hanging scroll mounted on panel; ink and color on silk

90.8 x 29.5 cm

F1904.132

cat. 125

River Landscape

1843

Signature: Hachijū-yon rō Manji hitsu

hanging scroll; color on silk

99.3 x 31.8 cm

F1901.165

Breaking Waves

1847

Signature: Hachijū-hachi rōjin Manji hitsu

hanging scroll; ink and color on silk

126.0 x 46.2 cm

F1905.276

cat. 131

Viewing Cherry Blossoms at Arashiyama

1839–47

hanging scroll mounted on panel; ink and color on silk

37.7 x 64.8 cm

F1902.2

Handscroll with Miscellaneous Subjects comprises approximately twenty-eight paintings. The paintings are not richly colored, but all are finished with meticulous care, demonstrating the charm of Hokusai's brushwork. The seal impression is very clear, and this work can be regarded as a standard for the seal in its early period of use. *Boy Viewing Mount Fuji* displays the coexistence of illusion and mystery, which was a distinctive feature of Hokusai's late paintings. Though characterized as strongly redolent of the modern era, these later paintings comprise a single unified world. The seal impression on *Boat and Rock* is indistinct, which is not surprising given that it is a fan painting. *River Landscape* (left, F1901.165) provides an excellent example of landscape painting from this period. The composition with an image of Shōki is somewhat cramped, and the work tends towards flatness, but in the forcefulness of the brushwork, it recalls the *Bunshōsei* (cat. 127) painting that Hokusai completed when he was eighty-four years old. It is in good condition, and the signature and seal are still clear. The subject of *Rats and Rice Bales* is an auspicious one. *River Landscape* is in light colors and is similar to *Boy Viewing Mount Fuji* and *River Landscape: Ferryboat and Mount Fuji. Rats and Rice Bales* (cat. 125) and *River Landscape* have the same signature: "Hachijū-yon [age eighty-four] rō Manji hitsu." Up until the year before these works were done, Hokusai most often wrote his age using the form "yowai [age] (sai)," but beginning in 1843 (Tenpō 14), he gave the number of years without the "yowai" or "sai" (for example, "Hachijū-yon [eighty-four]"). An exception is the signature on *Zhang Fei in Snowfall (Setchū Chōhi zu; cat. 126)*. After some consideration, it seems that this change represents an identifiable trend in the way Hokusai signed his paintings. *Breaking Waves* displays the seal in its last period of usage. *Viewing Cherry Blossoms at Arashiyama* has no signature and bears only a seal. It is composed in two layers: Arashiyama in spring fills the upper section, while a group of figures is placed in the lower section. Setting aside the question of quality, the painting does not seem especially incompatible with what Hokusai would have done, and "seal 3" is definitely impressed on the work.

This seal is found not only on extant paintings, but also on letters and other documents. It exists on the preface and postscript of the *Nisshin joma* album formerly in the Miyamoto collection, good evidence for Hokusai's use of the seal. The documents on which "seal 3" appears include a painting fee receipt addressed to the Kobayashi Sūzanbō dated the twenty-ninth day of the second month, a letter dated the eighteenth day of the third month and addressed to the Jūhachiya, a receipt from the Jūhachiya for a painting fee dated the twenty-third day of the third month, and four blank forms used for painting fee receipts. All these documents are presumed to date from the end of the Tenpō through the Kōka (1844–48) eras. The preface and postscript to the *Nisshin joma* album was written in 1847 (Kōka 4), when Hokusai was eighty-eight years old.

From the inscription of Hokusai's age on extant works, it is clear that at this stage "seal 3" was probably in use from 1839 (Tenpō 10), when Hokusai was eighty years old, to 1847 (Kōka 4), when he was eighty-eight years old.

Square seal: Fuji image
This seal bears a design in the shape of Mount Fuji. According to Nagata, it was carved in three sizes: large, medium, and small.[18] There is one work in the Freer with the small version:

Tree and Four Red Torii
1843
Signature: Hachijū-yon rō Manji hitsu
fan painting from ten leaves; color on paper
14.6 x 46.2 (upper border) / 22.5 (lower border) cm
F1898.135h

This seal is the same one found on *Portrait of Priest Saigyō* (*Saigyō hōshi zu*) in the British Museum.[19]

Square intaglio seal: Hyaku (One hundred)
The "Hyaku" seal was used during the last three years of Hokusai's life, from the age of eighty-eight until his death at the age of ninety. It appears on the following six paintings:

The Lute and White Snake of Sarasvati (*Benten*)
1847
Signature: Kōka yon hinoto hitsuji shigatsu hatsuka tsuchinoto mi no shirafude o kudasu, hachijū-hachi rō Manji
hanging scroll mounted on panel; ink and color on silk
35.3 x 44.6 cm
F1904.134
cat. 139

Thunder God
1847
Signature: Hachijū-hachi rō Manji hitsu
hanging scroll; ink and color on paper
129.9 x 55.4 cm
F1900.47
cat. 132

Traveler beside a Tree
1847
Signature: Hachijū-hachi rō Manji hitsu
hanging scroll mounted on panel; ink and color on paper
126.2 x 52.3 cm
F1904.186
cat. 138

Flower and Butterfly
1847
Signature: Hachijū-hachi rōjin Manji hitsu
fan painting from an album of ten leaves; ink and color on paper
18.2 x 46.0 (upper border) / 20.0 (lower border) cm
F1898.135d

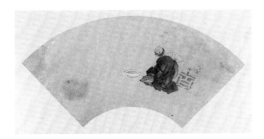

A Man with a Fan, Butterflies, and a Bowl of Water
1847
Signature: Hachijū-hachi rōjin Manji hitsu
fan painting; ink and color on paper
18.4 x 46.3 (upper border) / 20.3 (lower border) cm
F1898.135e

Fisherman and *Woodcutter*
1849
Signature: Kyūjū rōjin Manji hitsu
pair of hanging scrolls; ink and color on silk
right: 113.4 x 39.6 cm; left: 113.1 x 39.6 cm
F1904.181 and F1904.182
cat. 142

The Lute with White Snake is an eerie still life in bright colors. *Thunder God* is a famous masterpiece from the artist's last years. Small pieces of paper were joined together to form the painting surface for *Traveler beside a Tree*, suggesting the work was completed under particular circumstances. It is a profound work, expressive of a strong sense of loneliness. The two fan paintings have a similarly abbreviated brush style, indicating that they were probably done as impromptu works (*sekiga*). In the second fan painting, a piece of cut paper is magically transformed into a butterfly. *Fisherman and Woodcutter*, like *Thunder God*, is a late work known from early on.

The date given in the inscription on *The Lute with White Snake* indicates that the "Hyaku" seal was in use at least by the fourth month of 1847 (Kōka 4). The seal appears on the postscript of the *Nisshin joma chō* and was added at the same time as Katsushika "seal 3." Thus, one should consider the possibility that Hokusai continued to use "seal 3" even after he began to use the "Hyaku" seal. This will be a subject for further research.

WORKS WITH A SIGNATURE ONLY
There are two works that have no seal but are worthy of consideration. The first is a pair of hanging scrolls with a brushed seal-style signature called a *kaō* written in cursive style calligraphy and thought to read "Hoku."

New Year Custom: Makeup on the New Year Morning
New Year Custom: Wish for a New Year's Auspicious Dream
ca. 1806–11
Signature: Hokusai ga
hanging scrolls mounted on panels; ink and color on silk
each panel: 115.6 x 44.2 cm
F1903.52 and F1903.53
cat. 36

Also known as a "New Year Ritual," or paintings of customs of the new year, the above work is thought to be part of a set of three; the third, from a private collection, is a hanging scroll titled *Beauty with Mosquito Netting* (*Kaya bijin zu*).[20]

A Fat Old Man Sitting beside a Large Bell
1820–30
Signature: Hokusai aratame Iitsu hitsu
fan painting from an album of ten leaves; ink and color on paper
14.7 x 46.5 (upper border) / 22.6 (lower border) cm
F1898.135a

Below the signature in the above work is what appears to be a *kaō* in red ink (resembling the sign for infinity). Opinion is divided on whether or not this work is by Hokusai. The signature closely resembles those on paintings with Katsushika "seal 1." It is quite possible that Hokusai painted it while traveling and did not have his seals at hand.

WORKS WITHOUT A SIGNATURE OR SEAL
Other than rough sketches and preparatory drawings, there are two works by Hokusai that do not have a signature or seal:

Various Scenes
ca. 1810
two-panel folding screen; ink and color on paper
each panel: 70.2 x 79.8 cm
F1902.3
cat. 45

Birds, Animals, and Plants Representing the Twelve Months

ca. 1820–35
pair of six-panel folding screens; ink and color on paper
each screen: 179.5 x 376.0 cm
F1904.179 and F1904.180
cat. 86

The first is thought to be a work of the Bunka/Bunsei era, and the second a work of the Bunsei/Tenpō period. There are no signatures on either work, but they are excellent paintings and are, if anything, above the usual level of works ascribed to Hokusai.

It is quite likely that the following two paintings are by Hokusai:

Two Entertainers Strolling at the New Year
ca. 1798–1801
hanging scroll; ink and color on paper
115.0 x 51.6 cm
F1902.178
cat. 25

Standing Figure of a Tall Beauty
ca. 1801–04
color on paper
60.0 x 25.3 cm
F1904.173

Two Entertainers is thought to date from the latter part of the Kansei era (1789–1801), and *Standing Figure of a Tall Beauty* from the Kyōwa. Both are patched, so it seems that they were not originally mounted as hanging scrolls. It is unclear why they are unsigned, and they need to be thoroughly studied.

In addition, the Freer collection includes forty-one sheets of *hanshita-e*, final drawings for the woodblock print series "One Hundred Poets," and ninety-two sheets of rough sketches by the Hokusai school. That the former is extremely important as a product of Hokusai's "Manji" period needs no further explanation here. The latter set mixes drawings by Hokusai himself and those by the artists in his circle. As none are signed, judgment must be on the basis of the works themselves—a difficult job, to say the least.

I would like to conclude with an introduction to one of these sketches, a charming work titled *Hotei and Chinese Child Acrobats* (*Hotei to karako*; cat. 145). The work is related to the *Chinese Children and the Character Meaning "Long Life"* (*Juji to karako*) in the Museum of Fine Arts, Boston.[21] The instructions, "the Chinese boys should be drawn behind Hotei," are inscribed on the Freer sketch indicating that it must have been done as a model for Hokusai's students.

Translated by Carol Morland

1. Asano 1991.
2. Nikkei 2005, cat. 50.
3. Nagata 2000, no. 111; Nikkei 2005, cat. 477.
4. Illustrations of the works mentioned can be found in the following publications: *The Bird of the Capital*–Lane 1989, pls. 42, 43; Nikkei 2005, cat. 125. *Panoramic Views along the Banks of Sumida River*–Lane 1989, pls. 60-61, 56-57, fig. 185, 302; Nikkei 2005, cat. 130.
5. These works are illustrated in the following publications: *Pilgrims Worshiping the Great Buddha*–Nagata 2000, no. 27; Nikkei 2005, cat. 157. *Returning from a Foliage-Viewing Excursion*–Nagata 2000, no. 37.
6. Nagata 2000, no. 73.
7. Carpenter 2005, 161.
8. Images of the mentioned works can be found in the following publications: *The Story of Evil Foxes in Three Countries (Sangoku yōko den)*–Nagata 1985, 41. Actors on Stage (Yakusha shibai zu) ibid., 72.
9. Illustrations of the works mentioned can be found in the following volumes: *Matching Warriors of Japan and China for the Soramitsuya Circle*–Nikkei 2005, cat. 391. *Five Sibling Pictures of China and Japan for the Zakurogaki Circle*–ibid., cats. 392-93.
10. Nihon Art Center 1991, 11:1-55.
11. Nagata 1990, 2:no. 3; Nikkei 2005, cat. 495.
12. The author contributed research on Hokusai's seals for "Hokusai no nikuhitsuga no inshō ni tsuite" (Seals on Hokusai's paintings). *Siren, Bulletin of Chiba City Museum of Art,* no. 1 (March 1994). The English version is published in Carpenter 2005.
13. Nagata 1997; idem 2000.
14. Nagata 2000, no. 98 (bw).
15. The reading of this seal is not certain. Here, I use the conventional reading of "Katsushika."
16. Nagata 2000, 223-40.
17. Ibid., 235.
18. Ibid., 237-38.
19. Ibid., no. 280 (bw).
20. Nagata 1990, vol. 3, no. 5.
21. Nagata 2000, no. 286 (bw).

CATALOGUE

SHUNRŌ

1779-94

1 Shōki and Demon
ca. 1793-94
Signature: Kusamura Shunrō ga
Seal: kaō (handwritten seal)
hanging scroll; ink and color on paper, 53.6 x 26.0 cm
Katsushika Hokusai Museum of Art, Tsuwano
Literature: Fenollosa 1901, cat. 2; Nagata 1998, 75-76;
Nagata 2000, no. 3 (color); Nikkei 2005, cat. 46.
(1-133)

2 Women in Various Walks of Life
ca. 1793
two hanging scrolls; ink and color on paper, left: 106.8 x 52.7 cm; right: 107.0 x 52.5 cm
Katsushika Hokusai Museum of Art, Tsuwano
Provenance: Baron Funakoshi collection.
Literature: Asahi 1993, no. 1; Nagata 2000, no. 1 (color), 2; Nikkei 2005, cat. 45.
(1-3)

During the Kaiyuan era (713–41) of the Tang dynasty (618–907) in China, Emperor Xuanzong (r. 712–56) was suffering from an illness. Zhong Kui (J: Shōki), a scholar-official from Mount Zhongnan appeared in the emperor's dream and captured the small demons that were troubling him, thereby purifying him of evil. The emperor's illness was cured. When Xuanzong awoke from the dream he commanded the artist Wu Daoxuan to paint Shōki's portrait, which is said to be the origin for this type of image. Since that time Shōki has been venerated as a deity who subdues evil, and in Japan his image is typically made into dolls and painted onto banners and hanging scrolls for use at the annual Boys' Festival (Tango no sekku) on the fifth day of the fifth lunar month. It is also thought that the color red is effective in subduing evil, thus Shōki's portrait is often painted in that color. This work is a variant of the so-called "Red Shōki" (see cat. 134).

Here, Shōki is shown subduing a small demon painted in black. It is a powerful work that effectively contrasts the heroic Shōki with the helplessness of the demon. Nevertheless, the line quality is not particularly well ordered and the kind of effortless brushwork seen in paintings from Hokusai's "Sōri" period onward is not yet apparent. This work is very significant, however, as the only surviving painting bearing the Shunrō signature. As previ-

ously mentioned, it is likely that the painting was commissioned for the Boys' Festival. In the biography *Katsushika Hokusai den* written by Iijima Kyoshin in 1893, an episode about the artist's "Sōri" period is recorded that may be relevant:

One day a certain person requested a banner for the Boys' Festival. Sōri immediately prepared some red paint, did a picture of Shōki and gave it to him. The man was highly delighted and rewarded (the artist) with two gold *ryō*. For Sōri, who was suffering in poverty, these two gold *ryō* were riches beyond belief. It was thanks to this money that he was able to make a name for himself in later years (Iijima 1999, 9).

The handwritten seal (*kaō*) on this work is unique to the artist's "Kusamura Shunrō" period. The same seal is used on the fan print *Ebisu and Daikoku Performing a Manzai Dance* (Nikkei 2005, cat. 27) and also on *Party Hand-game*, a calendar print for the New Year in 1794. A handwritten seal of a slightly different form is found on works from the 1780s, such as *Fudō Myōō* (*hosoban* print) and *Blue-faced Kongō* (tall *hosoban* print; Nikkei 2005, cats. 6 and 7; Asahi 1993, nos. 10 and 11). It should also be mentioned here that yet a third type of handwritten seal is found on the printed illustration *Warbler in the Deep Mountains* (cat. 24) in the album *Miyama uguisu*, published in 1798. AS

Hokusai made his debut in the art world at the age of twenty, using the name Katsukawa Shunrō. He would continue to use this name for the next fifteen years. Throughout this period, he followed the style of his teacher, Katsukawa Shunshō, producing prints of actors and beautiful women and illustrated books. His early output also included paintings, but only a few examples have survived. The two scrolls here carry no signature or seal, but they are certainly among the rare extant paintings of beautiful women from Hokusai's early "Shunrō" period.

Eight women, who together represent a range of social classes, are shown here. The group includes denizens of the pleasure quarters, such as an apprentice courtesan (*shinzō*) and a courtesan dressed in white for the Hassaku Festival during mid-autumn, as well as a townswoman and lady-in-waiting from

a samurai household. The conception is the same as for *Five Beauties* (Seattle Art Museum), which was produced somewhat later, when the artist used the name Hokusai (Nagata 2000, no. 58 [color]).

In considering the style of this work, the first two things to note are the hairstyles, which are characteristic of the Kansei period (1789–1801), and the sweetly rounded faces, several of which clearly reflect the style of Katsukawa Shunshō. Hokusai used the Katsukawa style as a starting point, and then altered it to a certain degree. A similar style is shown in the painting of a beauty with an early "Sōri" signature (cat. 17) and in woodblock printed book illustrations with a "Shunrō" signature. There is good reason to believe that the paintings were produced at the end of Hokusai's "Shunrō" period, around 1793. NM

3 Fashionable Directions in the Eastern Capital: Myōkendō Hall of Hosshōji, Yanagishima
Fūryū Tōto hōgaku: Hosshōji Myōkendō no zu
ca. 1787–88
Signature: Shunrō ga
ink on paper; *hanshita-e*, 18.1 x 25.0 cm
Victoria and Albert Museum E.5087-1910
Literature: Nagata 2000 cat. 137 (bw), 2058; Keyes 2003, 16–17; Nikkei 2005, cat. 35.
(1-154)

4 Fashionable Directions in the Eastern Capital: Fudō at Meguro
Fūryū tōto hōgaku: Meguro Fudō
ca. 1787–88
ink on paper; *hanshita-e*, 17.1 x 25.1 cm
Victoria and Albert Museum E.5090-1910
Literature: Nikkei 2005, cat. 44.
(1-155)

5 Actor Nakamura Nakazō I as Tenjiku Tokubei, in Reality Sōkan
Tenjiku Tokubei, jitsuwa Sōkan: Nakamura Nakazō
1783 (eighth month)
Signature: Katsu Shunrō ga
color woodblock print; *hosoban*, 30.3 x 15.1 cm
Ōta Memorial Museum of Art
Literature: Asahi 1993, cat. 2.
(1-29)

6 Hares and Roses
ca. 1783
Signature: Katsu Shunrō ga
color woodblock print; *hashira-e*, 66.7 x 12.1 cm
The Art Institute of Chicago, Clarence Buckingham Collection 1925.2873
(1-99)

These two drawings are final sketches (*hanshita-e*) for a series of prints in the *aiban* format. Nishimuraya Yohachi published four of the color prints (Nikkei 2005, cat. 34, 59, 308). Ten designs are known through the final sketches in the Victoria and Albert Museum, the only extant drawings from the earliest phase of Hokusai's career when he worked in the studio of his teacher Katsukawa Shunshō. All the designs for this series were composed in the shapes of folding or flat fans. These drawings are very important for the insight they provide into Hokusai's brushwork, process of design, and artistic models, which included Chinese sources. For example, the background around the fans in some finished prints is black and the large-scale calligraphy, carved into the printing block, is white. This departure from conventional black on white inscriptions suggests that Hokusai was familiar with the appearance of rubbings of stone engravings of Chinese calligraphy inscriptions (Nikkei 2005, cat. 34). A two-character inscription in the Myōkendō drawing is written in the archaic Chinese seal script style.

The drawings also reveal aspects of Hokusai's own religious beliefs and practices and his familiarity with important sites in Edo and their significance to his contemporaries. Large-character calligraphy (reading from right to left), which gives the series title at the top and the title of the work below, surrounds the folding-fan format. The design shows

two women and a man visiting the Myōkendō, a hall at the Buddhist temple Hosshōji, which was dedicated to the bodhisattva Hokushin Myōken, the Buddhist deity of the North Star. Roger Keyes has interpreted this image in terms of the significance of North Star worship for Hokusai, whose name means "North [Star] Studio." Keyes considers the concentric composition of this image, which is centered on the white circle among the pine needles to the left of the young man's head, to be related to the star gazing practice associated with North Star worship, an important element of Hokusai's religious beliefs and practices. Keyes interprets the small white circle as a visual allusion to a name for the large pine tree, which was known as star descending pine (*hoshifuri matsu*), because it was believed that the North Star came down from the sky and appeared in it (Keyes 2003, 17).

Hokusai's drawing in the form of a flat fan, which has an oval shape indented at the top, is probably based on a Chinese form. The example shown here shows pilgrims bathing for purification in a waterfall at a site dedicated to the Buddhist deity Fudō Myōō (Alcalanatha). Near the center, a man squats as water pours over his head, dividing as it falls. A woman turns to look over her shoulder in a pose that Hokusai would frequently repeat in his paintings of beautiful women. AY

Hokusai designed this print early in his career, when he was a young artist in the studio of Katsukawa Shunshō, who specialized in actor prints. This print portrays Nakamura Nakazō (1736–90) in the role of Tenjiku Tokubei, a favorite character of kabuki and puppet dramas imaginatively developed from historical tales of the Japanese merchant Takamatsu Tokubei, who returned from India in 1633. Tokubei received instruction in toad sorcery. In this scene the magical toad sits beside the actor Nakamura Nakazō, who portrays Sōkan in the guise of Tokubei. The elaborate garden setting confines the actor in a tight foreground space, which increases the tension of his threatening pose. The landscape includes a waterfall splashing over rocks in stylized curls, an early manifestation of Hokusai's interest in depicting water in motion. AY

This print is a unique impression of a design of animals and flowers that Hokusai completed in his first years as a young artist of the Katsukawa school when he was known as Shunrō. Pillar prints (*hashira-e*) like this example were said to be designed for display on the supporting pillars of a Japanese commoner's house. The long, narrow format was especially effective for close-up views like this print of hares in a garden with roses in bloom. The work reveals Hokusai's deliberate control of composition and focus as well as his early interest in the natural world, a subject that ukiyo-e artists at the time rarely portrayed. He rendered the animals with strong three-dimensional forms in a space low in the foreground, while arranging the plants vertically along one side. Such contrasts between density and open space remained an important feature of Hokusai's compositions throughout his life. The limited palette of red and green recalls *benizuri-e*, prints published prior to the development of techniques for printing full-color prints (*nishiki-e*). AY

7 Eight Views of Fashionable Dandies: Evening Bell of Yazaemon
Fūryū otokodate hakkei: Yazaemon no banshō
ca. 1785
Signature: Shunrō ga
Publisher: Nishimuraya Yohachi
Publisher seal: Eijudō
Collector seal: "HV" (Henri Vever)
color woodblock print; *chūban*, 21.9 x 16.1 cm
Freer Gallery of Art, Smithsonian Institution,
gift of the family of Eugene and Agnes E. Meyer F1974.73
Provenance: Eugene and Agnes E. Meyer; Henri Vever.
Literature: Asano 1998, fig. 4.
(1-28)

8 Night Attack of the Forty-seven Loyal Retainers of Akō
Chūshingura uchiiri
ca. late 1780s
Signature: Shunrō ga
Publisher: Nishimuraya Yohachi
color woodblock print; *ōban* triptych, each sheet: 39.3 x 26.3 cm
Ōta Memorial Museum of Art
Literature: Edo Tokyo Hakubutsukan 1995, I-13.
(1-54)

This print is a unique surviving impression of a design from the series *Eight Views of Fashionable Dandies.* The series is one of many Japanese transformations of the *Eight Views of the Xiao and Xiang (Xiao-Xiang bajing),* a Chinese subject made famous in poetry and landscapes inspired by the scenery around the confluence of the Xiao and Xiang rivers. In Japan, Chinese ink landscape paintings of the theme became popular among elite warrior patrons and Zen Buddhist monks of the Kamakura (1185–1333) and Muromachi (1333–1573) periods. During the Edo period, especially in ukiyo-e, the subject was further transformed to the incongruous urban settings of Edo's floating world.

Today only six of the eight prints of young, flashy men from "Eight Views" are known. The subtitle of this print pairs the name Yazaemon with the imagery of an evening bell, which in the landscape series comes from a distant Buddhist temple. In contrast, this work portrays a young man gazing over his shoulder at a beautiful courtesan as he departs from a room decorated with a Chinese-style landscape and calligraphy that allude to the original poetic and artistic tradition of the "Eight Views." The figures in this design, which Hokusai created in his mid-twenties, reveal mastery of figure drawing, textile patterns, architectural settings, as well as his ability to understand the breadth of artistic knowledge — beyond the usual boundaries of the floating world — that his teacher, Shunshō, possessed. AY

This unusual *ōban* triptych created in Hokusai's youth portrays the final vendetta of the forty-seven masterless samurai (*rōnin*) against Kira Yoshinaka (1641–1702). The *rōnin* served the daimyo of Akō Castle, Asano Naganori (1665–1701). Asano was forced to commit suicide after drawing his sword in Edo castle against Kira, who had provoked Asano through his arrogant behavior. After failing to regain their master's domain, his loyal retainers lay in wait for two years before gathering on the agreed date, the fifteenth day of the twelfth month of the fifteenth year of the Genroku era (January 13, 1703) to avenge their master's unjust death. For their unsanctioned action, the forty-seven *rōnin* were ordered to commit suicide. The story became famous throughout Japan as a paradigm of samurai values, especially of the paramount importance of loyalty and honor.

Triptychs are rare among Hokusai's early prints, but in this larger format he created a complex architectural space that serves as a stage for many scenes of dramatic action as the *rōnin* storm Lord Kira's mansion in Edo. Hokusai's early experience as a book illustrator is apparent in his treatment of individual scenes, but the composition as a whole lacks the spatial and visual unity that he was able to achieve in his later designs. He must have been familiar with kabuki enactments of the scene, but this print conveys a sense of realism, and the vignettes within it have elements of pathos and even humor (as found in the courtyard scene of men in loincloths protecting their heads with basins) that appear often in Hokusai's book illustrations. AY

9 New Edition Perspective Picture:
Viewing Fireworks in the Evening
Breeze at Ryōgoku Bridge
*Shinpan uki-e Ryōgokubashi yūsuzumi
hanabi kenbutsu no zu*
ca. 1788–89
Signature: Katsu Shunrō ga
Publisher: Nishimuraya Yohachi
color woodblock print; *ōban*, 24.4 x 38.2 cm
The British Museum 1906.12-20.472
Literature: Oka 1974, fig. 7; Asahi 1993,
cat. 30; Calza 2003, fig. I.4A.
(1-27)

From midsummer through early fall, residents of Edo enjoyed the evening cool
(*yūsuzumi*) and fireworks displays sponsored by prosperous restaurants and
pleasure boat operators along the Sumida
River (Smith 1986, cat. 98). Hokusai's "perspective picture" incorporates techniques
of converging perspective that ukiyo-e
artists adopted as early as the 1730s from
the European art that Dutch traders
brought to Nagasaki. This picture focuses
on the busy vendors' stalls at the head of
the bridge and the crowds of people of
various social classes making their way to
and from the wide bridge. Pleasure boats
ranging from the large *yakatabune* (palace
boat) festooned with lanterns to smaller
covered boats and simple river ferries and
service vessels are depicted on the river.
Hokusai's focus on the crowds rather than
on the interiors of the shops — which in
pictures by other artists are often exposed
through the traditional Japanese device of
omitting the roofs of buildings that are
viewed from above — enhances the realism of his perspective view. Around 1830,
Yorozuya Kichibei published a later
reprint of this design with additional color
blocks and other modifications (Calza
2003, no. I.4B). AY

10 Actor Ichikawa Ebizō IV as the Monk
Mongaku
1791 (eleventh month)
Signature: Shunrō ga
Publisher: Tsutaya Jūzaburō
Publisher seal: Trademark of Tsutaya Jūzaburō
Censor seal: *kiwame*
color woodblock print; one sheet of
a diptych, *hosoban* 31.4 x 13.5 cm
The British Museum 1904.1.10.02
Literature: Asano 1998, fig. 3;
Forrer 1991, cat. Ia; Calza 2003, no. I.11.
(1-24)

11 Actor Sakata Hangorō III as Chinzei
Hachirō Tametomo
1791 (eleventh month)
Signature: Shunrō ga
Publisher: Tsutaya Jūzaburō
Publisher seal: Trademark of Tsutaya Jūzaburō
Censor seal: *kiwame*
color woodblock print; one sheet of
a diptych, *hosoban*, 31.4 x 13.5 cm
Museum of Fine Arts, Boston, William
Sturgis Bigelow Collection 11.1992
Literature: Forrer 1991, cat. Ib;
Asano 1998, fig. 2; Calza 2003, no. I.11.
(1-25)

This pair of prints depicts two prominent actors in a scene from the season-
opening kabuki play *The Golden Hilt
Ornament and Square Swordguard of the
Minamoto Family (Kin no menuki Genke
no kakutsuba)*, which was performed at
the Ichimura Theater in 1791. Hokusai
has followed the house style established
by his teacher, Katsukawa Shunshō, who
created a realistic style of portraiture
within the established genre of narrow
single-sheet actor prints. The actors
strike a *mie,* a fixed pose held at a dramatic climax in the performance. In this
scene, the monk Mongaku at left is disguised as a bandit while the warrior at
right is disguised as an itinerant monk.
AY

12 Water Seller
ca. 1793
Signature: Kusamura Shunrō ga
Seal: *kaō* (written seal)
color woodblock print; long *surimono*, 23.0 x 51.0 cm
Katsushika Hokusai Museum of Art, Tsuwano
Literature: Nikkei: 1998, 55–57; Asano 2005, 58–64; Ōta 2004, cat. 125; Nikkei 2005, cat. 29.
(1-41)

This *surimono* by Hokusai has been well
known in the West since the publication
of Edmond de Goncourt's *Hokousaï* in
1896, and it is one of the earliest extant
surimono by Hokusai. The signature,
Kusamura Shunrō, was one he used for a
brief period after the death of his
teacher, Katsukawa Shunshō, at the
beginning of 1793, the twelfth month of
the fourth year of the Kansei era, according to the Japanese lunar calendar.
Hokusai's name appears in this form on
privately commissioned *surimono* published between 1793 and late 1794, when
he began to use the name Sōri (Keyes
2003, 18). Beneath a magnificent old pine
tree, a young vendor of cold water rests
on the carrying-pole set across his water
buckets as he wipes his towel across his
body to cool himself. The majestic pine
and the open space to the left, an important feature in many of Hokusai's prints
and paintings, enhance the unassuming
charm of the youth. Asano Shūgō notes
that the symbol on his apron is the crest
of the *tokiwazu bushi*, musicians who
perform ballads. He also suggests that
the original complete *surimono* might
have included a *tokiwazu* program
(Nikkei 2005, 307). *Surimono,* especially
those that *haikai* and *kyōka* poets commissioned, provided a wider range for
Hokusai's artistic interests than commercially published prints with a narrower
range of subjects. AY

13 Various Moral Teachings for All Time
Kyōkun zō nagamochi
5 volumes, *dangihon* (moralizing tale)
1784
Signature: Katsukawa Shunrō ga
Author: Itō Tanboku (1680-1758)
Publisher: Nishimiya Shinroku and Kazusaya Rihei
color woodblock printed book; stitched binding (*fukurotoji*), 22.2 x 15.6 cm
The Art Institute of Chicago, gift of Martin A. Ryerson 4-1-18, 761.952H71 kyk, v.5, 26180
Literature: Toda 1931, 228-9;Hillier 1980, 19-20; Edo Tokyo Hakubutsukan 1995, cat. 17.
(1-146)

Illustrations for inexpensive fiction known as yellow-covers (*kibyōshi*) and other stories were an important source of income for the atelier of Katsukawa Shunshō, where Hokusai began working in 1778 as a young artist of nineteen. As an apprentice, Hokusai's assignments regularly included book illustrations. He designed illustrations for more than fifty titles during his fifteen years in the Katsukawa school, and Hokusai's books of this period provide important evidence for his work in the formative phase of his professional career.

This double-page illustration in the five-volume *Kyōkun zō nagamochi,* a book of moralizing tales, reveals Hokusai's increasing familiarity with a wide variety of artistic styles, as well as his talent for creating clear, focused compositions within the small format of book illustration. The scene illustrates a poor scholar who bought a hanging scroll of Hotei, a Zen Buddhist sage who became a popular deity, and dreamt that Hotei emerged from the painting to help him attain success. The principal figures are placed in the foreground, with the folding screen and lamp forming a vertical frame for the scholar as he listens attentively to Hotei. The hanging scroll in the display alcove (*tokonoma*) at left is blank, and Hotei, depicted in the broad brushstrokes of an ink painting, emerges from the scroll as a pattern of dots representing his imaginary appearance trace his path. Hokusai's mastery of a variety of brush techniques and painting styles can be seen in the pictures he incorporated within this scene. The folding screen at right shows a Japanese-style seascape with stylized waves and clouds. The door behind Hotei is painted with broad, expressive brushstrokes in techniques derived from Chinese painting. By incorporating paintings in various styles into his assigned work as a book illustrator and print designer, Hokusai was able to satisfy and express his interest in artistic styles beyond the more limited repertory of ukiyo-e. AY

SŌRI

1795-98

14 Plum Blossoms
ca. 1795-98
Signature: Hokusai Sōri ga
Seal: Kanchi
Inscription: See below.
Inscription signature: Yomo no Utagaki Magao
hanging scroll; ink and color on paper, 116.5 x 34.0 cm
The British Museum 1982.7-1.03 given by Dr. and Mrs. Michael Harari
Provenance: Ralph Harari; Janette Ostier; Louis Gonse.
Literature: Goncourt 1896, 291; Gonse 1926, no. 662; Hillier 1966, no. 6; Hillier 1970, no. 102; Clark 1992, no. 95; Lane 1994, no. 3.21, 61; Nagata 2000, no. 4; Keyes 2005, no. 20, 28-29; Nikkei 2005, cat. 132.
(1-80)

15 Blossoming Plum Branches
ca. 1795-98
Signature: Sōri ga
Seals: Hokusai, Sōri
Inscription: See below.
Inscription signature:
Hōkyō of Ōtorinodai
folding fan mounted on a panel;
ink and color on paper, 17.4 x 46.2 cm
Freer Gallery of Art, Smithsonian Institution, gift of Charles Lang Freer F1898.135b
Literature: Nagata 2000, no. 11 (bw).
(1-84)

Plum blossoms and the cries of the warbler (*uguisu*) are the harbingers of spring. Here white flowers bloom once again on the attenuated branches of an old, gnarled plum tree, symbolic of the eternal cycle of renewal. A verse hovers above the branches, like the absent warbler that we often hear but find so hard to spot. It reads:

Uguisu no	The first singing of the warbler
hatsune wa oya no iken yori	Is more impressive Than listening to parents' objections
kikeba mi ni shimu haru no asaoki	To getting up early On a spring morning. (Clark 1992, 145)

The leading poet of the time, Yomo no Utagaki Magao (1752–1829), composed this playful *kyōka* and wrote it directly onto the painting.

There has been debate in recent years as to whether this painting is by Hokusai or his pupil Tawaraya Sōri III to whom he passed on the Sōri name in the spring of 1798 (Lane 1994, 61; Keyes 2005, 22). The work bears a large round red seal with the name Kanchi, which Hokusai would also have passed on to his pupil, since some works clearly in the style of Sōri III bear the same seal. Hokusai passed on his names and seals to pupils several times during the course of his long career. In the case of the present painting, authorship hinges on whether the name

Hokusai may have been interpolated at a later date above a signature that originally read just "Sōri." After carefully observing the painting in a variety of lighting, there is no reason to doubt that the entire signature was not written at one and the same time. This should be regarded as a genuine work by Hokusai, which clearly relates to his other paintings of flowering plum trees completed around this time (see cat. 15).

The main branch thrusts forcefully in a diagonal across the bottom of the scroll, beginning a bravura display of ink painting in which Hokusai must have rapidly added the other, progressively smaller branches and twigs to form a complicated tangle. Next came the blossoms, each with a different shape and drawn at a different stage of bloom. The petals are filled with a wash of shell white (*gofun*) and, in the case of the open flowers, tiny stamens were added in pale yellow. Viewed in certain lights it is clear that there is a very light wash of pale blue across much of the background of the scroll — impossible to detect in a photograph — which must represent the early morning mist. Although quickly painted, the whole production was in fact carefully calculated in advance. Emblematic of this calculation is the way in which Hokusai deliberately allowed the hairs of the brush to split open as each branch was drawn, so that the areas of white reserve suggest the gnarled bark (and continuing vigor) of the venerable plum. TC

This work is a fan painting of plum blossoms, brushed in a rapid, abbreviated style. Several other fan paintings in similar style survive from the years after the artist began to use the name Hokusai. This work, however, dates from the previous "Sōri" period, around 1795 to 1798, when Hokusai also began to enthusiastically design *surimono* (privately commissioned woodblock prints).

The circumstances of Hokusai's succession to the name Sōri remain uncertain. He inherited the name from Tawaraya Sōri (fl. ca. 1764–80), one of the leading artists of the Rinpa school in Edo, but his style shows little influence from the two great early Rinpa masters in Kyoto, Tawaraya Sōtatsu (d. 1643) and Ogata Kōrin (1658–1716). However, Hokusai seems to have taken an interest in Rinpa subject matter at least, since such favorite Rinpa motifs as irises and plum blossoms begin to appear in his work at this time. In terms of its subject then, the present fan

painting contributes to an understanding of Hokusai's approach to his craft in the early stages of his career. The arching tree trunk, brushed in a single rapid stroke, is found in another, larger hanging scroll of the same subject in the collection of the British Museum (cat. 14). Nothing is known about the author of the inscription, other than his name Hōkyō and the fact that he was a resident of Ōtorinodai in Shimōsa Province (modern Chiba Prefecture). The inscription reads:

> After the many darling blossoms have fluttered down,
>
> the pure moonlight and one flower-laden branch
>
> express the joy of spring

NM

Translation of poem by Alfred Haft

16 Young Man
ca. 1795–98
Signature: Sōri ga
Seal: Kanchi
hanging scroll; ink and color on paper,
50.9 x 21.0 cm
Freer Gallery of Art, Smithsonian Institution,
gift of Charles Lang Freer F1903.130
Literature: Fenollosa 1901, pl. 6; Carpenter
2005, no. 9, 47.
(1-11)

From his "Sōri" period to his "Hokusai"
period, Hokusai produced a considerable
number of paintings brushed in shades
of ink with only occasional touches of
color. At first glance, the figure here
appears to be a woman, but the hairstyle
indicates that this is a handsome youth,
known during the Edo period as a
wakashu. The surcoat (*haori*) and bamboo hat (*kasa*) suggest that he is on an
outing about town. The composition and
the depiction of the figure in full profile
are quite typical of the artist's work during the late Kansei period (1789–1801),
when he used the name Sōri. The surface
of the painting is somewhat damaged. An
illustration in the catalogue of the
Hokusai exhibition organized by Ernest
Fenollosa in 1900 indicates that, extend-
ing from the right edge of the present
painting, there was once an additional
area that contained an inscription by a
certain Kitoku (Fenollosa 1901, pl. 6).
Presumably this section was trimmed off
during a later remounting. NM

17 Courtesan
ca. 1796–98
Signature: Hokusai Sōri giga (Informally painted by Hokusai Sōri)
Seal: Kanchi
hanging scroll; ink and color on paper, 70.9 x 24.0 cm
Freer Gallery of Art, Smithsonian Institution, gift of Charles Lang Freer F1903.129
Provenance: Kobayashi Bunshichi 1903; Honma Kōsō.
Literature: Fenollosa 1901, no. 20; Stern 1973, no. 84; Stern and Narazaki 1981, 16:no. 51; Nagata
2000, no. 8 (color).
(1-2)

In the middle of the night a courtesan
has left her bed to go to the bathroom.
Some seven hairpins support her
Katsuyama-style hair arrangement,
indicating that she is a high-ranking
courtesan in the Yoshiwara pleasure
quarter. She wears an outer robe over
her nightdress and is biting the collar.
Holding a roll of tissue, she walks in a
disheveled manner, and her expression
is distracted, with a hint of sadness.
The emphatically crooked pose,
whereby her body is bent forward at
the waist, is typical of Hokusai's work.
A sense of sadness and hopelessness
permeates her entire body, and Hokusai
is even able to suggest the still air of the
dead of night. The careful rendering of
the right collar of the overrobe so that
it appears to rise up as the courtesan
bites it, is indicative of an overall
scrupulous attention to detail.

This subject was also a specialty of
Kitagawa Utamaro (d. 1806), who was
then at the height of his career. Examples
include *Hour of the Ox*, from the series
The Twelve Hours in Yoshiwara (Asano
and Clark 1995, no. 151), *Hinazuru of the
Keizetsurō (Chōjiya)* from the series
Comparing the Charms of Beauties (ibid.,
no. 172), and *Ōgiya Hanaōgi* from a
series with picture-riddle titles (ibid., no.
213). *Hour of the Ox*, in particular, is similar in composition and mood, and it is
possible that Hokusai took Utamaro's
print as his point of departure and then
arranged the figure in his own way.

It is likely that this was a commissioned
work. The use of the term "informally
(or playfully) painted" in the signature
may reflect the artist's embarrassment
with respect to the vulgar subject of a
courtesan going to the toilet. AS

18 Woman Walking beneath a Willow Tree
ca. 1797–98
Signature: Hokusai Sōri ga (Painted by
Hokusai Sōri)
Seal: Tokimasa (or Tatsumasa)
hanging scroll; ink and color on paper,
99.7 x 28.0 cm
Hosomi Museum, Kyoto
Literature: Narazaki 1982, no. 3; Asahi 1993,
no. 5; Nagata 2000, no. 11 (color); Calza
2003, no. II-8; Carpenter 2005, no. 4, 37 and
no. 3, 107; Nikkei 2005, no. 136.
(1-12)

In essence, this is an ink painting. The
limited coloration means that, at first, it
conveys a somewhat murky impression.
Yet, close examination reveals it to be a
work of great interest.

A pale moon has begun its nightly
ascent, and bats flit through the gathering darkness. The branches of a willow
descend along one side, creating vertical
movement within the composition. In
the center, the tall figure of a beautiful
woman offers an echoing form, augmented by the ends of her sash, which
hang straight down behind her. Only the
umbrella tucked under her arm lends
variety, with its diagonal alignment.

Since the woman is seen from behind,
with her head covered by a towel, her
facial expression remains undisclosed.
Yet the viewer is able to supply the
emotional meaning of the picture, after
learning that the woman is a streetwalker, colloquially termed a "nighthawk"
(*yotaka*), the lowest type of prostitute in
the city of Edo. As a verse of the period
candidly expressed it:

19 The Chinese Immortal Yuzhi
Dragon with Qin
1798
Signature: Hokusai Sōri ga
Seal: Shizōka
pair of hanging scrolls; ink and color on paper, each scroll: 125.4 x 56.5 cm
Private collection
Provenance: Azabu Museum of Arts and Crafts, Tokyo; Hayashi Tadamasa.
Literature: Sansai 1985, no. 495; Forrer 1988, no. 86; Asahi 1993, no. 3; Kobayashi 1995, 6:nos. 54-55; Calza 1999, no. II.12; Nagata 2000, nos. 14-15 (color); Carpenter 2005, 16-19, 30; Nikkei 2005, cat. 140.
(1-129)

Hitome mo kusa mo Neither the public eye nor a patch of grass

itowanu wa causes her the least discomfort:

yotaka nari she's a nighthawk

The "nighthawks" of Edo would walk the streets in search of customers willing to pay the meagre sum of twenty-four *mon*. Hokusai's artistry has turned this coarse figure into an idealized beauty.

The signature "Hokusai Sōri" and seal "Tokimasa (Tatsumasa)" indicate that the picture was painted around 1797–98, during the latter part of Hokusai's "Sōri" period. The slender, elongated figure of the woman and the stillness of her pose characterize Hokusai's pictures of beauties during this period. Ink with light coloration is another feature of the numerous beauty paintings from the "Sōri" and early "Hokusai" periods. Eventually, though, in the subsequent "Hokusai" period, quite different figures—with neck bent forward or twisted body—became the norm. NM

Translation of poem by Alfred Haft

In this painting, the female immortal Yuzhi stands imposingly amid black clouds. Doubtless at her summoning, a coiling and writhing dragon comes flying through the clouds. It brings her musical instrument, a one-stringed zither (*qin*). According to ancient Chinese lore, Yuzhi (Japanese, Gyokushi; alternative name Taizhen Wang [Japanese, Taishin'ō] "Lady of Exulted Sublimity") was the third daughter of Xiwangmu (Japanese, Seiōbo), the "Queen Mother of the West." She often played her zither, at the sound of which one hundred birds would come flocking. Sometimes she would ride on a white dragon, sporting around the four oceans. Here Yuzhi and the dragon are shown on separate scrolls, originally mounted on the panels of a two-fold screen. This is an unusual variant on the normal iconography, which typically shows Yuzhi riding on the back of the dragon (Hokusai's pupil Hyakurin Sōri III painted such a standard version on a hanging scroll in about 1800; see Narazaki 1944, pl. 40).

Roger Keyes has written in detail on this painting and demonstrated that it must have been done about the second or third lunar month in the spring of 1798, just before Hokusai announced that he was changing his name from Sōri to Hokusai Tatsumasa, thereby affirming a new, independent identity as an artist (Carpenter 2005, 16–19, 30). Spiritual strength to support this bold transition was drawn from his veneration of the deity of the North Star, the bodhisattva Myōken. The dragon is a symbol of the North Star, and the art-name Hokusai itself relates to these beliefs.

Fundamental to such an interpretation of the present painting is Hokusai's use of the rare seal "Shizōka," which Keyes translates, inspiringly, as "My master is creation." A cosmic subject was called for at such an important juncture in Hokusai's career. Keyes also demonstrates that elements of Hokusai's painting derive from a monochrome book illustration in Kano style (1745), by the Osaka artist Tachibana Morikuni (1679–1748); although Hokusai made a bold and dramatic adaptation of this source image.

The winsome facial features, with a somewhat quizzical expression emanating from the slightly raised eyebrows, are familiar from the small *surimono* prints of beauties designed by Hokusai at this time. The scale here, however, is truly monumental, and this must be regarded as one of the most important works, if not the culminating one, of the artist's "Sōri" period. Apparently effortlessly, the expressive qualities of the brushwork constantly change, whether for fluid outlines of robes, patterns on drapery, spikes and spines on the face of the dragon, or for the diffuse forms of storm clouds. Shell-white is used to great effect as a significant color in its own right. Finally, rich black ink is spattered over the surface of both scrolls in energetic flourishes.

Accompanying the paintings is an additional scroll with an inscription by Hayashi Tadamasa, the major Japanese art dealer active in Paris at the end of the nineteenth century (dated April 11, 1890). In this, Hayashi dates the painting (spot on) to 1798 and describes some of Hokusai's subsequent changes of name. TC

20 Viewing Cherry Blossoms at Mount Asuka
Asukayama no sakura dai
Signature: Hokusai Sōri ga
color woodblock print; long *surimono*, 19.2 x 52.0 cm
Private collection
(1-40)

21 Grasshopper, Morning Glories,
and Taro Plant
ca. 1798
Signature: Sōri aratame Hokusai ga
(by Sōri changed to Hokusai)
color woodblock print; long *surimono*,
40.4 x 57.2 cm
Collection of Joanna H. Schoff
(1-63)

22 Artisan's Workshop from the *kyōka*
album, *Mists of Sandara*
Sandara kasumi
1798
Signature: Hokusai Sōri ga
color woodblock print from an album,
22.0 x 31.5 cm
The Art Institute of Chicago, Clarence
Buckingham Collection 1925.3205
Literature: Forrer 1991, cat. 114.
(1-14)

A cherry tree in full bloom overhangs a festive multicolored curtain where a gathering for poetry composition is taking place. Above three poems is an inscription in Chinese characters in the archaic seal script style that reads "cherry tree *dai* at Mount Asuka." The term *dai* was a topic or classification in Japanese poetry that also provided an organizational principle for anthologies (Miner 1985, 272). Poems on the seasons were the principal group of *dai*, and cherry trees by association are a seasonal subtheme associated with spring, just as red maples are representative of

autumn. The three poets whose names appear here are Hana no Edozumi, Zeniya Kinratsu, and Yomo no Magao. The title of this *surimono*, which was commissioned by a poetry club, sets the scene at Asukayama, a site on the outskirts of Edo that was famous for its spring cherry blossoms and for parties exempt from the usual regulations imposed by the shogun's government. Excursions to view the cherry blossoms and to enjoy such pastimes as sipping sake and reciting poetry were an annual highlight of the spring season in Edo. AY

Hokusai's artistry as a designer of *suri-mono* can be appreciated in this close-up image of a grasshopper clinging to a large taro leaf with morning glories and bellflowers in a garden setting. The exquisite block carving and printing that were possible in *surimono*, which were printed in very small editions, allowed Hokusai full expression of nuances of color and line that would have proved impractical in commercially published prints. The first edition of this print has poems printed in the space below the image and a silver full moon shrouded in mist behind the taro leaf. The image, without the moon, was reprinted with a program for a performance at the bottom. The printed sheet was intended to be folded horizontally so the writing could be read vertically from the top open edge to the fold. AY

This beautiful illustration of an artisan's workshop was published in the second edition of a *kyōka* album titled *Mists of Sandara (Sandara kasumi)*. Hokusai placed the woodturner's workshop in the foreground with a view of Mount Fuji appearing above mist in the distance. Hokusai's developing mastery of group figure compositions, color, and landscape are apparent in this image. Overprinting created several of the unusual hues, and the image features skillful gradations *(bokashi)* of color. Within the scene, a woman turns toward a traveler to offer tea while other women assist a craftsman who remains engrossed in his work. Behind them is a screen with a collection of prints and fan paintings. AY

23 *Shikinamigusa*
1 volume, *kyōkabon*
1796
Signature: Hyakurin Sōri ga
Compiler: Seiryōtei Kangi, preface by
Banshōtei
color woodblock printed book; stitched
binding; 22.5 x 16.5 cm
The British Library 16099.c.60.folio 7 verso
Literature: Hillier 1980, 25; Toda 1931, 234.
(1-56)

24 Warbler in the Deep Mountains
Miyama uguisu
1 volume, *kyōkabon*
1798
Signature: Hokusai Sōri utsusu (copied by
Hokusai Sōri)
Seal: *kaō* (written seal)
color woodblock printed book;
orihon, 19.4 x 26.3 cm
The British Museum 1979.3-5.0.410/JH 410
Literature: Hillier 1980, 31; Forrer 1991, no.
112; Calza 2003, 431-32.
(1-79)

This book of *kyōka* is illustrated with
imaginative pictures from tales and legends, often of distant lands. Illustrated
by Hokusai with New Year *kyōka* by
members of the Yomo poetry club, the
pictures show a variety of people from
distant and often imaginary places. This
page depicts the land of long-armed
people, with one figure playing a drum
and one holding aloft a ring with a performing monkey. Hokusai's art name
Sōri is coupled here with the name
Hyakurin, another early art name that
he used. AY

For a small album of *kyōka* verses,
Hokusai created a single ink print of a
plum branch in bloom, a symbol of late
winter and of literary pursuits. The
paper is blind printed with an uninked
block to create a texture that resembles
silk, a favored support for high-quality
paintings. Poets commissioned *kyōka*
albums for limited circulation among
members of their poetry clubs.
Illustrations for these books were commissioned from leading artists to
enhance the beauty of the verses. Often
more than one artist participated, and
because of their artistic quality, the illustrations were often removed from the
poems and collected as if they were single-sheet prints. Hokusai's inscription
indicates that it is based on a work by
Ogata Kōrin (1658–1716), for whom the
Rinpa school, first established in seven-
teenth-century Kyoto, was retrospectively
named. The simplicity of Rinpa paintings may have encouraged Hokusai's
interest in isolating single subjects such
as plants, animals, and even human figures, in open space. His artistic quota-
tion of Kōrin is evidence for Hokusai's
early familiarity with a wide variety of
painting styles. AY

25 Two Entertainers Strolling at the New Year
ca. 1798-1801
hanging scroll; ink and color on paper, 115.0 x 51.6 cm
Freer Gallery of Art, Smithsonian Institution, gift of Charles Lang Freer F1902.178
Provenance: Michael Tomkinson.
(1-39)

26 Woman with Umbrella beside a Willow Tree
ca. 1802-03
Signature: Gakyōjin Hokusai ga (Painted by Hokusai, Man mad about painting)
Seal: Tokimasa/Tatsumasa
hanging scroll; ink and color on silk, 83.5 x 25.0 cm
The Hokusai Museum, Obuse
Literature: Hokusaikan 1985, 11; Nagata 1990, 3:no. 8; Asahi 1993, no. 13; Kobayashi 1996, 5, no. 13 (Hokusai Museum); Calza 2003, no. III.17; Carpenter 2005, 206-07, no. 18.
(1-13)

This painting depicts a pair of street performers—the master *(tayū)* and his comic sidekick *(saizō)*—as they stroll from house to house on New Year's Day, bringing blessings and humor to the common people of Edo. The New Year's pine decoration in the painting symbolizes longevity. This type of street entertainment, known as "Mikawa Manzai," dates from the medieval period. The master carries a special fan called a *chūkei,* and his sidekick carries a drum. The two might dance and chant blessings in time to the drum, or they might engage in a comic dialogue; either way, Mikawa Manzai is an auspicious annual custom. Here, the two figures may be father and son, and the younger figure is playing with a puppy.

This quintessential New Year's subject, painted entirely in light colors, is occasionally found among other works of the artist's "Hokusai" period, for example the Manzai painting in the collection of Sumida ward, Tokyo (Nagata 2000, no. 26 [color]). Despite surface damage to the present painting, the style is readily identifiable as that of Hokusai. Nevertheless, since the work lacks a signature, the attribution must remain tentative. The painting dates from around the late Kansei (1798–1801) to early Kyōwa (1801–04) eras. NM

The young woman in this work is shown in a somewhat haughty pose, arching her back like a bow and glancing back over her shoulder. She carries a flamboyant "snake's-eye" umbrella and wears high clogs, which suggests a scene just after a rainfall. Upon close examination, there are certain details that indicate this is no everyday outfit, but perhaps the special costume of, say, a dance performer. For instance, the pronounced décolletage of the outer robe shows off her shoulder underneath; also, she seems to have tucked her long, hanging left sleeve into the back of her sash. Furthermore, the high clogs look to be painted with black lacquer and are decidedly top quality and impractical. Thus, Hokusai placed a woman who does not come from the ordinary, everyday world, on a country road beneath a willow tree.

The trunk and branches of the willow form a gentle curve, echoing the pose of the woman's body and enveloping her in their embrace. Elements of the composition are similar to Hokusai's earlier works: He used the same manner for depicting the trunk of the willow in *Oxen and Willow* (Katsushika Hokusai Museum of Art, Tsuwano), and the forms of the beauty and willow branches are reminiscent of *Woman Walking beneath a Willow Tree* (Hosomi Museum, Kyoto; cat. 18). However, this painting probably dates from a few years later and gives the strong impression that Hokusai has now become more confident in his handling. Here we see the beginnings of the extraordinary explorations of form that will become such a pronounced feature of Hokusai's works during the subsequent Bunka era (1804–18). The manner of depicting the figure can also be seen as the culmination of the sweet, fragile type of beautiful woman typical of the artist's earlier "Sōri" period. Space was left at the top of the scroll so that an inscription could be added. AS

27 Ono no Komachi
ca. 1798-1801
Signature: Hokusai ga
Seal: Tokimasa (or Tatsumasa)
Inscription: See below.
Inscription signature: Inscribed by Teishō at the practice hall of the Bashō school
hanging scroll; ink and color on paper, 109.1 x 38.0 cm
Private collection
Literature: Kaneko 1975, no. 12; Asahi 1993, no. 16; Nagata 2000, no. 23; Nikkei 2005, cat. 150.
(1-43)

This is a portrait of the mid-ninth-century poet Ono no Komachi (fl. ca. 833–57), the only woman among the Six Immortals of Poetry (*rokkasen*). Ki no Tsurayaki (ca. 868–945) mentioned the Six Immortals of Poetry in his famous preface (*kanajo*) to *Collection of Verses Ancient and Modern* (*Kokinshū*), the first imperially commissioned poetry anthology.

Tsurayuki described Ono no Komachi as belonging to "the same line as Soto'orihime of old. Her poetry is moving and lacking in strength. It reminds one of a beautiful woman suffering from an illness. Its weakness is perhaps due to her sex" (McCullough 1985, 7). Komachi is conventionally depicted as a ravishing beauty of the ancient imperial court. In this work, Hokusai followed that tradition, and he shows her admiring a row of distant cherry trees, perhaps in reference to Komachi's famous poem:

Iro miede   So much have I
utsurou mono wa   learned:
yo no naka no   the blossom that
hito no kokoro no   fades away,
hana ni zo arikeru   its color unseen,
     is the flower in the
     heart
     of one who lives in
     this world

This is one of several paintings that the artist produced during the late Kansei era (1789–1801), when he began to use the name Hokusai. The works are signed "Hokusai-ga" with the round red character seal "Tokimasa (Tatsumasa)." In this example, however, Komachi's

elongated face shows lingering traces of the artist's style from the previous "Sōri" period.

The inscription on the painting, which is written by Teishō, may be translated as:

On the street, I acquired the ceramic figure of a woman and brought her home. She keeps me company on sleepless nights. She never speaks or laughs, but also never succumbs to anger or jealousy. Although she coldly refuses to drink alcohol, she has grace enough not to consume food. She wears the same garment season after season, but what a relief that neither the winter's chill nor the summer's heat makes any difference to her! If she lives to be a thousand years, her figure will never change. And I will not have to worry about making her sad as I grow old, or leaving her a young widow.

> Far beyond my reach,
> those blossoms on the high peaks,
> there just for the looking.

I was asked to consider this inscription by Raizan and to provide my own. Having noticed a chrysanthemum floating by in the wind, I decided to add the following:

> Even the mountain hermit
> keeps a pale bride:
> the fragrant chrysanthemum.

Inscribed by Teishō at the practice hall of the Bashō school. NM

Translation of poem from McCullough 1985, 12
Translation of inscription by Alfred Haft

28 Shinto Priest, Three Women, and a Child
ca. 1799-1801
Signature: Tōyō Hokusai ga (by Hokusai, of Edo)
Seal: Gakyōjin
two-panel folding screen; ink, gold, and color on paper, 162.5 x 166.5 cm
Freer Gallery of Art, Smithsonian Institution, gift of Charles Lang Freer F1904.177
Provenance: Kobayashi Bunshichi, 1904; Honma Kōsō.
Literature: Stern 1960, no. 10; Stern 1973, no. 88; Stern and Narazaki 1981, 16:no. 52; Nikkei 1982, 7:no. 21.
(1-131)

In early summer each year, at the beginning of the fourth month, a curious festival was held at the Tsukuma Shrine in Ōmi Province (modern-day Shiga Prefecture). Local women attended the shrine and were expected to carry on their heads the same number of cooking pots as the number of men with whom they had had relations. Anyone who did not tell the truth risked incurring the wrath of the deity. The scene of this two-fold screen seems to depict that event.

Sheltered by a huge ancient tree within the precincts of the shrine, a Shinto priest waves sacred white paper streamers (*gohei*) in blessing over a group of three women and a child. Each of the three women carries a single pot on her head. The child dangles a small toy and tugs at the hand of his minder, who from her bent posture, plain clothing, and shaved eyebrows must be older than her two companions. The poses of the women as they try to retain appropriately solemn composure while balancing the pots on their heads are amusingly rendered, and the energetic forward stance of the priest and tugging of the boy both introduce movement to the composition. Perhaps the mighty tree trunk, painted in rich deep tones of ink, is included to give the sense that this same ritual had been repeated in the same sacred place, for

many hundreds of years. The clothing of the figures is rendered in brilliant color, in contrast to the subdued ink and wash used for the setting.

Along the central fold of the screen, the formations of ink wash that describe the ground plane do not match up. This suggests that during a remounting the panels were slightly reduced in size. The square seal with red characters that reads "Gakyōjin" (Man mad about painting) is thought to have been used by Hokusai for only a very few years around 1800, perhaps from 1799 to 1801 (Asano 2005, 114). "Tōyō" (meaning Edo) in the signature implies that either Hokusai was not in Edo when he painted the screen, or that the client was not from Edo. It is tempting to suggest that Hokusai might even have painted the screen at (and for) the Tsukuma Shrine, but there is currently no evidence that he traveled outside of Edo at this time. In fact, according to the illustrated guidebook *Famous Places in Ōmi* (*Ōmi meisho zue*, 1814), by that time younger girls (around ages eight to twelve), who wore hunting cloaks and court hats and carried substitute paper cooking pots on their heads, had replaced the adult women in the festival (Ikeda 1981, 11:98). That is the form the festival retains to this day. TC

29 Egret on a Bridge Post

ca. 1800–02
Signature: Gakyōjin Hokusai ga (Painted by Hokusai, Man Mad about Painting)
Seal: Kimō dasoku
hanging scroll; ink and color on paper, 85.9 x 25.0 cm
Freer Gallery of Art, Smithsonian Institution, gift of Charles Lang Freer F1898.95
Provenance: E. S. Hull 1898.
Literature: Nagata 2000, no. 31.
(1-94)

A white egret (*shirasagi*) perches on a metal ornament, which is shaped like a "sacred jewel" (*gihōju*) and decorates the top of a bridge post. With its legs stiffly vertical, feathers fluffed up, and head tucked down against its breast, the bird appears completely motionless. Perhaps after diving into the river below and swallowing a fish, it is drying its plumage while digesting its meal. A brief episode like this could well be described in a haiku poem.

The work was painted quickly and appears deceptively simple. The shape of the body was achieved entirely with "outside shading" (*sotoguma*) in pale gray ink, with deft touches of white on the plumage and breast. Broad, rough strokes in dark ink combine to capture the rounded shape of the metal ornament, which gives it convincing three-dimensionality. During this period, Hokusai normally used such an abbreviated ink wash style for fleeting depictions of beautiful courtesans and youths of the pleasure quarters. Thus, its use in the depiction of the subject here is quite unusual.

Very little damage around the edge of the "kimō dasoku" seal suggests a date early in its use, about 1800–02. The art-name "Gakyōjin" was also used in signatures from about 1800 onward. TC

30 Landscape

ca. 1801–02
Signature: Gakyōjin Hokusai ga (Painted by Hokusai, Man Mad about Painting)
Seal: Kimō dasoku
hanging scroll; ink and color on paper, 28.0 x 59.2 cm
Freer Gallery of Art, Smithsonian Institution, gift of Charles Lang Freer F1904.174
Provenance: Kobayashi Bunshichi 1904; Honma Kōsō.
Literature: Fenollosa 1901, no. 30; Stern and Narazaki 1981, 1: no. 13 (bw); Nagata 2000, no. 30 (color).
(1-107)

This ink-wash landscape is painted in the most abbreviated style. Houses, trees, and an embankment are depicted at water's edge facing toward a lake (or the sea) on the left. The land continues to the left side and in between is a plank bridge that is higher in the center than at the ends. This shape of bridge is seen quite often in works by literati (*bunjin*) painters in the Edo period and Hokusai would have been aware of such examples. Above and below the bridge, waves are painted in pale ink, against a wash of pale blue. A few mountains appear in the middle-ground and background of the upper part of the composition; the distant mountains are painted in pale blue to distinguish them from those in the middle. A large amount of empty space exists around the edge of the landscape, resulting in a light and stylish work.

Hokusai continuously explored new subjects and techniques and, although he did many paintings in ink technique, it is sur-prising that his ink landscapes are so rare. There is another example in the Freer collection: a horizontal composition painted on silk that, on the basis of the signature and seal, must date from around 1830. The brushwork used for the trees, mountains, and buildings in this second landscape is in the more forceful style characteristic of Hokusai's mature works. In comparison, the abbreviated ink-wash style of the present painting evokes a sense of clear and fresh airiness that is most appealing.

The rectangular, red-character "kimō dasoku" seal was the one Hokusai used most often from around 1801 to 1813. It is found on between fifty and one hundred surviving works. There is little damage to the outlines of the seal on this painting, suggesting it was created during the earliest period when the seal was used. AS

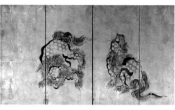

31 Chinese Lions

ca. 1801–04
Signature: Gakyōjin Hokusai ga (Painted by Hokusai, Man Mad about Painting)
Seal: Kimō dasoku
four-panel folding screen; ink on paper with gold leaf, 54.0 x 96.0 cm
Tokyo National Museum
Literature: Tokyo National Museum 1995, no. 42; Nagata 2000, no. 47; Calza 2003, III:48; Nikkei 2005, cat. 188.
(1-139)

Two Chinese lions, one seated and the other in motion, are painted against a gold-leaf background. Lions are not native to Japan, so Japanese artists of the pre-modern period depicted them as mythological creatures, almost as religious deities. Throughout his life, Hokusai produced numerous versions of this subject in the form of small paintings, sketches collected in the *Hokusai manga*, and, during his last years, painting exercises undertaken to bolster his spirits and preserve the vigor of his brush style when he was afflicted with palsy (the so-called *Daily Exorcisms [Nisshin joma]*). The style of the present painting has several elements in common with academic Chinese-style painting of the Kano school, notably the heavy outlines. The screen was probably produced as a decoration for the Boys' Festival on the fifth day of the fifth lunar month. It dates from the period when the artist used the "Gakyōjin Hokusai" signature, from the Kyōwa (1801–04) to early Bunka (1804–18) eras. NM

32 Carp
ca. 1801–10
Signature: Kōto Gakyōjin Hokusai ga
(Painted by Hokusai of Edo, Man Mad
about Painting)
Seal: Kimō dasoku
hanging scroll; ink and color on silk,
101.9 x 44.0 cm
Kōhōan Inoue Collection, The Museum
of Modern Art, Gunma
Literature: Calza 2003, III:77.
(1-102)

33 Woman Reading a Letter
ca. 1804–05
Signature: Kukushin Hokusai sekiga
(Painted at a gathering by Kukushin
Hokusai)
Seal: Kimō dasoku
ink and color on silk, diameter: 30.5 cm
Cincinnati Art Museum, The Thomas
Collection; Given by Mrs. Murat H. Davidson
in Honor of Her Grandfather, Joseph C.
Thomas 1982.14
Literature: Nagata 2000, no. 41; Nikkei
2005, cat. 196.
(1-18)

34 Profile View of a Standing Geisha
ca. 1806–08
Signature: Hokusai ga
Seal: Kimō dasoku
hanging scroll; ink and color on paper,
51.9 x 18.1 cm
Freer Gallery of Art, Smithsonian Institution, gift of Charles Lang Freer F1902.41
Provenance: S. Bing, 1902; Hayashi sale, no. 1599.
Literature: Stern and Narazaki 1981, 16:no. 112; Nagata 2000, no. 65 (bw).
(1-10)

Artists of the Maruyama-Shijō school, founded in the late eighteenth century by the Kyoto painter Maruyama Ōkyo (1733–95) produced the most noted depictions of this subject. In Maruyama-Shijō school works, the carp is generally depicted swimming at liberty in streams, marshes, and lakes. The term "painted from life" (*shasei*) usually conveys the essence of the Maruyama-Shijō style. The ukiyo-e artist Utagawa Hiroshige (1797–1858) is generally credited with absorbing the broad influence of the style. It is possible, however, to trace hints of the Maruyama-Shijō style in Hokusai's painted work, albeit only in his depictions of birds and flowers. A painting of freshwater trout, in an album produced during Hokusai's Manji period, is a good example (Nagata 2000, nos. 90–99).

The painting shows very little influence from other schools; rather, it is a forceful expression of Hokusai's individuality. His artistic interests are revealed most clearly in the swirling form and almost human expression of the carp. Similar fish are seen in *Carp and Turtles* (Saitama Prefectural Museum; Nagata 2000, no. 63), and in the set of paintings entitled *Six Tama Rivers* (cat. 89). NM

Although the title of this work is *Woman Reading a Letter*, the young woman with her hair arranged in Shimada-style is looking at a slim booklet. This may be a music book for practicing *nagauta* or *jōruri* chanting. She appears to be biting a winter cherry. It is clearly summer, since she wears a thin black gauze robe. She is of quite an innocent age, yet Hokusai gives her the full facial beauty of a mature woman. The signature includes the art name Kukushin, which also appears on a *surimono* of 1805 and was probably used only for a short period. This painting must therefore date from almost exactly that time. The term *sekiga* (painting done at a gathering) also appears in the signature, which implies that the work was done at one of the so-called "calligraphy and painting parties" (*shogakai*), where artists performed for an audience. However, the high level of finish — each line is unwaveringly painted and many colors are employed — suggests otherwise. There is another half-length portrait of a woman with the same *sekiga* notation titled *Picking Tea* (about 1807-08, Ōta Memorial Museum, Tokyo) with similar carefully applied colors. AS

A young woman in rich, elegant attire — thought to be a geisha — is shown from the side, her head in exact profile. Lifting one toe and leaning back slightly, there is the suggestion of motion; perhaps she responds to music playing at a party or simply makes a stylish entrance. Overall, the effect of the painting is light, deft, and spontaneous. The skirt of her robe seems to point upward, echoing and exaggerating her lifted toe. The front of her sash forms a similar rising shape. The pale blue robe is decorated with a pattern of young fern fronds and is lined with a silk starfish pattern in red. The stiff brocade sash that hangs down almost straight at the back has a pattern of clouds and lucky jewels.

Thickly swelling ink lines in a variety of tones describe the outlines and folds of the geisha's costume, a visual suggestion of the weight and sheen of the rich silk fabrics. The single most bravura line, done at some speed, snakes around to create the hem of the skirts. All the detailing of the head and face, from the tiny lines for eyebrow, eye, nostril, and lip, to the oiled hair that coils around the hairpins, is abbreviated, yet the result is vividly alive.

Breaks are visible in the outline of the "Kimō dasoku" seal in seven or more places, which, combined with the "Hokusai" signature suggests a date in the early Bunka era (1804–18). At this time Hokusai fully developed the complex ink-and-wash figure style that he had begun in the preceding "Sōri" period. TC

35 Five Women Examining Fabrics
ca. 1806–11
Signature: Katsushika Hokusai ga (Painted by Hokusai, Man mad about painting)
Seal: Kimō dasoku
Inscriptions: See below.
Inscription signature: Nōbutei Sankyū (Mimari) dai (Inscribed by Nōbutei Sankyū [Mimari])
Inscription seal: Sankyū (Mimari)
hanging scroll; ink and color on silk, 40.8 x 78.9 cm
Hosomi Museum, Kyoto
Literature: Nikkei 1967, no. 13; Narazaki 1982, no. 12; Ōta 1985, no. 533; Forrer 1988, no. 178; Asahi 1993, no. 44; Nagata 2000, no. 48; Nikkei 2005, cat. 202.
(1-4)

The women in this scroll are examining fabrics, probably the latest designs put on sale at the New Year. Two richly dressed young women stretch out a length of red fabric with a white tie-dyed pattern. There are two more bolts of cloth and a pair of scissors beside them. A third companion holds her head in her hands and looks intently at the cloth. The senior figure in the group is seated on a patterned mat, holding a pipe and with a smoking set and open brazier to her side. Judging from her shaved eyebrows, she is married, perhaps to a merchant. She looks over to the crouching woman who holds one hand to her mouth as she speaks and the two seem to be exchanging comments. Based on her apron, simpler hairstyle, and respectful posture, she is likely a maid.

Two poems are inscribed in the top-left corner. The first is a Chinese-style couplet, and the second is a *kyōka* signed Nōbutei Sankyū (Mimari), a name that is otherwise unknown. The content of both verses is crude in comparison to the refinement with which Hokusai painted the women, and it may be that someone unconnected with the original production of the work added the inscription later. The verses read:

Gachū gunjo	The group of women in the painting
kao [ni] yō [ga]	sport dimples on
moyōshi	their faces
gagai ippu	the solitary man outside the painting
kuchi [kara] sen [ga] izu	has drool coming from his mouth
Kimi ga tame	Because of you
me ni shōgatsu wa	my eyes are full of enjoyment
shidaretomo	nevertheless
kokoro ni okosu	my heart beats fast
bonbon bonnō	with desire

Wordplay that juxtaposes the auspicious New Year holidays with the early autumn Bon Festival, which celebrates returning spirits of the dead, is woven into the second poem.

Many breaks in the outline around the "Kimō dasoku" seal, resulting from increasing wear and damage, suggest a date between about 1806 and 1811; relatively late during the period when Hokusai used this seal. (From around 1810 to 1811 he began to use the name Taito, not seen here, and then in 1813 passed on the "Kimō dasoku" seal to his pupil Hokumei.) The figures feature the simple, fluid ink outlines, rich costumes, and delicate, slightly pinched facial features typical of Hokusai's paintings from this time. Five kneeling figures are skillfully balanced around two strong diagonals, which are placed on a ground plane and spread back convincingly into the painting. TC

Translation of poem by Timothy Clark

36 New Year Custom: Makeup on the New Year Morning
New Year Custom: Wish for a New Year's Auspicious Dream
ca. 1806–11
Signature: Hokusai
Seal: Handwritten seal (*kaō*)
hanging scrolls mounted on panels; ink and color on silk, each panel: 115.6 x 44.2 cm
Freer Gallery of Art, Smithsonian Institution, gift of Charles Lang Freer F1903.52 and F1903.53
Provenance: Siegfried Bing: Hayashi Tadamasa
Literature: Hayashi sale 1903, lot 1667; Stern 1960, 16; Stern 1973, nos. 85 and 86; Stern and Narazaki 1981, 16: no. 110.
(1-16)

At right, a woman is tying a picture of a lucky treasure ship to her pillow, so that her first dream of the New Year will be an auspicious one. In former times it was customary to refer to the first New Year dream with the phrase "One: Mount Fuji, two: hawk, three: aubergines" (*Ichi Fuji, ni taka, san nasubi*). There are various explanations for this phrase: One is that this is simply a list of the most famous things from Suruga Province (modern Shizuoka Prefecture). Another is that this is a list concocted by the first Tokugawa shogun Ieyasu (1542–1616) of the most important things in Suruga, in terms of their elevation and/or value. An additional theory is that this is an auspicious phrase that, on the basis of various associations and wordplay, means "succeeding in everything" (*monogoto o nashitogeru*). In any case, it is clear that during the Edo period, the first dream of the New Year encompassed an individual's most fervent hopes and wishes.

Judging by the large porcelain bowl, which was used for gargling, and the toothbrush on the wooden stand, the second painting captures a moment when a woman is engaged in her morning toilette. Therefore, both paintings feature a scene from daily life, but each woman is presented in quite a monumental manner.

What strikes the viewer first and foremost in both compositions is the flowing quality of the drapery lines, which are nonetheless a bit stylized. These lines almost look like written calligraphic characters that form a picture (*emoji*). They have a quality that is slightly at odds with the lines normally found in Hokusai's work. Yasuda Gōzō, in *Gakyō Hokusai*, has suggested that during the Bunka era (1804–18) a studio of pupils assisted Hokusai in his work (Yasuda 1971). This could account for the difference in line style. In view of the many demands on Hokusai at this time, perhaps some work was divided up among the pupils of his school, first and foremost the students Hokkei (1780–1850) and Hokuba (1771–1844). Regardless, the paintings clearly appear to date from the period when the artist was using the Hokusai name (in the early to mid-Bunka era), and the handwritten seal (*kaō*) is of a type that he is known to have used at this time. Therefore, these works warrant attribution to Hokusai. AS

37 The Courtesan Eguchi as the Bodhisattva
Fugen and the Monk Saigyō
ca. 1806–11
Signature: Katsushika Hokusai ga
Seal: Kimō dasoku
framed *shikishi*-format album leaf;
ink and color on silk, 26.4 x 21.5 cm
John C. Weber Collection
Literature: Ōta 1985, no. 534; Asahi 1993, no. 43;
Nagata 2000, no. 53 (color).
(1-142)

38 Preparatory sketch for *The Courtesan
Eguchi as the Bodhisattva Fugen and the
Monk Saigyō*
ca. 1806–11
ink on paper, 26.4 x 18.0 cm
Freer Gallery of Art, Smithsonian Institution,
gift of Charles Lang Freer F1904.423
Provenance: Kobayashi Bunshichi 1904.
Literature: Nagata 2000, 275.
(1-143)

39 Daikoku Carrying a Giant Radish
ca. 1806–13
Signature: Katsushika Hokusai hitsu
Seal: Kimō dasoku
hanging scroll; ink and color on paper,
58.4 x 25.0 cm
Katsushika Hokusai Museum of Art, Tsuwano
Provenance: Said to have come from the
collection of Edmond de Goncourt.
Literature: Nagata 1987, 128–29; Asahi 1993,
no. 41; Nagata 2000, no. 56 (col.).
(1-149)

In the thirteenth century, various tales in the collection of *Selected Stories* (*Senjūshō*), and the nō play *Eguchi* by Kan'ami (1333–84), featured encounters between holy men and prostitutes who finally reveal themselves to be manifestations of Buddhist deities. The version of the story that has endured almost to present times features a meeting and exchange of poems between the traveling monk-poet Saigyō (1118–90) and Eguchi, a courtesan of a brothel in a town of the same name. When Eguchi refuses Saigyō lodging, he protests:

yo no naka ni	Indeed it may be hard
itou made koso	to reject
kata karame	the world,
kari no yodori o	but you begrudge
oshimu kinu kana	a temporary lodging

To which the courtesan replies:

ie o izuru	Seeing you were the one
hito toshi mireba	who had left his home
kari no yado ni	I only thought
kokoro tomu na to	your mind should not dwell
omou bakari zo	on temporary lodgings

Eguchi implies that this world of illusion is nothing more than a "temporary lodging," and the monk should have "left his home" (and secular life) behind. In the climax of the *nō* play, the prostitute reveals that she is in fact a manifestation of the bodhisattva Fugen (Sanskrit: Samantabhadra) and ascends to the Western Paradise seated on the back of a white elephant.

The spiritual message is clear: One must look beyond appearances—even a prostitute might be a Buddha.

By Hokusai's day, the subject had been treated many times by earlier ukiyo-e artists, generally in a light-hearted manner that could even verge on comic. This was one of dozens of classical subjects considered appropriate for recasting in contemporary terms.

A preparatory drawing for the painting is in the collection of the Freer gallery (cat. 38). Apart from revealing many changes that Hokusai made to the sketch, the figures were drawn on separate pieces of paper suggesting that he probably moved them about relative to one another in order to decide their final positions. The finished painting creates a strong sense of separation between the mundane and spiritual worlds with the dignified, aged monk and the ethereal, beautiful woman literally facing each other down. The contrast between the crisp, angular drapery of the monk's robes and the seductive, flowing lines of the courtesan's costume further emphasize this point. Most of the outlines of the elephant were overpainted and thereby softened with white, to lend an otherworldly aspect to the lumbering beast. Small, crisp details were finally picked out in rich black.

The "Katsushika Hokusai" signature and the substantial damage to the outline of the seal suggest a date between 1806 and 1811. TC

These three small sketches pasted to a larger sheet of paper are important documents of Hokusai's methods for determining the exact placement of figures. The monk gazing upward and the beautiful woman seated on an elephant are the subject of a small full-color painting by Hokusai (cat. 37) depicting a famous encounter between the Buddhist priest and poet Saigyō and the courtesan Eguchi. The figures were sketched in brush and ink on thin paper, then cut out, moved into position, and pasted onto this sheet, which also includes a sketch of a courtier who may be another famous poet. A partial drawing of Saigyō's face is repeated to test a slightly varied expression. When Freer purchased this drawing in 1904, its significance as a preparatory study for a specific finished painting was not known. Today, it is recognized as a rare and valuable document of Hokusai's artistic technique. AY

The giant "two-legged radish" (*futamata daikon*) in this work is deliberately and humorously suggestive of a woman's body. Daikoku, one of the Seven Lucky Gods who bring wealth, stoops forward as he carries the radish on his shoulders. Rats served as messengers of Daikoku, and on "rat" (*kinoe-ne*) days, it was customary in merchant households to make offerings of radishes and other foods to Daikoku in the hopes of attaining success in business. This helps to explain the frequency with which the subject was painted in the Edo period; such scrolls must have been displayed as part of the ritual. Few artists, however, treated the theme with as much eccentric humor as Hokusai does here.

The painting was quickly and deftly done, and Hokusai gave the radish perky leaves in modulated ink that almost imbue it with personality. Daikoku has tucked his lucky mallet into the back of his belt in order to get a better grip on such an unwieldy burden. From the "Katsushika Hokusai" signature and worn outline of the "Kimō dasoku" seal, the painting can be dated to about 1806–11. TC

40 Gathering Shellfish at Ebb Tide
ca. 1806-11
Signature: Katsushika Hokusai
Seal: Kimō dasoku
hanging scroll; ink and color on silk, 54.3 x 86.2 cm
Osaka Municipal Museum of Art, Important Cultural Property
Provenance: Nakajima Shōichirō; Hosomi collection; Takeoka Tadao 1942, 1944; Takeoka Toyota 1923, Kobayashi Bunshichi.
Literature: Kyoto Imperial Museum 1923; Fujikake 1943, no. 482; Narazaki 1944, no. 148; Nikkei 1967, no. 19; Narazaki 1982, no. 20; Sansai 1985, no. 540; Forrer 1988, no. 179; Asahi 1993, no. 45; Calza 1994, no. 9.9; Nagata 2000, no. 108; Nikkei 2005, cat. 212.
(1-35)

41 Beauty Becoming Inebriated
ca. 1807
Signature: Katsushika Hokusai ga
Seal: Kimō dasoku
hanging scroll; ink and color on silk, 26.5 x 32.3 cm
Ujiie Ukiyo-e Collection, Kamakura Museum
Provenance: Hayashi Tadamasa.
Literature: Narazaki 1982, no. 14; Nagata 2000, no. 45 (color); Nikkei 2005, cat. 201.
(1-7)

With their boat drawn up to the rocky shore, a group of adults and children have come with baskets ready to harvest shellfish at low tide. Their sleeves are tied back with special cords (*tasuki*), and the skirts of their robes are pulled up in business-like manner. The three country women, in particular, are quite elegantly dressed and may be visitors from the city. A child draws their attention to a group of three more boys who have captured some kind of sea creature. In other depictions of the subject, the creature is almost always a flapping flat-fish, and it is curious that the fish was not drawn explicitly here. Shells, pebbles, and sea spray dot the mudflats and create visual excitement. The silk support of the painting has become quite toned; originally the unpainted areas would have appeared much more creamy white.

Various locations for this scene have been suggested, most recently somewhere around Edo Bay, which would mean that the far shores and mountains are the Miura and Izu peninsulas, crowned with a view of the distant snow-covered peak of Mount Fuji (Nagata 2000, 278). However, there is little sense that Hokusai painted the scene directly from life.

The painting is an accomplished amalgamation of Eastern and Western techniques and dates from Hokusai's mature period when he was approximately fifty years old. The brilliantly colored figures have the refined proportions typical of this period, and the baskets and other accessories are crisply executed. The figures are daringly set into a panoramic vista that demonstrates Hokusai's pragmatic absorption of European perspective techniques. Albeit that the emphasis is very much on the foreground scene of work, there is also the convincing — if not strictly mathematical — suggestion of recession deep into the seascape. "Muddy" (*doro-e*) effects in the sky, where matte shell white was mixed with all the other colors, also signal an imitation of European oil painting. The European influence may have been indirect, however, and Hokusai may have learned the technique from doctrinaire Western-style painters among his contemporaries, principally Shiba Kōkan (1747–1818; compare Kōkan's famous *Seven League Beach, Kamakura* [Kōbe City Museum]; Naruse 1995, 2:pl. 140).

A copy of this work with a forged signature and "Kimō dasoku" seal is in the collection of the Freer gallery (Stern and Narazaki 1981, 16:no. 53; Clark 1992, 36–38). TC

As can be surmised from the red-lacquered sake cup on the floor, the geisha in this work is drunk. She is slumped over the storage box for her shamisen (three-stringed instrument). The mark of three pestles in a lower corner of the box is the crest of the Kineya family, master shamisen players who accompanied Edo-style *nagauta* chanting. This suggests that the geisha has been trained in the Kineya school. A brocade bag lying on top of the box is for the plectrum used to play the shamisen. The arrangement with the woman's neck bent forward at a right angle is a common Hokusai specialty. The pose of the body is particularly beautiful, seeming to flow almost like mountain torrent down toward the bottom right, occasionally slowing along the way.

Notwithstanding its small size, this work is one of the most important of Hokusai's paintings of beautiful women. A middle-layer robe with cherry and tie-dyed patterns protrudes all around the line of the hem, serving as an anchor to the composition. This same pattern is used quite often in other paintings of beauties from the period, such as *Five Women Examining Fabrics* (cat. 35).

From about 1810, so-called "frilly" drapery lines became an important feature of Hokusai's paintings of beautiful women. Such lines are not yet apparent in this work, but can already be seen in a fan painting of a similar subject titled *Woman Leaning on a Shamisen Box* (cat. 42). AS

42 Woman Leaning on a Shamisen Box
ca. 1810–13
Signature: Hokusai ga
Seals: Toki, Masa
folding fan; ink and color on paper,
22.3 x 47.3 cm
Tokyo National Museum
Literature: Nikkei 1967, no. 20; Asahi 1993,
no. 34; Kobayashi, 1995 2:no. 110; Calza 1999,
no. III.66; Nagata 2000, no. 77 (bw); Nikkei
2005, no. 206.
(1-17)

A young woman of the townsman class, dressed in summer apparel, is leaning forward with her elbows resting on the lid of the large black storage box for a shamisen. Crossing her hands idly in front of her, she dangles a round fan and looks off to one side. It is almost as if Hokusai devised this highly complex pose—with the woman's knees pointing one way and her body turned the other way—in confident defiance of the small folding-fan format. The voluminous bustle of the thick brocade sash and the bold curve of the skirts of her checked cotton robe fluidly expand to the right, so as to balance the solid box positioned just to the left of center. Even the positions of the signature and seals were carefully calculated: They seem like a pile of weights that were placed above the skirts to anchor them further. Since the woman wears an apron and her hair is slightly disheveled, she is probably a serving woman who has escaped for a moment of respite from a busy party. A geisha performing at the party would have left the shamisen box behind. In contrast to the fragility and refinement of the figure style in his earlier "Sōri" period, in this work Hokusai is exploring a more voluptuous and sensual type of feminine beauty. The conception is very similar to another fan painting of a woman in summer clothing titled *Beauty Lost in Thought*, which has an identical signature and seal (Nagata 2000, no. 76). The two fan paintings may well have been done together. TC

43 Six Immortals of Poetry
ca. 1806–08
Signature: Katsushika Hokusai (Ōtomo no Kuronushi only)
Seal: Kimō dasoku
set of six hanging scrolls; ink and color on paper, 131.3 x 55.4 cm (Narihira),
131.1 x 53.4 cm (Kisen), 131.3 x 53.1 cm (Henjō), 131.4 x 53.2 cm (Yasuhide),
131.2 x 55.5 cm (Komachi), 131.1 x 533 cm (Kuronushi)
Freer Gallery of Art, Smithsonian Institution, gift of Charles Lang Freer
F1907.368, F1907.369, F1907.370, F1907.371, F1907.372, and F1907.373
Provenance: Yamanaka and Company, 1907.
Literature: Stern and Narazaki 1981, 16 :nos. 114-15; Nagata 1990, 5 :nos. 18-23; Nagata 2000, nos. 100-05 (bw).
(1-44)

The Six Immortals of Poetry (*rokkasen*) of the Heian period (794–1185) were Ariwara no Narihira (825–80), Sōjō Henjō (816–90), Kisen Hōshi (fl. ca. 810–24), Fun'ya no Yasuhide (fl. ca. 858–88), Ono no Komachi, and Ōtomo no Kuronushi (fl. ca. 885–97). In his famous preface for *Collection of Verses Ancient and Modern (Kokin waka shū)*, Ki no Tsurayuki refers to them as "people who have made a name for themselves in recent times" and gives critical assessments of each; the collective name Six Immortals of Poetry dates from that time. The Six Poets gradually became almost deified, and legends about them and pictorial depictions abound. However, apart from Narihira and Henjō, the biographies of the other four are almost unknown.

In ukiyo-e paintings and prints the Six Immortals of Poetry are almost always depicted in "parody pictures" (*mitate-e* or *yatsushi-e*). Hokusai did several versions of the subject in the genres of painting, single-sheet prints, and *surimono*, and this set of six hanging scrolls is the grandest. It is likely that the original format was a six-fold screen. The intended order of the paintings is unknown, but considering the various compositions and positions of the signatures and seals, the following order is proposed (right to left as arranged above): Narihira, Kisen, Henjō, Yasuhide, Komachi, Kuronushi. The scrolls are approximately the same width, apart from Narihira and Komachi, which are both more than two centimeters wider than the others (typically, the two outside panels of a six-fold screen are slightly wider than the four in the center).

The six scrolls are not "parody pictures": The figures are dressed in the fashions of the courtly Heian period (794–1185), even if the details of their costumes are not all historically accurate. Narihira appears in the formal attire of a military official with horsetail "fans" (*oikake*) on either side of his cap. Kisen Hōshi is shown from behind, wearing the black-dyed robes and brocade stole of a monk and carrying a stick. Henjō wears the brilliant red robes appropriate to a high-ranking Buddhist priest and carries a court fan. Fun'ya no Yasuhide, who looks away from the viewer, is dressed in a hunting costume with a bent-over court cap.

Komachi wears the scarlet divided trousers of a lady-in-waiting and carries a painted fan. Ōtomo no Kuronushi is dressed in formal black court robes with a vertical wave pattern and court crown; he is seated and is holding a "board of office" (*shaku*) upright. In the cases of Narihira and Kuronushi, a long undergarment in the form of a sash (known as a *shitagasane*) trails out from beneath their robes.

Each scroll is painted in the freewheeling, expansive brush style that typifies the artist's mature "Hokusai" period. Not yet apparent are the tremulous wavelike outlines that begin to appear in his paintings around 1810. Hokusai also designed a set of six *ōban*-sized prints of the Six Immortals of Poetry for the publisher Ezakiya Kichibei, although all six are seated portraits. A decorative pattern of dripped color is at the top of each scroll. On that set of prints there is a similar kind of decoration in gradated printing, even though the shape of the decorative pattern in these works is somewhat different. This suggests that the set of paintings and the set of prints are quite closely related. AS

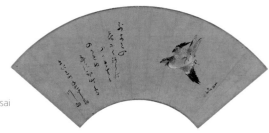

44 Flying Cuckoo
ca. 1809
Signature: Tōyō Hokusai
(Hokusai, of Edo)
Seals: Toki, Masa
folding fan mounted on panel; ink and color on paper,
17.8 x 50.4 (maximum width) / 22.8 (minimum width) cm
Inscription: See below.
Inscription signature: Bunka mi toki ni toshi nanajū ō Kawatsura (Kawatsura,
old man of seventy years in the snake year of the Bunka era [1809])
Freer Gallery of Art, Smithsonian Institution, gift of Charles Lang Freer F1904.187
Provenance: Kobayashi Bunshichi.
Literature: Nagata 2000, no. 97 (bw).
(1-85)

45 Various Scenes
ca. 1810
two-panel folding screen; ink and color on paper, each panel: 70.2 x 79.8 cm
Freer Gallery of Art, Smithsonian Institution, gift of Charles Lang Freer F1902.3
Provenance: Thomas E. Kirby, 1902.
Literature: Stern 1973, cat. 91; Stern and Narazaki 1981, 16:145-46.
(1-21)

A cuckoo in flight is painted onto a fan prepared with a shiny mica ground. Hokusai used tones of ink with additional white to create a simple depiction of the bird, and yet he convincingly and accurately captured the form of the cuckoo.

The comic *kyōka* poem inscribed on the left by Kawatsura reads:

Utayomi no   A struggling poet
hana ni kurou wa   who describes the
nogarete mo   flowers
nogarenu mimi ni   tries to escape but
hatsu hototogisu   cannot
           the cries in his ear of
           the first cuckoo

According to *Kyōka Portraits: Authors Classified* (*Kyōka gazō sakusha burui;* published in 1811) and *Edo Divided by Direction* (*Edo hōgaku wake*; compiled about 1818), the poet's common name was Fujita Min'an, his *kyōka* poetry names were Miyado Kawatsura or Yuigadō Kawatsura, and he lived in the Honjo district, alternatively at Moto-Odawarachō in Nihonbashi. He wrote the character "no" with the large, flat shape typical of the calligraphy of the famous *kyōka* poet Akera Kankō (1738–98), and he is therefore thought to be a member of the Akera poetry circle. In *Kyōka gazō sakusha burui,* he is included in the section "authors of around the An'ei (1772–81) and Tenmei (1781–89) eras," and in *Edo hōgaku wake* his name is given a mark that indicates

he was deceased. Therefore, he must have been close to the end of his life when he wrote the inscription in 1809 at the age of seventy. The most likely scenario is that Kawatsura added the *kyōka* inscription to this painting, which Hokusai had just completed, at a public poetry and painting meeting (*shogakai*).

The "Tōyō" of the artist's signature refers to the fact that Hokusai lived in Edo. This would not be necessary if the person who ordered the fan was also a native of Edo and the fan was painted in Edo. Therefore, either the fan was painted somewhere else, or someone from elsewhere requested it. If one imagines that the *shogakai* attended by Hokusai and Kawatsura was indeed held in Edo, then this would mean that someone from elsewhere requested the painting.

All of the images of cuckoos by Hokusai show the bird in a similar manner to the present painting. Examples include a hanging scroll from a private collection with an inscription by Ōta Nanpo from Hokusai's "Taito" period, an image in an album of paintings from his "Manji" period, and a *chūban* color woodblock print titled *Cuckoo and Dwarf Azalea* with an Iitsu signature (Nikkei 2005, cat. 373). In fact almost all the pictures of cuckoos by ukiyo-e artists of the late Edo period conform to this type. AS

Translation of poem by Timothy Clark

In this painting, a medley of miscellaneous subjects — a compositional technique commonly found in Hokusai's illustrated books and albums of sketches — is applied to a two-fold screen. The two panels, however, may originally have formed the front and back of a single freestanding screen (*tsuitate*). From right to left, the subjects of the painting are: a Japanese monk and perhaps a Korean ambassador conversing by writing, a dragon and clouds, a pet bird on a perch, a woman holding a pipe, a galloping horse, a teabowl and cherry blossoms, a shrine official

repainting a gateway, a pilgrim resting with his chin on his hand, and a plum branch with a mandarin duck. The panels are unsigned, but the brush style is completely consistent with the artist's "Hokusai" period. The famous printed volumes, *Hokusai manga* also began to be published during these years, and the similarity is readily apparent. If "sketching" in this context is understood as drawing various subjects for one's own enjoyment as they come to mind, then the various scenes shown here may be understood as sketches in "Hokusai" style. NM

46 Plum Tree in Bloom
ca. 1810-11
Signature: Hokusai hitsu
Seal: Raishin
Inscription: See below
hanging scroll; ink and color on silk, 115.09 x 41.59 cm
The Nelson Atkins Museum of Art, Kansas City, Missouri, Purchase: Nelson Trust 32-83/7
Literature: Calza 1999, no. III.16; Nagata 2000, no. 62 (color).
(1-81)

47 Nichiren Reading a Sutra
ca. 1806-13
Signature: Katsushika Hokusai Taito haiga (Respectfully painted by Katsushika Hokusai Taito)
hanging scroll; ink and color on paper, 40.6 x 20.3 cm
Inscription: Namu myōhō renge kyō, Nichiren Dai Bosatsu
Inscription signature: Anryūzan Nichiyō
Inscription seal: kaō (handwritten seal)
Hikaru Memorial Museum, Shiga Prefecture
Provenance: Nasu Royal Museum, Tochigi Prefecture
(1-135)

Flowering plum trees are associated with early spring and the first cries of the warbler (*uguisu*). The humorous inscription seems to suggest that the female warbler definitely does not listen to the cry of her mate:

Uguisu no	The warbler's
tsumadori sazo ya	female mate
kiki oranu	is not listening.

Branches of the white plum tree twist in all directions to completely fill the large painting. Hokusai had used the subject of a white plum many times in paintings, *surimono* prints, and book illustrations (see cats. 14, 15, and 24). Examples include a hanging scroll on silk, signed "Hyakurin Sōri ga" (private collection), and a small painting on paper, signed "Hokusai" (Chiba City Museum of Art; 1995, 10:no. 38). Here, the tree trunk is rendered in complex shades of gradated ink and is formed into arcs that ripple like waves and seem to be full of power. Countless smaller branches with white flowers separate off from this main trunk. This obsessive approach to form clearly represents a new departure in Hokusai's depiction of plum trees. AS

Translation of poem by Timothy Clark

The monk Nichiren (1222–82), founder of the important sect of Japanese Buddhism that bears his name, is shown seated on a large tree or rock, with a handscroll open in front of him. The entire background of the painting is rendered in a single shade of ink. The temple Anryūzan that Nichiyō mentioned in the inscription refers to the Jōonji Temple (present-day location 2-2-3 Moto Asakusa, Taitō-ku, Tokyo), also known as "the patriarch of the Dobudana district [Shintera machi in Asakusa] (Dobudana no O-shishi sama)," one of the three great Nichiren sect patriarchs of Edo. Nichiyō Shōnin (d. 1840) was the fifteenth abbot of the temple. According to *History of Anryūzan Jōonji Temple* (*Anryūzan Jōonji shi*), he was famous for restoring the fortunes of the temple after the fires of 1806 and 1830. It is possible that Hokusai, himself a fervent believer in the Nichiren sect, did the painting as a commission for another sect member, and that Nichiyō later inscribed the work with the incantation "Hail the wondrous Lotus Sutra, the great bodhisattva Nichiren."

The handwritten seal (*kaō*) that Hokusai inscribed after his signature is one he used during a ten-year period beginning in 1803. It is thought to be a transformation in cursive script (*sōshotai*) of the character "Hoku." AS

50 Turtles with Reflections
of Cherry Blossoms
1800
Signature: Tōyō Hokusai ga
Seal: Sankei
color woodblock print; long *surimono*,
19.1 x 51.2 cm
Ōta Memorial Museum of Art
Literature: Nagata 1990, 1:no. 55.
(1-103)

48 Woman Holding a Fan
ca. 1810–11
Signature: Katsushika Hokusai hitsu
Seal: Raishin
hanging scroll; ink and color on silk, 82.4 x 30.5 cm
Freer Gallery of Art, Smithsonian Institution, gift of Charles Lang Freer F1904.183
Provenance: Kobayashi Bunshichi 1904; Honma Kōsō.
Literature: Fenollosa 1900, no. 56; Stern and Narazaki 1981, 16:no. 111; Nagata 2000, no. 111.
(1-9)

49 Lady Holding a Cat
ca. 1810s
ink on paper, 23.0 x 19.9 cm
Freer Gallery of Art, Smithsonian Institution,
gift of Charles Lang Freer F1904.256
Provenance: Kobayashi Bunshichi 1904.
Literature: Stern 1960, cover; Stern 1973,
cat. 105, 277.
(1-37)

A young woman wearing a summer robe of black gauze and holding a folding fan turns round to look over her shoulder. The first line of what is probably a haiku poem inscribed on the fan can just be made out: "A heavy shower…" (*Hakuu ya…*). The woman's pose with her neck bent forward almost at a right angle is commonly found in Hokusai's paintings of beautiful women. A frilly, wavelike line is already visible on the collar of her dotted undergarment, and her sash is edged with a forcefully angled zigzag line. This manner of depiction would become an increasing feature of Hokusai's paintings in the 1810s, but here the use of wavering lines does not yet extend to all of the drapery.

Hokusai used the white-character "Raishin" seal around 1811 on the following works: a votive panel titled *Cherry Blossom* (Sasato-san Chōsen'in Temple, Saitama Pref; Nagata 2000, no. 116 [bw]),

dedicated in the third month, 1811; *Zhong Kui Painted in Red* (Museum of Fine Arts, Boston; Boston 2000, 3: no.63), dated the fifth day of the fifth month, 1811; and *Tametomo and the Inhabitants of Onoshima Island* (cat. 66), which has an inscription by Kyokutei Bakin dated winter of the same year. Hokusai is thought to have passed on the same seal, together with the "Hokusai" name, to his pupil Hokusai II in the fourth month of 1813. A date of about 1810–11 is proposed for the present work due to the form of the signature — "Katsushika Hokusai hitsu" — the fact that the seal does not appear to be any more worn than on other works dated 1811, and the general style. It should also be noted that there is a work by Hokusai II, *Beauty Reading a Letter* in the Museum of Fine Arts, Boston, in which the figure is almost identical to the present work and which must have been copied from it (Boston 2000, no. 87). AS

In this ink sketch, a woman wearing a kimono and an outer jacket embraces her cat in the folds of her garments. Her slim face, delineated with a slender brush, is typical of Hokusai's paintings of beauties. The contrasting lines of her garments are sharply angled around the neckline and flowing in the sleeves and skirt. This undated and unsigned drawing was one of a large group that Charles Lang Freer purchased from the Japanese art dealer Kobayashi Bunshichi. The drawing can be dated by comparison with Hokusai's paintings to about 1810, a period when Hokusai received many commissions for paintings of beautiful women. AY

This *surimono* depicts a strikingly naturalistic close-up view of a group of four turtles at the shore of a body of water. A fifth turtle appears to be swimming toward them. Overhead, faint images of cherry blossoms appear as if reflected at close range in the water. Of particular interest in this scene is Hokusai's articulation of the three-dimensional forms of the rocky landscape. His combination of brushstrokes and dots, which the block carver interpreted accurately, exhibits a mastery of brush methods from Chinese painting. The subject of turtles may have had a special meaning for Hokusai, who chose three turtles for a *surimono* that he designed to announce his name change in 1798 from Sōri to Hokusai Tokimasa (or Tatsumasa). Turtles were associated with the north direction, so for Hokusai, whose most famous name meant "North (Star) Studio," they were an appropriate symbol for his choice of a name associated with his belief in the North Star and its associated constellation and deities. AY

51 Fashionable Seven Habits:
Women with an Umbrella and Telescope
Fūryū nakute nanakuse
ca. 1800
Signature: Kakō ga
Publisher: Tsutaya Jūzaburō
Publisher seal: Publisher's trademark
color woodblock print with mica; *ōban*,
36.8 x 24.8 cm
Kobe City Museum
Literature: Oka 1974, fig. 11; Asano 1998, fig. 14.
(1-20)

52 Fashionable Seven Habits:
Women with a Handmirror
Fūryū nakute nanakuse
ca. 1800
Signature: Kakō ga
Publisher: Tsutaya Jūzaburō
Publisher seal: Publisher's trademark
color woodblock print with mica; *ōban*,
39.3 x 26.3 cm
Grabhorn Collection
Literature: Oka 1974, pl. 10; Yamaguchi 1995,
pl. 110.
(1-19)

53 Traveling Hat with Spring Greens
1801
Signature: Gakyōjin Hokusai sha
color woodblock print; long *surimono*,
18.0 x 52.2 cm
Ōta Memorial Museum of Art
Literature: Asahi 1993, pl. 25;
Mirviss 2003, pl. 14.
(1-64)

54 Mount Fuji with Cherry Trees in Bloom
ca. 1800-05
Signature: Gakyōjin Hokusai ga
color woodblock print; long *surimono*,
20.1 x 55.4 cm
Rijksmuseum Amsterdam RP-P 1980-6
Provenance: Louis Gonse Collection
Literature: Forrer 1991, pl. 92;
Calza 2003, no. III.61; Nikkei 2005, cat. 107.
(1-82)

Hokusai used the name Kakō as a pen name for his writings, but here he signed as Kakō for a series of prints that depict women engaged in various activities. Only two prints are known from this series, which should have comprised seven designs. Hokusai's publisher was Tsutaya Jūzaburō, a prominent Edo firm that also issued prints by Utamaro, the leading designer of *bijinga*. Close-up views of pairs of beauties were one of Utamaro's specialties. Here Hokusai portrayed beauties with the long, narrow faces identified with his unique style. Each pair is engaged in an activity such as gazing through a telescope or adjusting makeup while a companion holds a ground cherry (*hōzuki*) in her mouth. Both prints have the pearly mica backgrounds that appear on many prints of beauties and actors in the 1790s and early 1800s. AY

Hokusai realized the quality of artistic expression that could be achieved in *surimono*. The prints, which sophisticated patrons such as *kyōka* poets commissioned, encompassed a wide range of subjects and were printed with top quality, thick paper and materials by publishers who engaged master block carvers and printers. Still-life arrangements, such as this New Year design of edible plants gathered in an inverted straw hat, provided an endless variety of materials, colors, and compositions and a vehicle for creating the refined effects of painting in the print medium. Eighteen *kyōka* poets contributed verses for this *surimono*. AY

The snow-covered peak of Mount Fuji appears above a close-up view of cherry trees in full bloom. This landscape is an early manifestation of Hokusai's interest in Mount Fuji as a subject; his most famous series, *Thirty-six Views of Mount Fuji*, was designed some thirty years later. The light colors of the outlines of the petals enhance the impression of their fragility as they bloom briefly before falling in the slightest breeze like snow. Like many *surimono* of this format, the lower half of the sheet on which the poems would have been printed has been removed, and only the picture remains. Hokusai was well known among Edo poets, and he often received commissions for *surimono* designs to be published with poems by groups of poets who belonged to poetry clubs. AY

55 Dancers
1804
Signature: Gakyō Rōjin
Hokusai ga
color woodblock print;
double-length pillar
surimono, 119.2 x 14.1 cm
Ōta Memorial Museum of Art
Literature: Ōta 2004, pl.130;
Nikkei 2005, cat. 115.
(1-23)

A lively group of dancers fills the narrow format of this work, which is an unusually long double-length pillar print (*hashiraban* or *hashira-e*) with *kyōka* poems filling the upper half. Hokusai arranged the dancers with each one at a slightly higher level so they appear one behind the other. In this unusual and original composition, which is perfectly suited to the tall format, Hokusai applied to a group of human figures a principle for spatial representation found in Chinese landscape painting in which motifs placed higher in the picture are meant to appear more distant. Throughout his work, Hokusai altered conventional artistic practices to apply unique methods to unexpected subjects. In this case he arranged figures as if they are a receding range of mountains. Although the subject of this *surimono* has often been interpreted as an example of the *Bon odori* (dances performed in midsummer at the Festival of Lights for the spirits of the deceased), Asano Shūgō recently noted that several types of dances are mentioned in the poems above the dancers, for example, the Ise *ondo* dance, Daimoku *odori*, and Kamakura *odori*. The *surimono* was commissioned by the Asakusa club (Tsubo club) in the seventh lunar month of 1804 (Nikkei 2005, 317–18). AY

56a Jūnisō at Yotsuya
Yotsuya Jūnisō
ca. 1804-07
Signature: Hokusai egaku
color woodblock print; *chūban*,
14.4 x 22.6 cm
Private collection
Literature: Calza 2003, III.46.1.
(1-112)

56b Rowboat among Waves
Oshiokuri hatō tsūsen no zu
ca. 1804-07
Signature: Hokusai egaku
color woodblock print; *chūban*,
14.4 x 22.6 cm
Private collection
Literature: Calza 2003, III.46.3.
(1-113)

56c Viewing Noboto Beach at Low Tide from the Salt Coast at Gyōtoku
Gyōtoku shiohama yori Noboto no higata wo nozomu
ca. 1804-07
Signature: Hokusai egaku
color woodblock print; *chūban*,
14.4 x 22.6 cm
Private collection
Literature: Calza 2003, III.46.1.
(1-114)

These three prints come from an untitled series of *chūban* designs inspired by European paintings and engravings. To enhance the "Western" effect, Hokusai surrounded each scene with a framelike border and wrote the title and his signature in two lines of cursive *hiragana* phonetic script that is oriented horizontally from top at left to bottom at right, like European writing and reading. He also incorporated elements of Western style in the forms of the trees and clouds, the use of dark shadows to render three-dimensional forms, and the unusual palette that reflects the opaque tonalities of oil painting. Many of these elements recur in Hokusai's later paintings and prints, where they are integrated into an individualistic artistic style. Two of the scenes prefigure subjects of Hokusai's famous landscape prints from the 1830s. The scene of Jūnisō Shrine shows travelers crossing a bridge over a steep ravine near a scenic waterfall. The surging wave and boats are clearly related to Hokusai's "Great Wave," which he created nearly thirty years later. AY

57 Mallard with Two Clams, Abalone Shell, Plum Blossoms, and Parsley
ca. 1805-10
Signature: Gakyōjin Hokusai ga
Inscription: *Kyōka* by Yukinoya Torikane
Collector seals: Hayashi Tadamasa and Henri Vever
color woodblock print; *koban surimono*,
13.9 x 19.3 cm
Private collection
Literature: Mirviss 2003, pl. 15;
Croissant 2005, fig. 5, 220, 221.
(1-62)

This small *surimono* is illustrated with an elegant still life of a mallard lying beside ingredients for a stew. The poem inscribed above reads:

mizutori no	Just when water birds
hikkomu koro wa	are returning back north,
yukige shite	the snow starts to thaw
kishi no ashi mo	and reeds along the bank
arau shiranami	are washed by white-capped waves.

This *surimono* would have served as a New Year greeting, with the words of the poem interpreted in Hokusai's picture with an ironic twist. The bird will indeed be "washed," but for cooking, and the *ashi* (a homonym meaning both "reeds," as in the poem, and "feet") in the illustration are those of the bird. Hokusai's familiarity with contemporary poetry both as an artist and an illustrator brought him many commissions for *kyōka surimono* for which he could devise witty and unexpected pictorial interpretations of the poems. AY

Translation of poem by John T. Carpenter (Croissant 2005, 220)

58 The Bodhisattva Monju's
Teachings for Children
Chigo Monju osana kyōkun
originally 3 volumes, *kibyōshi*
1801
Signature: Gasaku Tokitarō Kakō
Author: Katsushika Hokusai
Publisher: Tsutaya Jūzaburō
woodblock printed book; each illustration
mounted flat, 23.0 x 16.0 cm
The Art Institute of Chicago,
gift of Martin A. Ryerson 4-1-44
Literature: Asahi 1993, 64-65;
Edo Tokyo Hakubutsukan 1995, 34.
(1-140)

This delightful story, which Hokusai
wrote himself, was once a printed book.
Each pair of illustrations forming an
opening of the book is now mounted
flat. The stories concern Chigo Monju,
the youthful bodhisattva Monju
(Manjushri), an enlightened Buddhist
deity associated with wisdom. In this
illustration, the 33,330 monkeys of the
Sannō shrine beseech Monju to make
them human. When their wish was
granted they endeavored to act like
humans, with amusing results. Monkeys
are popularly regarded as the messengers
to the deities of the Sannō shrine,
located at the Enryakuji of Mount
Hiei. AY

59 Songs of Itako
Itako zekku shū
2 volumes, *kyōkabon*
1802 (First edition)
Author: Fuji Karamaro
Publisher: Tsutaya Jūzaburō
color woodblock printed book; stitched
binding (*fukurotoji*), 19.4 x 13.2 cm
Smithsonian Institution Libraries,
Freer Gallery of Art and Arthur M. Sackler
Gallery Library, Special collection NE1325.K3
A693 1802
Literature: Toda 1931, 238; Oka 1974, 214-15;
Hillier 1980, 36-37; Asahi 1993, no.19; Edo
Tokyo Hakubutsukan 1995, II-48.
(1-53)

Zekku are a form of Chinese verse consisting of four lines of five or seven characters each. Chinese verses, printed at the
tops of the pages, have punctuation and
pronunciation guides for Japanese read-
ers. In this book, the Chinese poems are
interspersed with Itako *bushi*, boatmen's
songs associated with the river town
Itako in Hitachi Province where prostitutes sought clients. This illustration by
Hokusai carries a landscape with the
river in the distance across a full opening
of the book. A young man and a prostitute stroll together along the shore. The
trees in the landscape are placed in the
foreground and frame the couple. This
illustration demonstrates Hokusai's ability to create compositions that contrast
open space and denser placement of
motifs, as well as to focus on relationships between figures in a scene. AY

60 Mount Fuji in Spring
Haru no Fuji
1 volume, *kyōkabon*
1803
Signature: Gakyōjin Hokusai ga
color woodblock printed book; folding album
orihon, 22.0 x 16.0 cm
Smithsonian Institution Libraries,
Freer Gallery of Art and Arthur M. Sackler
Gallery Library, Special collection
NE1325.K3 A67 1803
Literature: Toda 1931, 242; Hillier 1980, 51.
(1-57)

This small *kyōka* album of New Year
poems contains three exceptionally
beautiful illustrations of early spring
subjects. The album can be opened flat,
and each illustration is simply folded at
the center, rather than printed on separate sheets and joined by stitching at the
center as would be the case in books
with *fukurotoji* bindings. In this format,
Hokusai created three contrasting illustrations, all with early spring associations: a coastal view of Mount Fuji and
Miho no Matsubara, a close-up view of
a blossoming plum branch with a silver
moon behind it, and a scene of young
women gathering early spring herbs. In
this period, Hokusai had turned away
from commercial prints to pursue commissions for *surimono*. The styles and
colors of these illustrations reflect
Hokusai's broad familiarity with Edo
artistic schools. Their varied subjects,
refined and unusual colors, and superb
printing prefigure Hokusai's great
period of commercial print design in
the 1830s. AY

61 Wrapper for *Illustrated Book of* Kyōka:
Range upon Range of Mountains
1804
Signature: Hokusai shujin ga (by Master
Hokusai)
Publisher: Tsutaya Jūzaburō
color woodblock print, 26.5 x 41.7 cm
The British Museum 1979.3-5.0.440.4
Literature: Calza 2003, no. III.40.1-2;
Asahi 1993, pl. 23; Nikkei 2005, cat. 128.
(1-50)

62 Illustrated Book of *Kyōka*:
Range upon Range of Mountains
Ehon kyōka yama mata yama
1804
three volumes, *kyōkabon*
Gakyōjin Hokusai (in preface)
Author: Ohara Teishujin
Publisher: Tsutaya Jūzaburō
color woodblock printed book,
26.5 x 18.0 cm
The British Museum 1979.3-5.0.440/JH440
Literature: Toda 1930, 241; Oka 1974, nos.
59-60; Hillier 1980, 58-59; Edo Tokyo
Hakubutsukan 1995, II-56; Calza 2003,
III.40.1-2; Nikkei 2005, cat. 129.
(1-51)

The subject of the three volumes of
Illustrated Book of Kyōka: *Range upon
Range of Mountains* is the scenery of
Yamanote, the high lands of Edo to the
north and northwest of the city that
included the Yotsuya, Ushigome, and
Koishikawa districts. The rare wrapper
for this book has a bold and amusing
design of the strong boy Kintoki and the
mountain woman (*yamauba*) who
raised him. Kintoki holds a brush that
was used to write the sign behind him,
which gives the title of the book and the
artist's name. Wrappers protected sets of
books like modern-day dustjackets.
Hokusai's image clearly shows the
woman holding the wooden signboard
with her and the boy's heads in front.
The large close-up view of their heads
follows the contemporary fashion of
ōkubi-e (head-and-shoulder pictures)
which artists such as Utamaro had made
popular. AY

TAITO

1810-19

63 "Early Ferns," Chapter 48
of *The Tale of Genji*
ca. 1810-14
Signature: Hokusai Taito hitsu
Seal: Fumoto no sato
hanging scroll mounted on panel;
ink and color on silk, 103.1 x 40.5 cm
Freer Gallery of Art, Smithsonian Institution, gift of Charles Lang
Freer F1904.184
Provenance: Kobayashi Bunshichi 1904; Honma Kōsō.
(1-48)

64 Woman Holding a Tobacco Pipe
ca. 1814-15
Signature: Hokusai aratame Taito hitsu
Seal: Fumoto no sato
Inscription: See below.
Inscription signature: Shokusanjin (Ōta Nanpo)
hanging scroll; ink and color on silk, 71.9 x 26.9 cm
Freer Gallery of Art, Smithsonian Institution, gift of Charles Lang
Freer F1898.107
Provenance: E. S. Hull, 1898.
Literature: Stern and Narazaki 1981, 16:no. 109; Nagata 2000, no. 72
(col.).
(1-8)

The Tale of Genji has been depicted countless times in painting since at least the late Heian period (794–1185). The novel, written by Lady Murasaki (d. 1014?) around 1000, centers on the romantic adventures and personal relationships of Genji, the "Shining Prince," and his descendants at the imperial court. The earliest known illustrated version dates to the mid-twelfth century. Artists of the "Yamato-e" (Japanese painting) lineage were the first to produce such works, which featured a brilliantly colored style. Later, members of the imperial court commissioned similar works from artists of the "Kara-e" (Chinese painting) lineage.

Depictions of the novel in ukiyo-e usually take the form of *mitate-e*, in which classical events are adapted to a modern setting. Occasionally, however, ukiyo-e artists produced images in a traditional style that directly evoked the life of the classical Heian court. This painting falls into the latter category. It depicts a scene from "Early Ferns," one of the ten "Uji chapters" that conclude the novel. Naka

no kimi is mourning the death of her elder sister Ōgimi. As a consoling gesture, the head monk of a nearby temple sends her a basket of young spring greens. A poem accompanies the gift:

Through many a spring we plucked these shoots for him.

Today, remembrance bids us do as well.

Hokusai produced at least two other hanging scrolls that depict scenes from *The Tale of Genji* in classical style. One, in the collection of the Ōta Memorial Museum, Tokyo, dates from the artist's "Hokusai" period; the other, in a private collection, dates from his "Iitsu" period (Nagata 2000, nos. 59 and 73). The Freer gallery painting, however, dates from the intervening "Taito" period, corresponding to the late Bunka era (1804–18). NM

Translation of poem by Edward Seidensticker in Murasaki 1977, vol. 2, 873

Toying with the tobacco pipe in her left hand, a woman gazes pensively upward and exhales deeply. Even without reference to the signature, the use of pale flesh tones rather than shell-white (*gofun*) for the skin of the face, hands, and breast indicates that this is a work from Hokusai's "Taito" period. The wave pattern (*tachimaki*) on the woman's sash is frequently encountered in Hokusai's paintings of beauties, and the subdued coloration suggests that the subject is a married woman. Women of worldly experience feature regularly in Hokusai's paintings of the "Taito" period; indeed, such works represent the ultimate among the artist's many paintings of women, in terms of their voluptuous sensuality. The painting dates from the late Bunka era (1804–18).

In keeping with the subject of the painting, the inscription, by Hokusai's friend Ōta Nanpo (1749–1823), is a brilliantly comic verse (*kyōka*) on the subject of tobacco. It reads:

Uzumibi no	How I long to see my leaf tobacco
jida ni sawarade	merely a breath's distance from the coals buried in the ash,
yawarakani	wooing them with
iiyoran koto no	tender words.
hatabako mo kana	

NM

Translation of poem by Alfred Haft

65 Daoist Immortal Liezi in the Wind
ca. 1810-13
Signature: Tōto Katsushika Hokusai Taito hitsu
(Painted by Katsushika Hokusai Taito of Edo)
Seal: Kimō dasoku
hanging scroll; ink and color on silk, 95.3 x 37.8 cm
Minneapolis Institute of Arts, Bequest of Richard P. Gale
Provenance: Gyokutandō.
Literature: Hillier 1970, 2:no. 197; Nagata 2000, no. 64 (color);
Nikkei 2005, 242.
(1-130)

66 Tametomo and the Inhabitants of Onoshima Island
1811
Signature: Katsushika Hokusai Taito hitsu
Seal: Raishin
Inscription: See below.
Inscription signature: Bunka kanoto hitsuji ryūtō joya Kyokutei Bakin dai (Inscribed by
Kyokutei Bakin on the last night of the year in deep winter, Bunka 8 [1811])
Inscription seals: Kyokutei, Bakin
hanging scroll; ink, color, and gold on silk, 54.9 x 82.1 cm
The British Museum JP 1479 (1881.12-10.01747)
Provenance: William Anderson; Box inscription by Hirabayashi Shōgorō III.
Literature: Anderson 1886a, pl. XXXVIII; Anderson 1886b, no. 1747; Goncourt 1896, 303;
Fujikake 1943, no. 481; Narazaki 1944, no. 149; British Museum 1948, no. 162; Hillier 1955, no.
77; Narazaki 1969, 3:no. 88; Narazaki 1982, no. 26; Nikkei 1987, 1:no. 140; Forrer 1988, no. 151;
Nagata 1990, 5:no. 32; Clark 1992, no. 96, Asahi 1993, no. 50; Calza 1994, no. 12.3; Calza 1999,
no. IV.27; Nagata 2000, no. 67 (color); Nikkei 2005, cat. 241.
(1-55)

Liezi (Japanese: Resshi) was a Chinese Daoist scholar of the ancient Zhou dynasty, who lived in reclusive study for forty years in the kingdom of Zheng. He was said to travel on the wind, a magic power that qualified him as an immortal (*sennin*). Hokusai included a very small figure of Liezi in a similar pose in volume three of the *Hokusai manga*, which was published in 1815, soon after this painting was done (Nagata 1986, 1:48). In this illustration he is just one of a group of thirty-five thumbnail sketches of named Chinese immortals.

Liezi hovers in the eye of the storm that sweeps down around him, the wind tossing maple leaves in all directions. His arms are stretched forward, long sleeves flapping in the wind, and he seems to bow in a gesture of worship to the powerful natural forces. Unusual for a paint-

ing on silk, the figure was quickly and powerfully worked in fluid ink and pale wash, and the maple leaves were rendered very sensitively as they are half obscured by the tempest. Hokusai used a similar technique at the end of his life in *Ducks in Flowing Water* (cat. 137) to suggest maple leaves sinking into water.

Hokusai is thought to have used the name "Taito" beginning in 1810: he relinquished the "Kimō dasoku" seal to his pupil Hokumei in the fourth month of 1813, giving parameters for the date of this work. The use of "Tōto" (possibly read "Edo") in the signature suggests that he was away from the Eastern capital at the time. In 1812, Hokusai made his first extended visit to Nagoya, where he stayed more than six months, perhaps with his pupil Maki Bokusen (Nagata 1985, 55–56). TC

The historical Minamoto no Tametomo (1139–77?) was said to be the strongest archer in all Japan. He was initially banished to Kyushu for his riotous behavior, and following his involvement on the losing side in the Hogen War of 1156, he was banished again to the island of Izu Ōshima. The image of him here derives from a long and hugely popular adventure story written by Bakin, which was dramatically illustrated by Hokusai. *Strange Tales of the Bow Moon* (*Chinsetsu yumihari-zuki*) was published serially in twenty-eight parts over the four-year period from 1807 to 1811. In the fanciful later parts of the tale, after leaving the Izu islands, Tametomo goes back to Kyushu and then far to the south to the Ryūkyū islands to quell a rebellion.

The scene depicted here comes from volume two of the second part of the novel, when Tametomo demonstrates his extraordinary strength to the inhabitants of the island of Onoshima. Not even three of them tugging together can bend

the arch or pull the bowstring of the bow that the warrior steadies in the grip of only one hand. As if to compensate pictorially for the immovability of the bow, Hokusai adds to the scene pine branches bending in a strong sea breeze and a pair of plovers that fly up squawking in alarm over waves that lap the shoreline. A similar, but reversed, printed image by Hokusai of two hairy figures pulling on the string of the great bow that Tametomo holds was featured in volume one of the first part of the novel, published in 1804. This is clearly an image emblematic of the novel as a whole.

A wealth of documentation surrounding the painting tells us much about how it came to be made. Bakin's account, which is found in his biographical study of Edo writers, *Edo Authors Classified* (*Edo sakusha burui*; compiled 1833–34) is the most detailed. He described how the runaway success of the novel earned three times the expected profits for the publisher, Hirabayashi Shōgorō, who in

67 Cormorant Fisherman
ca. 1817–18
Signature: Katsushika Taito hitsu
Seal: Yoshinoyama
hanging scroll; ink and color on silk, 96.8 x 36.1 cm
Inscription: See below.
Inscription signature: Gyokuchi hachijū-nana ō Sogai (Gyokuchi, old man of eighty-seven, Sogai)
MOA Museum of Art, Atami
Literature: Narazaki 1982, no. 25; Kobayashi 1994, 4:no.72; Nagata 2000, no. 137 (bw); Nikkei 2005, cat. 249.
(1-31)

the spring of 1811 gave Bakin an extra ten gold *ryō* in addition to the agreed author fees. Hirabayashi also commissioned the present painting from Hokusai and had Bakin inscribe it in celebration. A handwritten note by the publisher's descendent Shōgorō III (dated the ninth month of 1854), which is pasted inside the bottom of the wooden storage box for the painting, provides a summary of the basic facts to which he adds that he has remounted the painting; likely with the same brocade mounting it retains to this day. It was some three decades later that William Anderson acquired the painting during his stay in Tokyo from 1873 to 1880, where he worked for the Meiji government as principal of the Naval Medical College in Tsukiji.

The auspicious Chinese-style inscription at top left is dated "the last night of the year in deep winter, Bunka 8 (1811)" and is filled with fitting military metaphors that celebrate the success of the project and his friendship with the publisher, while also punning the names, title, and themes of the novel. It reads:

Ichigo ai-yorokobu	A word gives great pleasure
dankin ri su	and friendship profits
profihaigun ima ni itarite kunshin o shiki su	The distribution of forces at this time

Hachirō byōshoku su tōkai no sho nao amari tōnen tokutaku fukashi/ kumo no matou	Observes the wishes of the lord On the island in the Eastern Sea where Hachirō [Tametomo] holds court
kokoro no Onigashima harete	Truly this year blessings are so profuse that
yumihari-zuki no	The clouds of the devil-ridden heart clear away
kage ōku nari	And the light of the bow moon shines bright

With the figures and the basket of fish (bottom left) painted in Hokusai's most rich and brilliant technique, and with an extensive use of cut gold-leaf to enliven the background areas, it is clear that this was a "no-expenses-spared" commission from the publisher, for which the artist must have been handsomely rewarded. The near-certain date of the work to 1811 provides a very important benchmark for Hokusai's use of the "Taito" name (which he first adopted in 1810) and "Raishin" seal (used from about 1810 to 1812). TC

Translation of poem from Clark 1992, 146

A cormorant fisherman holds up a pine torch in his right hand and with the left skillfully controls a cormorant on a string, as it catches sweetfish (*ayu*). The river current flows through the darkness, winding broadly like a snake, an effect that the swift motion of the cormorant echoes, as it chases fish. The wing of the bird, which is stretched out over the surface of the water, creates a wonderful accent. Hokusai masterfully handles the complex forms of the boat, cormorant, and fisherman brandishing the torch. These elements embody almost spiritual qualities that are reminiscent of Hokusai's other works, such as *Woodcutter and Spring and Autumn Landscapes* (Fukui Prefectural Museum of Art), and *Fisherman and Woodcutter* (cat. 142), painted in the year that he died.

Tani Sogai (d. 1823), who added the inscription, lived in the Otama-ga-ike district of Kanda in Edo, and one of his art names, Gyokuchi, comes from an alternative reading of the characters of that place-name. He was an important haiku (*haikai*) poet of the Edo Danrin school. He is known to have died in 1823, and his age at death is given as ninety (alternatively, ninety-two). This would mean that the inscription was written in either 1818 or 1820. By 1820, however, Hokusai had already changed his name to Iitsu, indicating that the date of the inscription does not coincide with the artist's signature here. Therefore, Sogai must have died at age ninety-two, and this inscription must have been written in 1818. The inscription reads:

Ono ga hi ni	I light them skillfully
terasu ya satsuki	with my torch
yami no waza	in the fifth month darkness

AS

Translation of poem by Timothy Clark

68 Portrait of a Courtesan Walking
ca. 1815-19
Signature: saki no Hokusai Taito hitsu (Painted by Taito, the former Hokusai)
Seal: Yoshinoyama
hanging scroll; ink and color on silk, 110.4 x 41.7 cm
Freer Gallery of Art, Smithsonian Institution,
Purchase F1954.119
Provenance: Yamanaka and Co., 1954.
Literature: Stern 1960, no. 5; Stern 1973, no. 87;
Stern and Narazaki 1981, 16:no. 113.
(1-15)

69 Mandarin Ducks (*Oshidori*)
beneath Blossoming Plum
1813
Signature: Hokusai aratame Taito
(on poem)
Poets: Hokusai II, Heishi, Kōchō, Toseki,
Taigadō, Taizai, Toen (Hokusai changed to)
Taito, Taito, and Tobun
color woodblock print; double long
surimono, 40.1 x 54.4 cm
Harvard University Art Museums, courtesy
of the Arthur M. Sackler Museum, gift of
the Friends of Arthur B. Duel 1933.4.2450
(1-58)

70 Famous Places on the Tōkaidō
at a Glance
Tōkaidō meisho ichiran
1818
Signature: Katsushika saki no
Hokusai Taito hitsu
Seal: Taito
Publisher: Kadomaruya Jinsuke
color woodblock print; *ōban*, 43.0 x 58.0 cm
Katsushika Hokusai Museum of Art, Tsuwano
Literature: Edo Tokyo Hakubutsukan 1995, cat.
IV-4; Forrer 1991, cat. 7; Calza 2003, IV.29.1-2;
Ōta 2004, cat. 68; Nikkei 2005, cat. 219.
(1-115)

In the Yoshiwara pleasure quarter in Edo, the highest-ranking courtesans were respectfully referred to as *oiran*. This painting shows the formal procession (*oiran dōchū*) of one such courtesan. A typical procession would also include a young male servant from the brothel who would carry a long-handled parasol, the courtesan's teenage apprentice (*shinzō*) and child servant (*kamuro*), as well as the brothel madam (*yarite*). Here, however, the courtesan is featured alone. It is unusual for such a pose — the right hand slightly lifting the skirts of her robes and the right foot raised high to step forward — to be captured in a painting, and we should assume that it depicts the actual stylized manner of procession from the period. The woman's complex hairstyle, known as "sideways Hyōgo style" (*yoko Hyōgo-mage*), is done in a manner unique to courtesans and is supported by hairpins of extremely elaborate workmanship. She wears a surcoat with a pattern of pine clusters and decorative cords that look like the sacred ropes (*shimenawa*) used as New Year decorations. These in turn have smaller tassels hanging from them that evoke sacred paper decorations (*kamishide*). These elements are indicative of the trend from this period onward when courtesan fashions became more and more luxurious and increasingly divorced from the clothing of everyday life.

This painting is similar to *Woman Holding a Fan* (cat. 48), except that the tremulous, wavelike outlines that are such a feature of Hokusai's beauties have here expanded to encompass every single piece of fabric in her costume. This increases the sense of fantasy and eroticism in the work. AS

This large *surimono* is a rare masterpiece from Hokusai's "Taito" period, when he focused mainly on painting manuals. The pair of mandarin ducks beneath a blossoming plum branch, which signifies the winter season, reveals Hokusai's mastery of realistic renderings of birds in natural settings, a subject that he returned to often in his later paintings and prints. Printed in columns at the left of the image are poems by Hokusai himself, whose name is given as "Hokusai changing to Taito," and others in his artistic circle, including Hokusai II. The keyblock used to print the birds for this privately commissioned *surimono* was later reused in 1814 for an image of mandarin ducks in snow in *Hokusai's Album of True Pictures (Hokusai shashin gafu)* in 1814 (cat. 71). AY

This oversized print presents a topographic composite view of the Tōkaidō, the principal road between Edo and Kyoto, the imperial capital where the emperor resided. The road, which ran for the most part along the eastern coast of Japan and was famous for its scenery and its fifty-three post stations (towns a few kilometers apart that provided food and lodging for travelers), became a popular subject for print designers beginning in the early nineteenth century. The terminal points are at the right side of the print. The shogun's Edo castle and the Nihonbashi Bridge are at the lower right; Kyoto is at the upper right corner. Dominating the picture is the sacred peak of Mount Fuji with the sun rising behind it. Labels identify points of interest along the route as well as the distances between the stations. The print was originally sold in a wrapper imprinted with the title and the artist's name. Hokusai designed a similar large topographic print of the scenic inland route between Edo and Kyoto, the Kisokaidō, which was published in the following year. AY

71 Hokusai's Album of True Pictures
Hokusai shashin gafu
1 volume, *edehon*
1814
Publisher: Tsuruya Kiemon
color woodblock printed book; *orihon*, 26.0 x 17.0 cm
Smithsonian Institution Libraries, Freer Gallery of Art and
Arthur M. Sackler Gallery Library, Special collection NE1325.K3 A684 1819
Literature: Hillier 1980, 89-95; Edo Tokyo Hakubutsukan 1995, 107; Nagata 1990, 92-93;
Kerlen 1996, no. 550, 241; Nikkei 2005, cat. 225.
(1-97)

72 Illustrated Album of Three
Styles of Painting
Santai gafu
1 volume, *edehon*
1816
Signature: Hokusai aratame
Katsushika Taito (Hokusai changing to
Katsushika Taito)
Seal: Fuji no yama
Publisher: Kadomaruya Jinsuke
color woodblock printed book;
stitched binding, 23.0 x 15.7 cm
Smithsonian Institution Libraries,
Freer Gallery of Art and
Arthur M. Sackler Gallery Library,
Special collection NE1325.K3 A75 1816
Literature: Hillier 1980, 142;
Edo Tokyo Hakubutsukan 1995, 110.
(1-86)

73 Random Sketches by Hokusai
Denshin kaishu Hokusai manga
15 volumes, *edehon*
1814-49 and 1875-78
volume 7, 1817
volume 12, 1834
Signature: Hokusai aratame Katsushika
Taito (volume 7); saki no Hokusai Iitsu
(volume 12)
Seal: Fuji no yama (volume 7)
Publisher: Eirakuya Tōshirō
color woodblock printed book;
stitched binding, 23.0 x 16.0 cm
Smithsonian Institution Libraries, Freer
Gallery of Art and Arthur M. Sackler Gallery
Library, Special collection 754.7.H8 C3 vol.12
Literature: Hillier 1980, 95-111; Edo Tokyo
Hakubutsukan 1995, 94-104; Calza 2003,
453-54.
(1-26)

This folding album of prints is a rare and important document of Hokusai's growing interest in a variety of subjects, and in designing prints that demonstrated his skill and versatility in creating realistic images mainly of the natural world. The book is an extraordinarily rare example of the first edition (1814). In 1819, Tsuruya Kiemon published a reprint, but the printing and color do not equal the first edition, which has no colophon. For one of the illustrations of a pair of mandarin ducks, the keyblock from a *surimono* by Hokusai (cat. 69), a tour de force of fine block carving, was reused with different background printing to represent snow. This rare album contains sixteen illustrations. One depicting a pheasant leaving footprints on the ground recalls the story of an incident ten years before when the shogun had called a painting contest between Hokusai and Tani Bunchō, and Hokusai had dipped the feet of a chicken in paint and let it run across a long scroll painted with light blue brushstrokes. He then declared that the painting represented "maple leaves on the Tatsuta River." Another illustration depicts a close-up view of the heads of irises that prefigures Hokusai's famous "Large Flowers" series of the 1830s. One scene shows a man bending to paint the pillar of the red gate of a Shinto shrine, an image that resembles one on a small folding screen in the Freer Gallery of Art (cat. 45). Other illustrations include a winter landscape and a monochrome print of the bodhisattva Kannon riding a dragon reflecting Hokusai's interest in a wide variety of sources and painting styles. AY

By the time he reached fifty, Hokusai's reputation as an artist was well established, and he attracted many students as well as informal followers. He illustrated a number of *edehon* that were intended not only to demonstrate techniques for drawing a vast array of subjects, but also to record and make known his individualistic painting style. In *Santai gafu*, each subject is rendered three times, in styles that in calligraphic terms would be called *shin*, *gyō* (semicursive), and *sō* (cursive). For each subject, the most detailed rendering is marked with a square, the more abbreviated style with a triangle, and the most freely brushed style with a circle. AY

The full title of the famous series known in the West as the *Manga* begins with the words *Education of Beginners through the Spirit of Things (Denshin kaishu)*. The *Manga,* which include a vast range of subjects, natural and supernatural, were as influential as Hokusai's famous prints of the 1830s in establishing his reputation as an important artist in Japan and the West. The *Manga* were published and republished for more than three decades during Hokusai's lifetime, and three volumes were published posthumously. The Nagoya publisher Eirakuya Tōshirō launched the series in collaboration with Kadomaruya Jinsuke of Edo. AY

74 Broadsheet for Hokusai's Painting
Performance of a Giant Bodhidharma
Hokusai sokusho taiga hikifuda
1817 (fifth day, tenth month)
Signature: Hokusai Taito hitsu
Seal: Gakyōjin
woodblock print; large *ōban*, 47.2 x 35.3 cm
Nagoya City Museum of Art
Literature: Edo Tokyo Hakubutsukan 1995,
cat. IV-27; Calza 2003, no. IV.8.
(1-144)

During a stay in Nagoya in 1817 on the
fifth day of the tenth month, Hokusai
painted a giant picture of Bodhidharma,
the Indian patriarch of Zen Buddhism.
The size of the portrait was the area of
one hundred twenty *tatami*, or about 230
square meters. This illustrated broadsheet announces the painting by the
"visitor from the Eastern capital [Edo]
Hokusai Taito." The amazing size of
the image is described in the notes at
the lower right: "the eyes six feet (1.8
meters), nose nine feet (2.7 meters)
the mouth seven feet (2.1 meters)."
In 1804, Hokusai had painted a giant
Bodhidharma at the Gokokuji in Edo. AY

75 Sketch Book of an Impromptu Painting
Performance by Hokusai
Hokusai taiga sokusho saizu
1 volume
1817
by Kōriki Tanenobu (1756–1831)
Signature: Enkōan
color on paper; stitched binding,
24.4 x 18.2 cm
Nagoya City Museum of Art
Literature: Edo Tokyo Hakubutsukan 1995,
105.
(1-145)

Kōriki Tanenobu, whose art name was
Enkōan, wrote and hand-illustrated this
book, which records the public event
Hokusai staged when he painted a giant
image of Bodhidharma during a visit to
Nagoya. *Sekiga,* spontaneous paintings
for private or public audiences, became
increasingly popular during the Edo
period. Artists created *sekiga* upon
request to entertain patrons or one
another. They often painted such works
while traveling, and the images they produced in turn increased their fame.
Hokusai's huge Bodhidharma measured
one hundred twenty *tatami* mats, each
mat approximately three by six feet.
Hokusai designed a poster with a printed
reproduction of his painting (cat. 74) AY

76 Excellent Paintings at a Glance
Shūga ichiran
1 volume, *edehon*
1818
Signature: Katsushika Hokusai hitsu
Publisher: Hishiya Kyūbei
color woodblock printed book;
stitched binding, 26.0 x 16.9 cm
Smithsonian Institution Libraries,
Freer Gallery of Art and Arthur M.
Sackler Gallery Library,
Special collection NE1325.K3 A762 1818
Literature: Hillier 1980, 111–19; Edo Tokyo
Hakubutsukan 1995, 111; Asano and Yoshida
1998, 47–53.
(1-38)

Like Hokusai's popular *Manga* series,
Shūga ichiran presented a variety of
images but was printed in full color. A
similar book printed in ink was published under the title *Mirror of Paintings
Transmitted from Mind to Mind
(Denshin gakyō).* A wide variety of subjects are included in this book, which
was one of the early examples of
Hokusai's work imported to Europe in
the nineteenth century. Jan Cock
Blomhoff, Kapitan of the Dutch Factory
at Deshima from 1818 to 1823, brought
home an example of this book. AY

77 Rough Sketches by Hokusai
Hokusai soga
1 volume, *edehon*
1820
Signature: Katsushika Taito hitsu
Publisher: Minoya Iroku
woodblock printed book;
stitched binding, 27.0 x 17.7 cm
Smithsonian Institution Libraries,
Freer Gallery of Art and
Arthur M. Sackler Gallery Library,
Special collection NE1325.K3 A685 1820
Literature: Hillier 1980, 150–57.
(1-127)

Hokusai's delight in portraying human
activity is expressed in the book *Hokusai
soga.* Here a rainy scene is printed in pale
tones to replicate the misty atmosphere
during a sudden rain shower. A group of
traveling peasants unfurl umbrellas, and
one holds a mat over his head for shelter.
The quality of Hokusai's printed pictures
reveals not only his skillful draftsmanship, but also the high standards his
printers were able achieve. AY

IITSU

1820-33

78 Pounding Rice for *Mochi*
ca. 1822
Signature: Fusenkyo Iitsu hitsu
Seal: Katsushika (type one)
Inscription: See below.
Inscription signature: Hinamaro
hanging scroll; ink and color on silk, 54.3 x 85.0 cm
Freer Gallery of Art, Smithsonian Institution, gift of Lawrence and Sonia Klein F1992.24
Literature: Calza 2003, no. 50, 63.
(1-34)

Preparing rice for *mochi* is a long-standing Japanese custom at New Year. Friends and family gather together and take turns pounding rice that is placed in a large mortar. Today, as in the Edo period, the custom brings home the feeling that the old year is about to end, and the new one to begin.

Here, the figures struggling with the sticky rice dough correspond closely to figures depicted in a similarly humorous style in the *Hokusai manga*. Sometimes called *Toba-e* (Toba pictures), these amusing images were a Hokusai specialty. They convey a sense of delight in all aspects of human existence, and their satirical qualities invite a smile from the viewer, without any sense of crudeness.

This painting is signed "Fusenkyo Iitsu," a name Hokusai used during the mid-Bunsei era (1818–30). In the past, the term "fusenkyo" has been interpreted as "not settled in one place" (literally, "not permeated by habitation"). Recently, Kōno Motoaki has noted that *fusen* is a Buddhist term meaning "untouched by worldly passions" (literally, "unstained"). Thus interpreted, Hokusai's art name would mean, "living untouched by worldly passions."

The inscription on the painting reads:

wakō narishi	At the advent of spring
kao miru haru ni	we prepare offerings
utsuru tote	of rice cakes,
mochi wa kagami ni	round as a mirror,
torasekeru kana	in which the season finds reflected
Hina maro	her own youthful countenance.

NM

Translation of poem by Alfred Haft

79 Shōki (Zhong Kui)
1826 (prior to the fifth month)
Signature: Saki no Hokusai Iitsu hitsu (by the brush of Iitsu, formerly
Hokusai)
Seal: reading unclear
hanging scroll; ink and color on silk, 102.2 x 30.4 cm
Kumamoto Prefectural Museum of Art
Provenance: Totsuka Yakichi.
Literature: Nagata 2000 no. 142 (bw), 187 and 284.
(1-152)

80 Peddler of Fortune-telling Poems
1827 (first month, second day)
Signature: Hokusai Iitsu keiga (Respectfully painted by Hokusai Iitsu)
Seal: Katsushika (type one)
Inscription: Bunsei jū hinoto i nen/shōgatsu futsuka fude-hajime
(First use of the brush on the second day of the first month, boar
year, Bunsei 10 [1827])
hanging scroll; ink and color on paper, 124.2 x 50.5 cm
The British Museum 1913.5-1.0317 (Japanese Painting 1450).
Given by Sir. W. Gwynne-Evans, Bt.
Provenance: Arthur Morrison.
Literature: Morrison 1911, 2:pl. XXVI; British Museum 1948, no. 163;
Hillier 1955, no. 80; Narazaki 1982, no. 32; Forrer 1988, no. 327; Clark
1992, no. 100; Asahi 1993, no. 59; Calza 1994, no. 12.8; Nagata 2000,
no. 143 (bw); Nikkei 2005, no. 437.
(1-46)

The Chinese Popular deity Zhong Kui, known in Japan as Shōki, was believed to have the power to dispel demons, especially those who caused illness and epidemics. Banners and hanging scroll paintings portraying Shōki as a large muscular figure wearing the robes of a Chinese scholar were hung annually for the Boys' Festival in May and also during outbreaks of illness, especially smallpox. Hokusai's earliest known painting (cat. 1) portrays a red figure of Shōki with his sword drawn against an unfortunate demon. Several other known paintings of Shōki by Hokusai indicate that he received a number of commissions for this subject throughout his career.

Although many of Hokusai's paintings of Shōki are entirely red, a color regarded as efficacious in dispelling illness, the figure in this hanging scroll is rendered entirely in black ink. Two horizontal bands of dark blue across the top of the scroll give the appearance of a banner. In contrast to the dynamic action in his earlier image of Shōki, Hokusai's later paintings of the exorcist often present him, as in this example, with his sword concealed in a pose of contained but terrifying strength. Facing directly toward the viewer, Shōki stares menacingly and appears as if he is about to emerge from the painting. Contrasts of dark shading alternating with unpainted highlights that exaggerate the unnatural musculature create the striking volume of the figure.

An inscribed note on the back of the mounting of this scroll dated the fifth of the ninth year of the Bunsei era (1826) provides the name of the owner as the fourth-generation Totsuka Yakichi. This record of the date when Totsuka took possession of the painting clearly sets the date of execution of the painting before the fifth lunar month of 1826 (Nagata 2000, 284). AY

A "poem diviner" (uta-ura) in the medieval period was an itinerant seller of classical poems, which were used to tell people's fortunes. Hokusai included a similar figure in volume eleven of Hokusai manga, with the comment "this type originated with Watarai no Tayū." This seems to refer to the nō play Utaura, written by Kanze Motomasa (1400–32) in the early fifteenth century, in which the principal character Watarai Ietsugu of Ise travels around the land selling his poems. Therefore, this painting may depict Watarai wearing the white robes of a traveling priest and with the verses he sells written on long poem-cards (tanzaku) attached to the string of his bow.

One intriguing aspect to the painting is whether it could be considered in any way a self-portrait of the artist. Evidence for this would be its similarity, to a degree, to a surimono print of a fisherman seated on a rock. This surimono bears poems by both Hokusai and his daughter Ōi, and because of the signature, "self painted and inscribed" (jigasan), some scholars believe it is a self-portrait. The nose of the figure in the print is much shorter, and his features are generally coarser in comparison to the fine, serious expression here, which is appropriate to the noble character. If this is indeed a kind of self-portrait, then Hokusai, fascinatingly, has projected his own features onto a character from classical literature. The downcast expression appears reflective, and the warm smile seems tinged with a certain melancholy.

The signature and accompanying inscription have considerable documentary importance. Hokusai writes, "respectfully painted by Hokusai Iitsu" and "First use of the brush on the second day of the first month, boar year, Bunsei 10 [1827]," meaning the first use after a pause to observe the New Year holiday. The use of "respectfully" could be a mark of Hokusai's respect for the literary character portrayed. Another explanation, however, would be that this work was created for a patron of rank, which would make the possible inclusion of a self-portrait even more intriguing. Stylistically, this is a bravura performance, with lines of many different characters and tonalities combined boldly and at speed to form the figure. The simple background of broad horizontal strokes of wash and the fact that the painting is on paper further supports that this work was "done at a gathering" (sekiga) by special request. A very similar background and ink technique is seen in the painting Wild Boar under a Full Moon (Museum of Fine Arts, Boston), which has the signature "saki (no) Hokusai Iitsu hitsu" and the same type one "Katsushika" seal seen here (Boston 2000, 3:no. 66). Eighteen hundred twenty seven (Bunsei 10) was a year of the boar according to the traditional zodiac, making a wild boar an appropriate subject for a New Year painting. Therefore, it is possible that the two paintings were completed very close in time to one another. TC

82 Night Attack at the Horikawa Mansion
ca. 1820-33
Signature: Hokusai aratame Iitsu hitsu
Seal: Katsushika (type one)
Inscription: See below.
Inscription signature: Ōhira
hanging scroll; ink and color on silk, 106.3 x 37.6 cm
Private collection
Provenance: Manno Art Museum, Osaka; Tamura Ichirō, 1919.
Literature: Takeoka 1919; Ōta 1985, no. 555; Naitō 1995, no. 10, 20; Kobayashi 1996, 7:no. 51; Nagata 2000, no. 144 (bw); Nikkei 2005, no. 438.
(1·47)

81 Mount Fuji and Enoshima
ca. 1825-31
Signature: Katsushika saki no Hokusai Iitsu ga (Painted by Iitsu, Katsushika the former Hokusai)
Seal: Katsushika (type one)
pair of two-panel folding screens; ink and color on paper, each screen: 163.2 x 157.2 cm
Freer Gallery of Art, Smithsonian Institution, gift of Charles Lang Freer F1904.175 and F1904.176
Provenance: Kobayashi Bunshichi, 1904; Honma Kōsō.
Literature: Stern 1960, no. 11; Stern 1973, no. 90; Stern and Narazaki 1981, 16:no. 147; Calza 1994, nos. 2, 3, and 6-8.
(1·111)

This painting depicts the seashore with the pristine white peak of Mount Fuji rising in the background. The larger island is probably Enoshima, near Kamakura, and the smaller island to the left is probably Ubajima, popularly called "Court-Hat Rock" (Eboshi-iwa). In any event, the scene appears to be treated imaginatively, with quite a few differences from the actual landscape. The expansive view creates an impression entirely different from that of the "Enoshima" print in Hokusai's series *Thirty-six Views of Mount Fuji*, while the brush style and coloration are also highly unusual. Certain aspects of the style thus warrant further close study, but overall the pair of screens should be regarded for now as a product of the master's hand. They are currently mounted as a pair of folding screens, but the outlines of holes for old door-pulls are visible, strongly suggesting that they were originally a set of sliding doors. The artist used the signature "saki no Hokusai Iitsu" from the Bunsei (1818–30) to early Tenpō (1830–44) eras. NM

This work depicts a well-known episode from the life of the warrior hero Minamoto no Yoshitsune (1159–89), a brilliant but ultimately tragic figure who assumed legendary status in later periods. Notwithstanding the succession of military victories he secured over the rival Taira clan, Yoshitsune was persecuted in his last years by his increasingly jealous and suspicious elder brother Yoritomo (1147–99), who was the founder of the Kamakura shogunate. According to the various medieval war chronicles, in 1185 Yoritomo ordered Tosanobō Shōshun (Shōzon) to attack Yoshitsune at his mansion at Horikawa in Kyoto. Here, Yoshitsune's beautiful lover Shizuka offers up to him his great sword as the young warrior dresses to respond to the surprise attack at night. Judging from the pattern of the Buddhist wheel of the law on his robes, the alert older warrior at the bottom of the painting who scowls out ferociously in defiance must be Yoshitsune's faithful retainer, the monk Benkei.

Hokusai arranged the three figures into a complex and brilliantly original continuous snaking arrangement, which subliminally emphasizes their unity of purpose in the face of the alarm. Overall the composition might be described as forming an "S" curve, however the horizontal sword, the coiling skirts of Shizuka's black surcoat, and the spreading cloth of Benkei's long ceremonial trousers all interrupt this and add compositional weight and interest. The turn-ing, stretching, and crouching bodies of the three figures radiate dynamism even though each is hidden within voluminous clothing. In his "Taito" and "Iitsu" periods, Hokusai frequently used crinkled, nervous lines to edge the draperies of his female figures. This type of line is very evident in Shizuka's costume and contrasts with the more angular, but nevertheless characterful lines used for the robes and armor of the two male figures. Details such as the fabric patterns and sword fittings are finely done, in rich, saturated colors embellished with bright touches of yellow and gold.

Motoori Ōhira (1756–1833) inscribed a *kyōka* verse onto the top of the painting. Ōhira was the pupil and adopted son of the great scholar of national learning (*kokugaku*) Motoori Norinaga (1730–1801); therefore, the painting must have been done before Ōhira's death in 1833. The poem likens Yoshitsune, fated to be last in his line, to the end of a pine branch and weaves in the place names of Kamakura, the center of Minamoto family power, and Ichinotani, the site of a great Yoshitsune victory in 1184. It reads:

Kamakura no	The mountain wind
matsu no sueeda no	of the branch tips
yamakaze zo	of Kamakura
Ichinotani yori	comes racing in
ichihayaku shite	from Ichinotani Valley

TC

Translation of poem by Timothy Clark

83 Crustaceans
ca. 1825-30
Signature: Hokusai aratame Iitsu hitsu (Painted by Iitsu, changed from Hokusai)
Seal: Jinkō
hanging scroll mounted on panel; ink and color on silk, 47.7 x 60.1 cm
Freer Gallery of Art, Smithsonian Institution, gift of Charles Lang Freer F1902.254
Provenance: Kobayashi Bunshichi, 1902.
Literature: Fenollosa 1901, no. 160; Stern 1973, no. 95; Stern and Narazaki 1981, 16:no. 108;
Calza 1994, no. 2.4; Nagata 2000, no. 74 (color)
(1-100)

84 Cormorant on a Rock
late 1820s-early 1830s
Signature: Katsushika saki (no) Hokusai Iitsu hitsu (Painted by Iitsu, Katsushika the former Hokusai)
Seal: Katsushika (type one)
hanging scroll; ink and color on silk, 41.3 x 71.3 cm
Hayashibara Museum of Art, Okayama
Literature: Nikkei 1967, no. 46; Ōta 1985, no. 556; Nagata 1990, 5:no. 5; Asahi 1993, no. 57; Calza 1994, no. 3.8; Nagata 2000, no. 77 (bw).
(1-92)

85 Flowering Pumpkin Vine and Horsefly
ca. 1825-33
Signature: saki no Hokusai Iitsu hitsu (Painted by Iitsu, the former Hokusai)
Seal: Katsushika (type one)
hanging scroll mounted on panel; ink and color on silk, 34.3 x 53.8 cm
Freer Gallery of Art, Smithsonian Institution, gift of Charles Lang Freer F1898.111
Provenance: E. S. Hull 1898.
Literature: Nagata 2000, no. 141.
(1-105)

It was not unusual for Hokusai to decide on a theme and then mobilize his rampantly fertile imagination to explore it in all its manifestations. The most famous example is of course the forty-six prints in his *Thirty-six Views of Mount Fuji* (cats. 96–100), followed with the more than one hundred prints in the three-volume illustrated book *One Hundred Views of Mount Fuji* (cat. 162). Just around the same time that he was working on the Fuji print series, Hokusai must have decided to paint one hundred views of crabs in this single composition. (Actually there are about one hundred six crabs.) In his printed illustrated album of 1819, *Hokusai's Painting Method (Hokusai gashiki)*, there is a composition of crabs and water plants that anticipates aspects of this painting (Nagata 1990, 1:no. 59). As was often the case during his career, Hokusai worked his way up to something spectacular after quite a long period of gestation.

Literalist viewers might argue that the soft fronds of the seaweed, delicately modulated, seem to be in deep water, whereas the crabs appear to be standing on land. One could account for this by suggesting that we are looking down into a rock pool, still filled with a certain reservoir of seawater after the tide has retreated.

Surely the (hopeless) desire to explain literally this wonderfully eccentric painting stems from the fact that each creature—most of them tiny, while others are alarmingly large—is painted in such a vivid way. They look so full of life that one feels the need to read the whole painting realistically. So why do the teeming crabs suddenly stop in the top left corner? Is this the edge of the water? Whatever the reason, the decision to leave this area unpainted creates an exciting tension within the work, and makes the viewer even more aware of the intricate shapes around each of the spiky creatures.

Hokusai mobilized an extraordinary array of colors, ink washes, and lines of different kinds, especially for the bodies of the seven largest crabs grouped in the center. This quality is entirely typical of Hokusai's work. It is almost a truism to say that every single line of his original brushworks is of a different character. He was also careful to make the eyes of each crab visible. Which leads to a startling realization: They are all looking out at us.

There has been debate about the correct reading of the unusual seal on this painting. Here it is read tentatively as "Jinkō" (man-made). TC

A solitary cormorant crouches close to rocks, as spray from a foaming sea merges into the sky. Excited ink strokes representing moss jump into the air, increasing the drama. Perhaps the bird had just dived in the water and is now drying its spiky plumage in the stiff sea breeze. The contemporary Nagasaki school of painting, derived from China, also specialized in detailed renditions of birds set against pale blue skies. But the contorted pose and sparse setting in this work are quite unique, and the single, staring eye of the bird seems, frankly, to challenge. During his last two decades Hokusai would create many eccentric birds and beasts, all with strong personalities that project outward to engage the viewer.

An almost identical expression is found in the painting *Cormorant and Morning Glory* (Clark 1992, no. 98), which must be close in date to the present work. However, the bird in that painting bends its neck back, the plumage is less detailed, and overall the work is less dramatic.

The combination of the "saki (no) Hokusai Iitsu" signature and "Katsushika" (type one) seal suggests a date in the late 1820s or early 1830s. The addition of "Katsushika" at the beginning of such a signature is also found in books published at the New Year, 1834 (Nagata 1985, 85). TC

Hokusai chose this subject many times from his "Iitsu" period onward and the painted versions include: *Pumpkin Flowers and Insects* (1843, Sumida Ward, Tokyo), *Pumpkin Vine and Horsefly* (1847, Sumida Ward, Tokyo), *Album of Models for Painting* (1843, Ōta Memorial Museum, Tokyo), and *Handscroll with Miscellaneous Subjects* (cat. 118; Nagata 2000, nos. 112, 288 [bw], 262–76 [bw]). Hokusai probably enjoyed the challenge of painting the semitransparent wings of the flying insect and the complicated patterns and play of light and shade of the pumpkin leaves and flowers. And his patrons, too, must have been impressed by Hokusai's extraordinary technical skill in such works.

The seal used on this work is the earliest type of "Katsushika" seal (referred to as "type one"). Based on the known period of use of this seal and the similarities in the signatures, this work must have been completed around the same time as *Cormorant and Morning Glory* (British Museum; Clark 1992, no. 98) and *Hanshan and Shide* (Sumida Ward, Tokyo; Nagata 2000, no. 150 [bw]). AS

87 Cock and Hen
ca. 1827–33
Signature: saki no
Hokusai Iitsu hitsu
(Painted by Iitsu, the
former Hokusai)
Seal: Katsushika
(type one)
hanging scroll;
ink and color on silk,
134.0 x 46.4 cm
MOA Museum of Art,
Atami
Literature: Narazaki 1982,
no. 24; Calza 1994, no. 2-2;
MOA 1997, no. 73; Nagata
2000, no. 76 (color);
Nikkei 2005, no. 433.
(1-95)

86 Birds, Animals, and Plants Representing
the Twelve Months
ca. 1820–35
pair of six-panel folding screens; ink and
color on paper,
each screen: 179.5 x 376.0 cm
Freer Gallery of Art, Smithsonian
Institution, gift of Charles Lang Freer
F1904.179 and F1904.180
Provenance: Kobayashi Bunshichi, 1904;
Honma Kōsō.
Literature: Stern 1960, nos. 30-31; Stern
1973, no. 92; Stern and Narazaki 1981,
16:nos. 119-30; Calza 1994, nos. 2-12.
(1-104)

By the late Edo period, Japanese artists of several different schools were producing folding screens that depicted animals and plants representing the twelve months of the year. Such paintings first emerged from the workshops of the Maruyama-Shijō school artists in Kyoto. This school advocated the practice of "painting from life" (*shasei*), as formulated by the founder of the school, Maruyama Okyō (1733–95). Sakai Hōitsu (1761–1828), who was an advocate of the Rinpa revival of the early nineteenth century, brought the subject to Edo. By synthesizing elements of the Maruyama-Shijō and Rinpa schools, Hōitsu in fact forged his own style. He is particularly known for his exquisite depictions of seasonal animals, birds, fish, insects, and plants — many examples of which survive today.

The present pair of screens — a truly refined version of the subject that the works of the Maruyama-Shijō school probably inspired — is extremely unusual within Hokusai's oeuvre. In accordance with Japanese custom, the subjects follow seasonal order from right to left, beginning with the first lunar month and ending with the twelfth lunar month: the right screen depicts a crane and snow-covered tree trunk, fish and cherry blossoms, a fox and mustard flowers, a cuckoo and an iris, turtles and duckweed, and a heron and lotus; the left screen illustrates Bantam fowl and kudzu vine, swallows and loquat, ducks and chrysanthemums, a pheasant and autumn leaves, wild geese and thistle, and finally puppies and snow-covered nandina.

Many of the individual motifs differ from those found in comparable paintings by artists of the Maruyama-Shijō and Rinpa schools. This difference is to be expected from Hokusai, an artist known for his independent nature. On the other hand, the Maruyama-Shijō style clearly permeates the way he rendered the puppies, the wild geese, and the freely swimming fish. It is generally agreed that, among ukiyo-e artists, Utagawa Hiroshige (1797–1858) felt the influence of the Maruyama-Shijō school most profoundly. But since artists of that school had a following in Edo, Hokusai undoubtedly had a chance to view their works. And even though he seems to have possessed quite a superiority complex, he could not entirely disregard the style of the school, which went on to form the basis for modern *nihonga* (Japanese-style painting).

Although the screens are unsigned and have no seal, there is no question that Hokusai painted them. There is also no question that they are superb works, the artist's only known version of the subject. Their date, however, remains uncertain. The panel depicting Bantam fowl closely resembles a painting of the same subject in the MOA Museum of Art (cat. 87), which dates to the artist's "Iitsu" period. The panel with fish and cherry blossoms, on the other hand, recalls a leaf in an album that Hokusai's workshop produced early in the period when he signed his work "Manji." Provisionally, then, the screens may be dated to around the years when Hokusai used the name Iitsu (ca. 1821–33), but further study is warranted. NM

Puffed up with pride, a Bantam cock momentarily halts the minute movements of his head and warily eyes the viewer. The hen appears to support her mate by casting a similarly disdainful, sidelong glance. Both cock and hen convey a fierce individualism, the sort of independence that can find no satisfaction in doing things the ordinary way. Many of Hokusai's paintings of animals share this sort of personified individualism.

Here groups of curving leaves painted in different shades of ink stretch down from the top right, like hands giving cover to the two birds. Hokusai painted the feathers and legs with great care. The method differs from "painting from life" (*shasei*), which the Kyoto artist Maruyama Ōkyo (1733–95) had formulated several decades earlier. Rather, Hokusai's unique method of exaggeration and abbreviation produces an inimitable world, so characteristic of his paintings. Hokusai's modeling frequently shows evidence of calculated distortion, a technique that lends immediate visual interest to his work.

A number of scenes of Bantam fowl are among the fan prints that Hokusai produced in his last years. This painting, however, is his finest version of the subject, with an unforgettable quality all its own. Hokusai used the name Iitsu from the age of sixty until his early seventies. This painting may be assigned to the latter part of that period, corresponding to the early Tenpō era (1830–44). NM

88 Country Scenes
ca. 1830-32
Signature: saki no Hokusai litsu hitsu (Painted by litsu, the former Hokusai)
Seal: Katsushika (type one)
pair of six-panel folding screens; ink, gold, and color on paper, each screen: 150.7 x 350.8 cm
Freer Gallery of Art, Smithsonian Institution, gift of Charles Lang Freer F1902.48 and
F1902.49
Provenance: Ernest F. Fenollosa and Mrs. Lisa Fenollosa, 1902.
Literature: Fenollosa 1901, no. 170; Stern 1960, nos. 34-35; Stern 1973, no. 93; Stern and
Narazaki 1981, 16:no. 144.
(1-110)

89 Six Tama Rivers
1833
Signature: toki ni toshi nanajūyon, saki no Hokusai litsu hitsu (Painted by litsu, the former
Hokusai, aged seventy-four)
Seal: Katsushika (type two)
pair of six-panel folding screens; ink and color on paper, each panel: 132.0 x 47.8 cm
Freer Gallery of Art, Smithsonian Institution, gift of Charles Lang Freer F1904.204 and F1904.205
Provenance: Kobayashi Bunshichi 1904; Honma Kōsō.
Literature: Stern 1960, nos. 32-33; Stern and Narazaki 1981, 16:nos. 131-42; Nagata 2000, nos.
78-79 (color).
(1-49)

During the Edo period, ukiyo-e artists were considered mere "painting artisans" (*gakō*). They produced mainly prints and small-scale paintings. Large-scale works, such as folding screens or sets of sliding doors, remained the preserve of officially employed artists and certain designated "townsman painters" (*machi-eshi*). This situation even held true in the case of Hokusai, whose relatively large output includes only a limited number of screens. It comes as something of a surprise to discover that most of Hokusai's large-scale works are now found in the collection of the Freer Gallery of Art, reflecting Charles Lang Freer's determination to build what has become the finest Hokusai painting collection in the world.

Hokusai created a landscape with Mount Fuji rising in the distance, a true genre scene that extends on an exceptionally grand scale across a pair of folding screens. The work most likely dates from the period when Hokusai was designing the famous print series *Thirty-six Views of Mount Fuji* (cats. 96–100). Even if the sacred mountain itself were not included, there are many points of similarity with that series, in terms of the pictorial composition, the figures of the farmers, and the style of the trees. Figures comparable to those scattered across the screens can be seen in the *Thirty-six Views of Mount Fuji* series, in the *Hokusai manga* printed sketchbooks, and in other prints. The screens are a carefully executed, deluxe production—the extravagant use of sprinkled gold dust suggests a commission from a wealthy patron. In fine condition, they are a major work in which Hokusai's considerable artistic prowess is at its peak. NM

Located in different regions throughout Japan, the Six Tama (Jewel) Rivers have long served as a conventional theme (*utamakura*) in classical Japanese poetry. The rivers are: Ide Tama River in Yamashiro Province, Noji Tama River in Ōmi, Noda Tama River in Mutsu, Kōya Tama River in Kii, Chōfu Tama River in Musashi, and Mishima Tama River in Settsu. When the theme occurs in painting, a specific motif represents each river: Ide Tama River, the mountain rose (or kerria, *yamabuki*); Noji, bushclover; Noda, plovers; Kōya, a waterfall; Chōfu, country women bleaching cloth; and Mishima, country women fulling cloth.

This pair of screens depicts landscape features and legendary figures associated with the six rivers, together forming a collection of twelve related paintings. The artist is known to have painted another version of the subject during the late Kansei era (1789–1801), when he used the name Hokusai. On that occasion, he produced a set of six hanging scrolls, one to represent each river (five of the set are currently known and are located in different collections). The Freer pair of screens is thus exceptional because two motifs are depicted for each river. It is not possible to explore in detail here the choice of motifs, but they may be listed as follows: for the Ide, *yamabuki* and a court servant with carp; for the Noji, bushclover blossoming by a stream and the figure of Minamoto Toshiyori (ca. 1055–1129), a classical poet and author of the best-known poem about the Noji Tama River contained in the *Senzai wakashū* anthology (the pose, gazing up at the moon, may also evoke another famous poet, Abe no Nakamaro (ca. 700–70); for the Noda, plover birds and the haiku poet Matsuo Bashō

(1644–94), who is known to have visited the region; for the Kōya, a waterfall and a woodcutter; for the Chōfu, women bleaching cloth and a scene of the river; and for the Mishima, women fulling cloth and a classical court lady.

Formerly in the collection of Honma Kōsō, the screens were displayed to the public for the first time in a Hokusai exhibition that Ernest Fenollosa organized in 1900. However, the sequence of the panels was different from their current order. At that time, the pairs of motifs described above were placed alongside one another in a sequence of six pairings.

One unexplained puzzle is why the title, *Six Tama Rivers* (*Tamagawa rokkei*), the signature, "painted by Iitsu, the former Hokusai" (*saki no Hokusai Iitsu hitsu*), and "Aged 74" (*Jinen nanajūyon*) were all inscribed on the same single panel depicting the woodcutter. Screens are very rare in Hokusai's oeuvre, and the pair should be highly appreciated as the last masterpiece of the artist's "Iitsu" period. NM

90 Various Faces
ca. 1830
ink on paper, 23.7 x 33.1 cm
Freer Gallery of Art, Smithsonian Institution, gift of Charles Lang Freer F1904.268
Provenance: Kobayashi Bunshichi, 1904.
Literature: Stern 1960, cat. 12, 21; Stern 1973, cat. 114, 296-97.
(1-33)

Surrounding two rapidly and roughly sketched figures are drawings of faces of men and women seen from various viewpoints and rendered in contrasting styles ranging from realistic to stylized and abbreviated like a modern cartoon. The randomness of this spontaneous group of sketches resembles some pages of the *Hokusai manga*, the artist's most popular series of sketchbooks. Among the several images of elderly men on this sheet is one near the center with a short inscription, "Katsushika no okina" or "Old man Katsushika." This probably refers to Hokusai, and it is possible that the image was a self-portrait. AY

91 Fisherman Tossing Bait
ca. 1830
ink on paper, 15.5 x 26.2 cm
Freer Gallery of Art, Smithsonian Institution, gift of Charles Lang Freer F1904.264
Provenance: Kobayashi Bunshichi, 1904.
(1-32)

Like many of Hokusai's sketches of human figures, this image of a fisherman who is about to toss his net into the surging waves includes two renderings of the head in different positions. Hokusai's preliminary sketches often feature tests of different poses. As his drawings became more final, like the painstaking full-scale final versions (*hanshita-e*) for his prints, Hokusai occasionally cut out areas to be revised and carefully patched in his revision. In this sketch, Hokusai sketched the figure seated on the rocks and indicated roughly the configuration of the crests of the ocean waves, a prominent subject of his prints, illustrations, and paintings in the last two decades of his life. AY

92 Genroku Shell Match: The Leg Shell
Genroku kasen kai awase: ashigai
1821
Signature: Getchi Rōjin Iitsu hitsu
color woodblock print;
shikishiban surimono, 20.3 x 17.8 cm
The Art Institute of Chicago, Clarence Buckingham Collection 1925.2924
Literature: Asano 2003, 58-64; Calza 2003, V.7-2; Asano 1998, 33-50.
(1-59)

This *surimono* is one of thirty-six Hokusai designed under a title that refers to poetry competitions held on the New Year in which different types of seashells were matched to verses composed on the occasion. The series was created for the Yomo poetry club, whose members composed the humorous *kyōka* printed at the tops of the small sheets. The exceptional quality of block carving, color printing, and embossing and the luxurious effects of silver, gold, and mica enhance the elegant designs. This image, a masterpiece of the series, shows a flock of cranes in front of waves that are rolling toward the shore where they tend their young. AY

93 Horses of Every Fashion: Jinmesō
Seaweed
Umazukushi: jinmesō
1822
Signature: Fusenkyo litsu hitsu
Collector seal: Henri Wimiwater
color woodblock print; *shikishiban suri-
mono* 20.8 x 18.5 cm
Collection of Joanna H. Schoff
Provenance: Henri Wimiwater.
Literature: Mirviss 2000, cat. 9; Asano 1998,
33–50; Asano 2003, 58–64; McKee 2006, 95.
(1-60)

94 Horses of Every Fashion: Products of
Arima Province
1822
Signature: Fusenkyo litsu hitsu
color woodblock print; *shikishiban surimono* 20.4 x 18.1 cm
Collection of Joanna H. Schoff
Literature: Mirviss 2000, cat. 11; Asano 1998,
33–50; Asano 2003, 58–64.
(1-61)

95 Group of Hens and Roosters
1835
Signature: saki no Hokusai litsu hitsu
Publisher: Tsujiya Yasubei
Publisher seal: Tsuji
Censor seal: *kiwame*
color woodblock print; *uchiwa-e*,
22.5 x 29.0 cm
Tokyo National Museum,
Important Art Object
Literature: Nagata 1990, 1:17; Calza 2003,
v.50; Nikkei 2005, cat. 356.
(1-93)

The *Umazukushi* series of *surimono* commissioned by the Yomo club of *kyōka* poets was published in 1822, the Year of the Horse. It includes poems by Manmansai Manga, Waseiken Imaru, and Shichinsha Manpō. The title is printed as a red seal in the form of a gourd, an allusion to the Chinese immortal who carried a gourd from which he brought forth a horse that could be magically expanded to full size whenever it was needed. In one design of a New Year offering, a lobster rests atop a golden bundle of *jinmesō* seaweed commonly known as *hondawara* (sargasso) but also called "shrine-horse" seaweed after the sacred horses kept at Shinto shrines. Below the New Year ornament is a bundle of *gohei*, paper offerings to Shinto deities (Mirviss 2000, 57). AY

In another still life from the series, allusions to horses are more difficult to discern. Products of Arima, a name that means "there are horses," are arranged on a colorful cloth. Cutlery, in the form of scissors and a paper knife, rest atop a paper wrapper. Brushes with bobbing paper doll heads, another product of Arima, rest on the handle of the portable inkwell, which is wrapped with a purple cord lying to one side like a horse's bridle. The poem by Chikushien Itoyori mentions the bath girls of Arima and the green "bamboo grass" tone of their lip makeup, which was fashionable at the time (Mirviss 2000, 59–60).

Arimyama   At Mount Arima
Yuna mo sasabeni as the bathhouse
Kewai shitsu   girls apply
Ide soyosoyo to   "bamboo grass rouge"
soyogu harukaze   The spring winds rise
                    To blow it back and
                    forth.

AY

*Translation of poem by Daniel McKee,
Mckee 2006, 91.*

A group of seven hens and roosters is tightly intertwined at the center of this print in the form of a round flat fan (*uchiwa*). Prints of this type were often mounted on fans, which were used through the summer and discarded when they became worn. Few fan prints by Hokusai are known (Forrer 1991, cat. 67). In Hokusai's unusual composition, the black, brown, and white plumage of the birds forms striking patterns over the three-dimensional bodies and heads. In this design, Hokusai demonstrates his mastery of naturalistic representation and three-dimensional form and arranges an original composition with effective use of color as a design element, while imbuing each bird with a powerful gaze and expression. Recently scholars have dated the publication of this print to 1835 (Calza 2003, v.50; Nikkei 2005, 350), although a date of 1823 has also been proposed (Nagata 1990, 1:17). AY

Thirty-six Views of Mount Fuji

Hokusai's most famous series of landscape prints was published in the early 1830s when the artist was in his seventies. His images of the sacred mountain had meaning beyond their artistry for Hokusai and his contemporaries, many of whom worshiped Mount Fuji and made pilgrimages to its slopes. The soaring peak of the mountain, which is white with snow in winter, emerging from mist or banded with clouds, was visible from much of Edo. Worship of Mount Fuji was associated with the bodhisattva Sengen, and was believed to protect one from epidemics and to bring peace and prosperity to the country and its people (Clark 2001, 17). When Japanese prints caught the attention of Western artists and collectors in the second half of the nineteenth century, Hokusai's prints of Mount Fuji elicited admiration for their striking designs and colors and their expression of the power and beauty of nature. Some of the designs provide close-up views of the mountain itself, while others depict distant views and include human activity. Light and atmosphere representing different times of day are a focus of the series, which features simple but unusual coloration, including keyblocks printed in blue rather than the usual black ink. Ten additional prints under the same title and with keyblocks printed in black were added to the initial series of thirty-six, which was so successful that some of the most popular designs, such as the "Great Wave" were reprinted repeatedly. AY

96 Thirty-six Views of Mount Fuji: South Wind at Clear Dawn
Fugaku sanjūrokkei: Gaifū kaisei
ca. 1830–31
Signature: Hokusai aratame Iitsu hitsu (Painted by Iitsu, changed from Hokusai)
Publisher: Nishimuraya Yohachi
color woodblock print; *ōban*, 26.0 x 38.1 cm
Private collection
Provenance: Werner Schindler; Louis Gonse.
Literature: Forrer 1991, cat. 12; Calza 2003, no. V.35.2A.
(1-118)

This strikingly simple close-up view of Mount Fuji is commonly known as "Red Fuji." The conical form of the mountain has the red color that it takes on when illuminated by morning sunlight. A blue sky filled with horizontal bands of clouds that reflect Hokusai's assimilation of ideas from his earlier study of Dutch copperplate engravings further accentuates the shape and color of the sacred peak (Forrer 1991, cat. 12).

This print was once in the collection of the French collector and writer Louis Gonse, whose book *L'Art Japonais* (1883) included a chapter devoted to Hokusai. AY

97 Thirty-six Views of Mount Fuji: Beneath the Wave off the Coast at Kanagawa
Fugaku sanjūrokkei: Kanagawa oki namiura
ca. 1830–31
Signature: Hokusai aratame Iitsu hitsu (Painted by Iitsu, changed from Hokusai)
Publisher: Nishimuraya Yohachi
color woodblock print; *ōban*, 26.1 x 38.5 cm
The Mann Collection, Highland Park, Illinois
Literature: Forrer 1991, pl. 11; Calza 2003, V.35.1.
(1-117)

The arc of a huge breaking wave dominates this print, which is one of the most famous images in world art. Commonly known as "The Great Wave," the work is widely regarded as Hokusai's masterpiece. Three boats riding on the surging waves are filled with oarsmen who huddle to brace themselves against the impending crash of the wave. In contrast to the urgent human drama in the foreground, Mount Fuji in the distance is still and impassive, a symbol of the eternal in the midst of transience and mutability. Of particular interest in this print is the representation with broken lines and color tones of the complex and constantly changing movements of water as the waves form and break. AY

98 Thirty-six Views of Mount Fuji: Ushibori in Hitachi Province
Fugaku sanjūrokkei: Jōshū ushibori
ca. 1831
Signature: saki no Hokusai Iitsu hitsu (Painted by Iitsu, the former Hokusai)
Publisher: Nishimuraya Yohachi
color woodblock print; *ōban*, 26.3 x 39.3 cm
The Mann Collection, Highland Park, Illinois
Literature: Forrer 1991, cat. 19; Ōta 1994, no.70, Calza 2003, no. V.35, V.35.20.
(1-120)

This print is a rare early impression of this tranquil scene that is printed entirely in tones of blue and from perfectly intact printing blocks. From a boat moored in a marsh near the shore of a lake, a man pours overboard as others rest in the dim light before dawn. This print is exceptional for the control of the tonal gradations of the monochromatic color printing and for the finely carved lines of the keyblock. In later impressions, colors such as green, yellow, and pink were added (Forrer 1991, cat. 19). AY

99 Thirty-six Views of Mount Fuji: In the Mountains of Tōtōmi Province
Fugaku sanjūrokkei: Tōtōmi sanchū
ca. 1831
Signature: saki no Hokusai Iitsu hitsu (Painted by Iitsu, the former Hokusai)
Seals: Eijudō (publisher), *kiwame* (censor)
Publisher: Nishimuraya Yohachi
color woodblock print; *ōban*, 25.6 x 38.5 cm
Arthur M. Sackler Gallery, Smithsonian Institution, The Anne van Biema Collection
S2004.3.211
Literature: Yonemura 2002, 292-93; Calza 2003, V.35.19.
(1-119)

In this famous design, the timbers supporting a large tree trunk frame Mount Fuji as two workmen, one above and one below, saw it into boards. Nearby, a man seated in front of a simple straw-mat shelter hones the blade of another saw. This fine early impression shows particular refinement in the tonalities of the smoke that billows upward and disperses, echoing the path of the clouds encircling Mount Fuji. AY

100 Thirty-six Views of Mount Fuji: Viewing the Evening Sun at Ryōgoku Bridge from Onmayagashi
Fugaku sanjūrokkei: Onmayagashi yori Ryōgokubashi no sekiyō o miru
ca. 1832
Signature: saki no Hokusai Iitsu hitsu (Painted by Iitsu, the former Hokusai)
Seals: Eijudō (publisher); *kiwame* (censor)
Publisher: Nishimuraya Yohachi
color woodblock print; *ōban*, 25.7 x 37.3 cm
The Metropolitan Museum of Art, Rogers Fund, 1922 (JP1331)
Literature: Forrer 1991, pl. 26; Calza 2003, V.35.22.
(1-121)

A ferry in the foreground carries passengers across the Sumida River from Onmayagashi to Honjō. In the distance is the long span of the Ryōgoku Bridge, a busy crossing that could be traversed on foot. River ferries were the taxis of their day, and they were the swiftest and most efficient way to move people and baggage across distances in the crowded city. Mount Fuji appears deep blue in the fading daylight, matching the dark tone of the waves, which form a striking pattern in the foreground. Passengers from various walks of life settle in for the crossing as the boatman turns for a last view of the mountain before nightfall. AY

101 Traveling around the Waterfalls in the Provinces: Amida Waterfall on the Kisokaidō Road
Shokoku taki meguri: Kisoji no oku Amida ga taki
1833
Signature: saki no Hokusai Iitsu hitsu (Painted by Iitsu, the former Hokusai)
Publisher: Nishimuraya Yohachi
color woodblock print; *ōban*, 38.7 x 25.9 cm
Courtesy David R. Weinberg Collection
Literature: Forrer 1991, cat. 42; Asano 1998, fig. 28; Calza 2003, V.48.3.
(1-123)

The eight prints of Hokusai's "Waterfalls" series, published after *Thirty-six Views of Mount Fuji*, were the first to focus on water as the principal subject. Hokusai's interest in depicting running and splashing water had begun early in his career, but in this series he expresses the innate power and sacred associations of water as it flows from sources deep in the mountains. The links between the human, natural, and spiritual worlds are present in all the prints in this series, which includes images as memorable and original as the "Great Wave."

In this strikingly abstract work, water falls straight down a dark gorge from a circular pool. The linear pattern of the ripples in the pool resembles the effects created by floating ink on marbled paper used for calligraphy. On a cliff at the left, a group of travelers rests as a servant heats water for tea. Their presence heightens the sense of the awesome grandeur of the waterfall, which falls from a hollow that was believed to resemble the perfect eye of Amida, the Buddha of Infinite Light (Forrer 1991, cat. 42). AY

102 Traveling around the Waterfalls in the Provinces: Kirifuri Waterfall at Mount Kurokami in Shimotsuke Province
Shokoku taki meguri: Shimotsuke Kurokamiyama Kirifuri no taki
1833
Signature: saki no Hokusai Iitsu hitsu (Painted by Iitsu, the former Hokusai)
Seals: Eijudō (publisher); *kiwame* (censor)
Publisher: Nishimuraya Yohachi
color woodblock print; *ōban*, 38.1 x 25.8 cm
The Mann Collection, Highland Park, Illinois
Literature: Forrer 1991, pl. 39; Calza 2003, no. V.48, V.48.8.
(1-122)

The Kirifuri waterfall north of Edo was located along the route to the Tōshōgū shrine at Nikkō. The forceful energy of the water breaking into torrents as it rushes down the rocky mountain is rendered in striking ropelike patterns that break into spray at the base. A group of travelers gazes upward while two others climb along an overhanging ridge. References to Hokusai's publishing firm, Eijudō, are inscribed on the hats that the travelers carry. This print reveals Hokusai's unsurpassed ability to visualize and render in line and color the constantly changing appearance of flowing water. AY

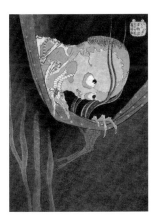

103 One Hundred Ghost Tales:
Kohada Koheiji
Hyaku monogatari: Kohada Koheiji
ca. 1831–32
Signature: saki no Hokusai hitsu
Publisher: Tsuruya Kiemon
color woodblock print; *chūban*, 25.8 x 18.5 cm
The Art Institute of Chicago, Clarence
Buckingham Collection 1943.602
Literature: Edo Tokyo Hakubutsukan 1995,
cat. V-13; Asano 1998, fig. 35; Ōta 2004,
pl. 119; Calza 2003, V.38.3.
(1-151)

104 One Hundred Ghost Tales:
House of Broken Dishes
Hyaku monogatari: Sarayashiki
ca. 1831–32
Signature: saki no Hokusai hitsu
Publisher: Tsuruya Kiemon
color woodblock print; *chūban*, 25.4 x 18.3 cm
Arthur M. Sackler Gallery, Smithsonian
Institution, The Anne van Biema Collection
S2004.3.210
Literature: Asano 1998, fig. 36; Ōta 2004,
cat. 118; Edo Tokyo Hakubutsukan 1995, cat.
V-14; Nikkei 2005, cat. 386, 238, 353.
(1-150)

105 Poppies
ca. 1833–34
Signature: saki no Hokusai Iitsu hitsu
Publisher: Nishimuraya Yohachi
Seals: Eijudō (publisher); *kiwame* (censor)
color woodblock print; *ōban*, 25.0 x 37.2 cm
Musée national des arts asiatiques–Guimet,
Paris E01637
Literature: Nagata 1990, 1:58; Forrer 1991,
cat. 57; Calza 2003, V. 45.
(1-88)

106 Chrysanthemum and Bee
ca. 1833–34
Signature: saki no Hokusai Iitsu hitsu
Seals: Eijudō (publisher); *kiwame* (censor)
Publisher: Nishimuraya Yohachi
color woodblock print; *ōban* 26.3 x 38.9 cm
The Art Institute of Chicago, Clarence
Buckingham Collection 1925.3373
Literature: Nagata 1990, 1:fig. 67, 54; Forrer
1991, cat. 58; Calza 2003, V.45.1.
(1-87)

From the title, *One Hundred Ghost Tales*, it is likely that a series of one hundred might have been planned, but only five designs are known. The title reflects a popular Edo custom of gathering at night to tell stories, and then putting out a candle at the end of each tale. When the last light was out, it was thought that strange specters would appear. Hokusai's *chūban* prints present eerie images of unhappy spirits whose own terrible fates have caused them to seek retribution. In this print, the skeletal ghost of Kohada Koheiji, who was drowned by his wife's lover, pulls back the mosquito net where the guilty couple sleeps. The composition, which frames the head above the border of the curtain and conceals the figure behind it, enhances the startling appearance of the specter. AY

The profile of a female ghost rises from an abandoned, overgrown well in the dark of night. The ghost is the spirit of Okiku, who was killed by her husband and thrown into the well after she accidentally broke his prized ceramic dish. At night her voice emanated from the well, counting broken dishes. Hokusai has created an image of Okiku with a body in the form of porcelain plates, creating the illusion of a snakelike form. Nagata Seiji notes the humor in the ghostly breath that Okiku seems to exhale like tobacco smoke (Nikkei 2005, 353). AY

The untitled series known in the West as "Large Flowers" comprises ten prints presenting close-up views of blossoming plants. Hokusai's strong compositions, expressive line, and color in the series were influential to Western artists and designers in the late nineteenth and early twentieth centuries (Calza 2003, 485). The poppies in this print bend as if caught by a strong breeze. Jagged, even rough lines prevail in this dynamic image, which echoes the composition of "The Great Wave" from the *Thirty-six Views of Mount Fuji* series (Forrer 1991, cat. 57). AY

A dense cluster of various chrysanthemums forms a living bouquet of rich color and texture. This print, a favorite of European artists and collectors, reveals Hokusai's ability to create complex and crowded arrangements while maintaining the integrity, legibility, and aesthetic distinction of each element. AY

107 Landscape with One Hundred Bridges
ca. 1832
Signature: Hokusai aratame Iitsu hitsu
(Painted by Iitsu changed from Hokusai)
Publisher: Nishimuraya Yohachi
color woodblock print; *ōban*, 41.3 x 56.4 cm
Ōta Memorial Museum of Art
Literature: Forrer 1991, cat. 33.
(1-116)

A dream that Hokusai describes in the
inscription at the top of this print
inspired the imaginary landscape. The
high vantage point provides a panoramic
view of the landscape of steep, rocky
mountains surrounding lakes and rivers.
Bridges of all kinds built of earth, stone,
and wood pass across water and steep
gorges. The style of the landscape is
based on Chinese models. AY

108 True Mirrors of Chinese and Japanese
Poetry: Li Bo
Shiika shashin kyō: Rihaku
ca. 1833
Signature: saki no Hokusai Iitsu hitsu
Publisher: Moriya Jihei
Publisher seal: Mori
color woodblock print; *nagaban*, 51.9 x 23.1 cm
Honolulu Academy of Arts, gift of James A.
Michener, 1969 (21,892)
Literature: Forrer 1991, cat. 70;
Asano 1998, pl. 29; Calza 2003, V.43.1.
(1-65)

Hokusai's lifelong interest in Japanese
and Chinese poetry inspired this series
of ten prints in the *nagaban* format that
resemble in smaller scale the proportions
of a hanging scroll painting. In Hokusai's
original rendering of the famous scene
of the Chinese poet Li Bo viewing a
waterfall at Mount Lu, the waterfall
bisects the image, forming an abstract
pattern of vertical lines. Rather than
standing at the base of the waterfall, as
he is conventionally portrayed, the poet
views the waterfall from a high vantage
point, supporting himself with a walking
stick as his two young pupils cling to
him. All the elements of this composition enhance the focus on the engagement between the poet and the waterfall
that inspired him to compose a poem.
AY

109 True Mirrors of Chinese and Japanese
Poetry: Minister Tōru
Shiika shashin kyō: Tōru no Otodo
ca. 1833
Signature: saki no Hokusai Iitsu hitsu
Seals: Mori (publisher); *kiwame* (censor)
Publisher: Moriya Jihei
color woodblock print; *nagaban*,
50.6 x 22.7 cm
The Art Institute of Chicago, Clarence
Buckingham Collection 1925.3332
Literature: Forrer 1991, pl. 68; Calza 2003,
no. V.43.
(1-66)

In this peaceful, moonlit scene, three
courtiers pause beside a lake. Minamoto
no Tōru (822–95), the son of Emperor
Saga, was a poet who was included
among the Thirty-six Immortals of
Poetry. His magnificent garden on the
grounds of his palace on the bank of the
Kamo River in Kyoto included a lake,
which Hokusai has imagined as a vast
expanse of water with a view of mountains in the distance. The composition of
this scene reflects Chinese-style landscapes. The exquisite color and printing
of this impression exemplify the high
aesthetic quality of Hokusai's finest commercial print designs. AY

110 One Thousand Pictures of the Ocean:
Whaling off Gotō Island
Chie no umi: Gotō kujira tsuki
ca. 1833–34
Signature: saki no Hokusai Iitsu hitsu
Publisher: Moriya Jihei
color woodblock print; *chūban*, 19.0 x 25.7 cm
The Art Institute of Chicago, Kate S.
Buckingham Endowment 1983.582
Literature: Forrer 1991, pl. 47;
Calza 2003, V.44.4.
(1-124)

The ten prints in the series *One
Thousand Pictures of the Ocean* focus on
fishing and shellfish gathering — the
activities of human labor that take place
in the sea surrounding the islands of
Japan. The Gotō (Five Islands) in
Nagasaki Prefecture were an important
locale for whaling. Hokusai may have
based this image of a whale on a sketch
or eyewitness description rather than on
his own experience. Nagata Seiji suggests
that a possible source might have been
Saiyu ryodan (1794), with illustrations
by Shiba Kōkan (1747–1818) (Nikkei
2005, cat. 321). The black whale in
churning foam, represented by dots of
unprinted white paper and two tones of
blue, dominates the scene. Like the large
birds in Hokusai's prints and paintings,
the whale seems to stare from the picture as the small fishing boats in a
wedge formation surround it. AY

111 One Thousand Pictures of the Ocean: Chōshi in Shimōsa Province
Chie no umi: Sōshū Chōshi
ca. 1833–34
Publisher: Moriya Jihei
Publisher seal: Mori
color woodblock print; *chūban*, 18.9 x 25.8 cm
The Art Institute of Chicago, Kate S. Buckingham Endowment 1983.583
Literature: Forrer 1991, pl. 48; Calza 2003, V.44.2.
(1-126)

112 One Thousand Pictures of the Ocean: Fishing by Torchlight in Kai Province
Chie no umi: Kōshū hiburi
ca. 1833–34
Seal: *Kiwame* (censor)
Publisher: Moriya Jihei
color woodblock print; *chūban*, 18.8 x 26.0 cm
The Art Institute of Chicago, Kate S. Buckingham Endowment 1983.581
Provenance: J. T. Spaulding, F. W. Gookin, Colonna, and Garland collections.
Literature: Forrer 1991, cat. 49; Calza 2003, V.44.1.
(1-125)

113 Grosbeak and Four O'Clocks
Ikaru, oshiroibana
1834
Signature: saki no Hokusai Iitsu hitsu
Seals: Eijudō (publisher); *kiwame* (censor)
Publisher: Nishimuraya Yohachi
color woodblock print; *chūban*, 29.3 x 19.0 cm
Tokyo National Museum
Literature: Calza 2003, V.46.
(1-89)

114 Bullfinch and Weeping Cherry
Uso, shidarezakura
1834
Signature: saki no Hokusai Iitsu hitsu
Seals: Eijudō (publisher); *kiwame* (censor)
Publisher: Nishimuraya Yohachi
color woodblock print; *chūban*, 25.1 x 18.2 cm
Honolulu Academy of Arts, gift of James A. Michener, 1991 (21,988)
Literature: Forrer 1991, cat. 64; Calza 2003, V.46.1.
(1-90)

Oarsmen turn their boat into a churning wave that crashes against the shore at the right. In the distance, beyond the sea spray, another boat is carried toward the shore. In this close-up view of the sea the boat nearly fills the foreground, and it appears as if the water will carry it off the edge of the picture. Precise alternations of two tones of blue and fine keyblock lines delineate the rushing water. AY

This night scene depicts fishermen holding torches near the surface of a river to lure fish while others prepare to catch them in baskets. An unusual feature of the scene is the black night sky with white stars left unprinted.

Conventionally, printing a gradated band at the top of the page indicated night scenes, although Hokusai had previously experimented with dark skies in the night attack scenes in some of his early *Chūshingura* series (Forrer 1991, cat. 49). AY

In 1834, Hokusai designed ten prints of birds and flowers known as the "Small Flowers." Composed in the midsize *chūban* format, the prints have the proportions of album pages. Hokusai's images of birds and flowers recall Chinese paintings, but also include distinctive elements of the artist's innovative style.

The bright colors of the birds and flowers and the use of gradated or solid colors in the background enhance the visual impact of this series. AY

This bullfinch is seen from below as it perches on a branch of a weeping cherry tree. Although at first glance it appears that the bird is hanging upside down, the picture makes the most sense if one imagines looking upward toward an overhanging branch. Hokusai set the rosy-breasted bullfinch and the delicate pink cherry blossoms against a deep blue background that represents the sky but also provides a striking contrast to the graceful pendant forms of the bird and branch. The poem reads:

Tori hitotsu nurete   One single bird, wet with dew,

dekeri asazakura   Has come out: The morning cherry.

AY

Translation of poem from Forrer 1991, cat. 64

115 Wagtail and Wisteria
Sekirei, fuji
1834
Signature: saki no Hokusai Iitsu hitsu
Seals: Eijudō (publisher); *kiwame* (censor)
Publisher: Nishimuraya Yohachi
color woodblock print; *chūban*, 24.8 x 18.2 cm
Arthur M. Sackler Gallery,
Smithsonian Institution, The Anne van
Biema Collection S2004.3.213
Literature: Yonemura 2002, 314;
Calza 2003, V.46.8.
(1-91)

This beautiful impression of a print
featuring a wagtail beneath wisteria
blossoms exemplifies the finesse of the
color printing in Hokusai's "Small
Flowers" series.

Two lines of a Chinese poem by Qian Qi
(ca. 722–780) appear in semicursive calligraphy to the left of the bird's upturned
tail. The poem reads:

  Stretching creepers
  emerge from cloudy trees

  Their dangling ropes
  cover the nesting crane.

AY

Translation of poem by Stephen D. Allee

116 One-brushstroke Picture Book
Ippitsu gafu
1 volume, *edehon*
1823
Signature: saki no Hokusai Taito sensei
Publisher: Eirakuya Tōshirō
color woodblock printed book; stitched
binding, 22.8 x 15.8 cm
The British Museum 1979.3-5.0.433 JH 433
Literature: Hillier 1980, 189–92; Edo Tokyo
Hakubutsukan 1995, 114; Calza 2003, 464.
(1-98)

Although Hokusai used more than one
brushstroke to create many of the
sketches in this book, he demonstrated
repeatedly that form could be rendered
with a minimum of separate elements.
Cranes standing, in flight, and holding
their heads in several positions could all
be rendered with a single stroke for the
beak, head, neck, and body. Hokusai
designed this book in 1817, at the peak of
his production of art manuals, but it was
not published until 1823. The preface
indicates that the book is based on
sketches by Fukuzensai (Niwa Kagen),
which Hokusai had seen in Nagoya
(Nikkei 2005, cat. 430). AY

117 Hokusai's Women's Precepts
Hokusai onna imagawa
1 volume
published in 1844, designed ca. 1828
Author: Sawada Kichi
Publisher: Eirakuya Tōshirō
woodblock printed book; stitched binding,
22.8 x 15.8 cm
Smithsonian Institution Libraries, Freer
Gallery of Art and Arthur M. Sackler Gallery
Library, Special collection 754.7H8f c.2
Literature: Hillier 1980, 202–05;
Edo Tokyo Hakubutsukan 1995, 191; Calza
2003, 467.
(1-22)

The extraordinary quality of line and
printing in the illustrations of this book
can be seen in this uncolored early edition. Hokusai's illustrations show his
mastery of composition, line, texture,
and narrative focus. The pages illustrated
here contrast in expression and mood. In
the dramatic scene of the maid Iwafuji
beating the virtuous Onoe with a sandal,
Hokusai places the figures in the immediate foreground. Onoe's posture conveys her humiliation, with her head low-
ered and her body compressed. The tree
trunks framing the open space above in
a stagelike setting heightens the focus on
her figure. In the tranquil scene of a
woman seated on the veranda and enjoying a cool breeze, the woman sits in an
elevated position that highlights her
beauty, which is the object of admiration
of the unseen man who is gazing
through the brushwood fence. AY

GAKYŌ RŌJIN MANJI

1834-49

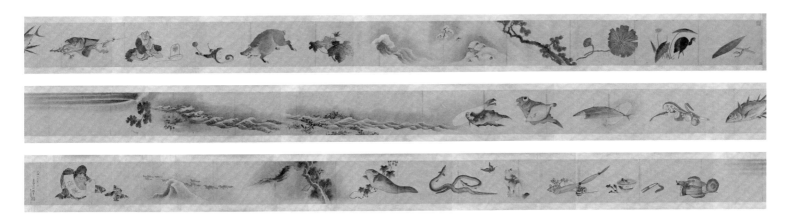

118 Handscroll with Miscellaneous Subjects
1839
Signature: Tenpō jū tsuchinoto i no fuyu, Gakyō rōjin Manji hitsu, yowai hachijū (Winter of
the boar year, Tenpō 10 [1839], painted by Manji, old man mad with pictures, aged eighty)
Seal: Katsushika (type three)
handscroll; ink and color on paper, 26.7 x 1365.0 cm
Freer Gallery of Art, Smithsonian Institution, gift of Charles Lang Freer F1902.42
Provenance: Siegfried Bing; Hayashi Tadamasa, 1902.
Literature: Stern 1960, no. 9; Stern 1973, no. 97.
(1-106)

A handscroll of miscellaneous subjects that Hokusai painted in "semicursive" (semiabbreviated) style (gyōtai), which probably served as a model for one of his pupils. He must have painted many such works, but very few have survived. The only other known examples are an unsigned pair of handscrolls in ink titled *Miscellaneous Subjects and Comic Paintings of Figures* (Museum of Fine Arts, Boston) and *Album of Models for Painting* (Ōta Memorial Museum, Tokyo), which is inscribed with the age of eighty-four and is in abbreviated style (sōtai) with light colors (Boston 2000, 3, nos. 74–75; Nagata 2000, nos. 262–76 [bw]). In comparison to those works the present handscroll is longer and more varied in its subject matter and also more carefully colored. It is a most important work for demonstrating Hokusai's freedom of artistic expression at the very height of his career.

It is admirable that Hokusai decided to date the handscroll, "winter of Tenpō 10

(1839)" at the end. The seal is the third type of the "Katsushika" seal, which is thought to have been used from this year onward, and this is one of the most important works on which it appears.

The scroll illustrates a piece of dried bonito, dried anchovies, and red and white paper cords for a gift; a moorhen and candock; a lotus; a pine tree; a snowy landscape; rough waves; a pumpkin plant; a wild boar; an aubergine and wasabi; a fox monk and badger monk; salted salmon-head and white plum; bonito and dwarf bamboo; Chinese taro and narcissus; filleted mackerel and a bottle; a scorpionfish and flounder; a pufferfish and radish; waves, plants, and flowers; maple leaves on the Tatsuta River; Li Bo viewing a waterfall; scissors; a blue-and-white porcelain bowl; lotus root, an arrowhead bulb, and other vegetables; a cat and butterfly; a yam and an eel; a gourd plant and catfish; a small hut under a tree; foxes crossing the ice; and finally, the lucky god Fukurokuju

and a Chinese boy (the characters taibi, "the end," are written on the scroll that Fukurokuju holds).

Naturally these various motifs appear in many other works by Hokusai. The dried anchovies (gomame, used for stock) are identified as such in an inscription in the *Album of Paintings to Serve as Models* mentioned above. The wild boar is exactly the same style as the one in the hanging scroll titled *Wild Boar under the Moon* (Museum of Fine Arts, Boston; Boston 2000, 3:no. 66). Hokusai painted partly peeled aubergines many times, and they are included in the *Album of Paintings to Serve as Models*. Fox monk and badger monk was also a Hokusai speciality, and they are the subject of a pair of hanging scrolls (cat. 140), as well as another combination with the legend of the teakettle that turned into a racoon (bunbuku chagama). There are many examples of the head cut from a salted salmon with a cord attached, including

one in the *Album of Paintings to Serve as Models*. The Chinese taro and narcissus are included as separate motifs in the same album. The Chinese taro (tō no imo) is just a kind of ordinary taro, but it is recorded with this special name in the album. Li Bo viewing the waterfall is significant as an earlier example of a subject to which Hokusai returned in a painting from the last year of his life (Museum of Fine Arts, Boston; Boston 2000, 3:no. 67). There seems to be some humorous intention in the composition of a yam and eel, in which the bottom half of the eel's body changes into the yam. An unsigned series of small format prints of *Types of Fish* recognized as works by Hokusai also includes a similar design. The section in which a pack of foxes run across the ice is filled with an indescribable sense of the supernatural. The lucky god Fukurokuju accompanied by Chinese boys is another Hokusai speciality. AS

119 Boy Viewing Mount Fuji
1839
Signature: Gakyō rōjin Manji hitsu yowai hachijū (By Manji, old man mad about painting, aged eighty)
Seal: Katsushika (type three)
hanging scroll; ink and color on silk, 36.2 x 51.2 cm
Freer Gallery of Art, Smithsonian Institution, gift of Charles Lang Freer F1898.110
Provenance: E. S. Hull, 1898; Honma Kōsō, 1892.
Literature: Kobayashi 1892; Goncourt 1896, 305; Stern 1960, no. 1; Stern 1973, no. 96; Stern and Narazaki 1981, 16:no. 116; Forrer 1988, no. 392; Calza 1994, no. 2.11; Carpenter 2005, 138–40.
(1-30)

A young boy seated in the bend of a willow trunk is playing a flute as he gazes at the majestically curving slopes of Mount Fuji that rise up toward the very top of the painting. Beside him, a large woven basket hangs from the tree; beneath him, a river comes cascading toward the viewer. The space between the foreground motifs and background mountain is left empty, save for a wash of pale green that subtly changes to pale gray across the lower slopes, and then transforms to deep gullies of darker ink, pocketed with snow on the right side of the mountain. On the left slope and at the summit, the unpainted silk suggests the heavy blanket of snow that covers most of Mount Fuji for all but the summer months. The inclusion of a ragged cloud of deep blue (most likely Prussian [Berlin] blue) that fills the top left corner gives additional depth to the composition. The distinctive technique of pooling, or puddling (*tarashikomi*) wet ink and blue creates the mottled bark of the tree, which is enlivened by dots of moss in black and green. Finally, dots of white above the river were either sprayed or flicked on with the brush to create, quite literally, spray.

The use of horizontal bands of color and ink across the mountain that subtly fade into one another is very similar to the special wiped printing effects (*bokashi*) that were a feature of certain designs in Hokusai's most famous color woodblock series *Thirty-six Views of Mount Fuji* (cats. 96–100). In between that print series and the present painting, Hokusai had of course designed the first two volumes of his illustrated book *One Hundred Views of Mount Fuji* (cat. 162) in which his depictions of the sacred mountain were often startlingly eccentric. Here, the small boy is cleverly pitted against the giant peak, thanks to his elevated perch and the lack of any intervening motif. Because the boy's face is not shown, the viewer is encouraged to join him in the uninterrupted contemplation of the beautiful mountain. His flute-playing is presented as an appropriately lyrical response, augmented visually by the gently waving fronds of the willow that towers even higher than Fuji.

It is surely this strong content of sentiment—which some might characterize as sentimental—that has caused certain scholars to doubt the work as a genuine product of Hokusai's hand. Also, the empty, even stark, composition of the painting also causes them to doubt that this work is one of Hokusai's time. Nevertheless, the workmanship is undeniably accomplished and the signature and seal seem to be quite genuine. (For the earliest dated use of the type-three Katsushika seal, see the handscroll *Miscellaneous Subjects* [cat. 118], done in the winter of Hokusai's eightieth year, 1839.) Thus, the painting makes us expand our notions of the emotional and stylistic ranges of which Hokusai was capable.

In 1892 the work was recorded in the collection of Honma Kōsō of Sakata, a relative of Hokusai's pupil Hokuyō (1822–68). Before 1896, Edmond de Goncourt saw it reproduced in the *Magazine of Japanese Art*. TC

120 Poet Semimaru with His Lute in a Bag
1839
Signature: Gakyō rōjin Manji hitsu, yowai hachijū
(Painted by Manji, old man mad about painting, aged eighty)
Seal: Katsushika (type two)
hanging scroll mounted on panel; ink and color on paper, 91.4 x 18.4 cm
Freer Gallery of Art, Smithsonian Institution, gift of Charles Lang Freer F1902.27
Provenance: Thomas E. Kirby, 1902.
Literature: Fenollosa 1901, no. 187; Stern and Narazaki 1981, 16:no. 15; Nagata 2000, no. 260 (bw).
(1-42)

A blind musician holds a *biwa* (a kind of lute, played vertically) in its brocade bag. Two famous blind biwa-players are typically depicted in paintings, Semimaru and Hyūga Taira no Kagekiyo. Due to the inclusion of distant mountains at the top of the painting and similarities to an illustration entitled *Semimaru* in *Hokusai manga*, one can assume that Semimaru is depicted here.

Semimaru is a legendary figure, said to be the fourth son of Emperor Daigo (r. 897–930) who was sent to Mount Ōsaka because he was blind. The following is a description of him in a headnote to the imperial anthology *Later Selected Poetry Collection* (*Gosen wakashū*, compiled in 951):

121 Young Man Writing a Letter
1840
Signature: Gakyō rōjin Manji hitsu yowai hachijū-ichi (From the brush of Manji, old man mad about painting, aged eighty-one)
Seal: Katsushika (type three)
hanging scroll; ink and color on silk, 73.3 x 32.7 cm
Ujiie Ukiyo-e Collection, Kamakura Museum
Literature: Kaneko 1964, no. 6; Nagata 2000, no. 108 (color); Nikkei 2005, no. 470.
(1-5)

122 Young Man Seated on a Bench
1840
Signature: Gakyō rōjin Manji hitsu yowai hachijū-ichi (From the brush of Manji, old man mad with pictures, aged eighty-one)
Seal: Katsushika (type three)
Inscription: See below.
Inscription signature: Yakko
hanging scroll; ink and color on silk, 80.4 x 32.7 cm
The British Museum 1913.5-1.318 (Japanese Painting 1451). Given by Sir W. Gwynne-Evans, Bt
Provenance: Arthur Morrison.
Literature: British Museum 1948, no. 170; Tokyo Toritsu Bijutukan 1990, no. 31; Clark 1992, no. 101; Asahi 1993, no. 67; Calza 1994, no. 12.9; Nagata 2000, no. 107 (color); Nikkei 2005, 469.
(1-6)

He built a cottage at the Osaka Barrier and observed the comings and goings of the people there:

Kore ya kono   This is it!
yuku mo kaeru mo   that going, to, and
                    coming, too,
                    continually separat-
wakarete wa   ing those known
                    and those unknown
shiru mo shiranu mo meet at the Barrier
Ōsaka no seki   of Osaka.

Myths and legends about him continued to appear after this, and they formed the basis for the medieval *nō* play *Semimaru*. In the Edo period he was featured as a character in puppet plays and kabuki dramas.

The abbreviated ink landscape at the top of the painting must be the mountain barrier of Osaka. The illustration in *Hokusai manga* depicts Semimaru playing his instrument. Perhaps the decision here to show him holding the *biwa* in its bag and gazing at the distant mountain is meant to emphasize his saintliness.

The seal used on the painting is tentatively read as "Katsushika." Hokusai used three versions of this seal and the one here is classified as "type two," which he used during the period from about 1833 to 1839. AS

Translation of inscription from Mostow 1996, 171

Already from the beginning of the tradition of ukiyo-e figure paintings, as represented by scrolls of beauties of the Kanbun era (1660–73), a small number of works survive that showcase alluring young men (*wakashu*) in a manner equivalent to the many more numerous paintings of female courtesans. Popular literature from around the Genroku era (1688–1704) regularly features debates about whether young men or young women made better lovers for (male) patrons of the pleasure quarters.

The young men portrayed in these works still have the adolescent forelocks that will be formally shaved off at the ceremony by which they will enter manhood (*genpuku*; held as a rule before the age of sixteen). The long, hanging sleeves (*furisode*) of their robes, which are consciously shown off to the viewer, may imply that they are prostitutes from a male brothel (*kagema*). Both youths are gentle and refined, their poses curled in on themselves. They wear dreamy expressions on their delicately inclining faces. The Chinese-style poem inscribed on the right scroll confirms that viewers of the time would have indeed interpreted this body language as coquettish. In the poem, one who calls himself "your servant" (*yakko*) addresses a youth called "young Sessen" (or Yukibune):

Shunpū shun'u kyōshi o utsushi	Spring breezes and spring rains imitate his lovely form
tsuyu toka ni omoku ichiryōshi	The dew sits heavy on a branch or two of blossoms by the wayside
nan zo nin kajin no	To so many things
omou tokoro ōku	I would liken this beautiful one
moha namida o obi shō ni yoru toki ni	[My eyes] brim with tears like waves
Sessen kun no tame ni daisu	As he rests there on the bench I inscribe this for young Sessen

The cherry-blossom pattern of the right youth's robe, which is skillfully modulated so that it can be seen through his gauze overrobe, indicates that he is probably enjoying an outing to admire the spring blossoms. He wears striped divided trousers (*hakama*) over his otherwise feminine robes and carries a single sword passed through a narrow sash.

The youth in the left scroll sits pensively, hand under chin and with one elbow and the other sleeve-covered hand resting on a raised knee. His brown robe also has

an early spring motif of stylized plum blossom and cracked ice. A roll of letter paper, a writing set, and a brush wait ready alongside. A pile of books in a carrying cloth behind him hint at literary interests. Perhaps the implied narrative is that he is daydreaming about an absent lover and is about to compose a letter graced with quotes from his favorite literary classics.

The near identical forms of the signatures and seals positioned on the far right and far left, as well as the similar sizes of the paintings and their subjects leaves no doubt that the two scrolls, each in different collections, were originally intended as a pair. Several small paintings of handsome youths by Hokusai are known among his early works; the large scale, high technical finish, and relatively late date of this pair imply a special commission.

One of the earliest dateable uses of the type-three "Katsushika" seal is found on *Handscroll with Miscellaneous Subjects* (cat. 118), inscribed "winter 1839," when Hokusai was eighty years old. This pair has the same seal and, in view of the seasonal patterns on the youths' costumes, were probably completed in the following spring of 1840. TC

Translation of poem from Clark 1992, 151

123 Four Fans Mounted on a Screen
four fans mounted on a two-panel folding screen; ink and color on paper
Freer Gallery of Art, Smithsonian Institution, gift of Charles Lang Freer
F1904.178
Provenance: Kobayashi Bunshichi, 1904; Honma Kōsō
Literature: Fenollosa 1901, no. 106; Stern and Narazaki 1981, 16: no. 118; Nagata 2000, no. 66.
(1-83)

From right:
Frog on Lotus Leaf
ca. 1814-15
Signature: Hokusai aratame Taito hitsu (Painted by Taito, changed from Hokusai)
Seals: Toki, Masa
17.5 x 48.4 (maximum width) / 20.9 (minimum width) cm

Scholar in a House
ca. 1801-03
Signature: Gakyōjin Hokusai ga (Painted by Hokusai, man mad about painting)
Seals: Toki, Masa
14.3 x 46.5 (maximum width) / 22.5 (minimum width) cm

Landscape
ca. 1825-30
Signature: Hokusai Iitsu hitsu (Painted by Hokusai Iitsu)
Seal: Jinkō (?)
17.2 x 49.5 (maximum width) / 22.2 (minimum width) cm

Boat and Rock
1841
Signature: Hachijūni rō Manji hitsu (Painted by Manji, old man of eighty-two)
Seal: Katsushika (type three)
14.3 x 49.3 (maximum width) / 25.7 (minimum width) cm

124 River Landscape: Ferryboat and Mount Fuji
1842
Signature: Gakyō rōjin Manji hitsu, yowai hachijū-san sai (Painted by Gakyō rōjin Manji, aged eighty-three years)
Seal: Katsushika (type three)
hanging scroll mounted on panel; ink and color on silk, 84.8 x 42.2 cm
Freer Gallery of Art, Smithsonian Institution, gift of Charles Lang Freer F1903.109
Provenance: Matsuki Bunkyo, September 1903.
Literature: Stern 1973, no. 98; Forrer 1988, no. 438; Calza 1994, no. 8.9.
(1-109)

The bottom of the two-fold screen has carved wooden panels with a pierced design of waves. When fully open the width is 166 centimeters. Two fan paintings by Hokusai are pasted on each panel of the screen, giving a total of four. The dates of production of the four fans stretch over a forty-year period and it is likely that they were assembled onto the present screen some time after Hokusai's death. Three of the fan paintings have folds, indicating that they were once mounted on spines and were actually used as folding fans; only *Landscape* has no folds and was mounted onto the screen before it was ever used. All four works are painted in ink in just one or two colors on paper specially prepared with shiny ground mica, and they were probably produced at public poetry and painting meetings (*shogakai*).

In *Frog on Lotus Leaf,* a lively looking frog is shown sitting on the back of a lotus leaf that has begun to wither. The lotus plant fills the entire space of the fan. The signature "Hokusai aratame

Taito hitsu" (painted by Taito, changed from Hokusai) is extremely rare and otherwise unknown on paintings. The same signature is found only on two other words: a *surimono* print in square *shikishi* format, *Pine Tree Where the Deity Myōken Appears, at Yanagishima* (Koishikawa Ukiyo-e Bijutsukan, Tokyo), which was published in the spring of 1814 (Nikkei 1998, no. 89); and a picture calendar (*egoyomi*) of the same date, *Courtesan Greeting a Client.* Therefore, the present fan painting was probably done at about the same time. Hokusai began to use the "Taito" art-name in about 1810 and continued to use it for a few years in combination with the name Hokusai. He then passed the Hokusai name and his "Raishin" seal on to a pupil, one Suzuki. The date when this occurred is not absolutely certain but, based on the existence of the above *surimono*, it was probably just before the New Year of 1814. This fan painting is probably one of the very few works to have survived from the end of 1813.

In *Scholar in a House,* a Chinese scholar who has left the mundane world far behind is shown peacefully reading in a thatched cottage. All around him are trees covered in creeper and thick clumps of grass. Above him, geese pass in front of the moon on their way home. The combination of the signature "Gakyōjin Hokusai ga" and the seals "Toki" and "Masa," and the relatively small amount of wear to the seal, suggest that the fan was painted around 1801–03.

Landscape shows two thatched cottages buffeted by wild wind and rain. The cottages are painted with a particular sense of form unique to Hokusai.

In *Boat and Rock* there is a brilliant contrast between the almost emotional depiction of the craggy rocks and the tension in the sailing ship, the form of which looks almost like the slender body of a ballerina. The painting has additional significance as one of the only known works by Hokusai from his eighty-second year. AS

Two energetic boatmen pole a ferryboat across a river toward a small hamlet of farmhouses on the far shore. Two cargo boats are farther up the river, and Mount Fuji is in the distance. Eight passengers in the boat share the narrow space with two horses laden with cut reeds, both of which, amusingly, are shown from the rear. The people look to be a mixture of ordinary travelers and farmers. Hokusai had already combined a boatload of passengers with a distant view of Mount Fuji in one of the most satisfying prints in the series *Thirty-six Views of Mount Fuji* (cat. 96–100). Here it is not possible to suggest a specific location and overall there is the feeling that a collection of generic motifs have been combined to make a pleasing composition. Nevertheless, Hokusai used a scrupulous sense of balance to divide the pictorial space into fore-, middle-, and background and to structure the motifs into a convincing visual recession. The curves of the sides of the boats and the waves in the water direct the eye with assurance toward the attenuated slopes, while also mimicking the elegant shape

126 Zhang Fei in Snowfall
1843
Signature: Yowai hachijū-yon sai Gakyō rōjin Manji hitsu
(Painted by the Old Man Mad about Painting, aged eighty-four)
Seal: Katsushika (type three)
hanging scroll; ink and color on silk, 132.6 x 43.9 cm
Ujiie Ukiyo-e Collection, Kamakura Museum
Literature: Narazaki 1982, no. 88; Nagata 2000, no. 114;
Nikkei 2005, cat 474.
(1-45)

of Mount Fuji. This use of repeating shapes in the composition was also a feature of the earlier Fuji print series.

The painting is in remarkably good condition, and the silk still retains the pale ivory color it would have had when it was new. TC

125 Rats and Rice Bales
1843
Signature: Hachijū-yon rō Manji hitsu
(Painted by the eighty-four-year-old man Manji)
Seal: Katsushika (type three)
hanging scroll mounted on panel; ink and color on silk, 90.8 x 29.5 cm
Freer Gallery of Art, Smithsonian Institution, gift of Charles Lang Freer F1904.132
Provenance: Michael Tomkinson, 1904.
Literature: Nagata 2000, frontispiece and no. 278 (bw).
(1-148)

Over the centuries, there have been numerous depictions of rats and stacked bales of rice, but the version of the theme in this scroll is especially inventive. One senses that the four white and two mixed-colored rats at the bottom of the picture are about to chase after the single black rat at the top. The painting thus conveys an underlying tension derived from the anticipated struggle for survival. Bales of rice have traditionally symbolized an abundant harvest, while rats have symbolized numerous offspring. In combination, the two subjects are ordinarily considered highly auspicious, but, typical of Hokusai's art, this picture reaches beyond long-established conventions. The work also shows the artist's habitual interest in compositional experimentation: The repeated forms of the single species of rat create an effect reminiscent of modern animation. Hokusai made frequent use of this device. He painted the picture in 1843, at the age of eighty-four, the same year he produced the famous sketches of mythical lions, the so-called *Daily Exorcisms* (cat. 148). NM

A Chinese warrior stands in the snow, holding up his traveling hat and staring at the sky. Although the figure is clearly Chinese, the pose recalls that of an actor on the kabuki stage.

Zhang Fei, one of the three heroes of the Chinese novel *Romance of the Three Kingdoms* (*Sanguozhi*) is depicted here. In the famous opening chapter of the novel, Zhang Fei pledges an oath of brotherhood with Guan Yu, Liu Bei, the commander of the state of Shu, and the future emperor. The author describes Zhang Fei as standing "eight feet tall, with a head like a leopard, eyes like wheels, a face like a swallow, the beard of a tiger, a voice like thunder, and the vigor of a galloping horse." In the novel he is depicted as a brave warrior, worthy of his weapon — a dragon-headed halberd (*shemao*) measuring eighteen feet in length. He is a match for ten thousand men, striking fear into the hearts of his enemies, and winning countless military victories. Yet, as the book progresses, he invariably deals out harsh punishments and treats his subordinates roughly. Liu Bei reprimands him frequently, but he pays no heed, and consequently meets an untimely death at the hands of an angry subordinate.

This painting depicts the violent Zhang Fei, as envisioned by an artist with a strong interest in China. The reference may be to a famous chapter in which Liu

Bei, accompanied by Zhang Fei and Guan Yu, treks through the snow three times in order to meet the military strategist Kongming at his hut. (Alternatively, it has recently been suggested that the figure depicted is Lin Zhong, a character from another Chinese novel, *The Water Margin* [*Shuihuzhuan*]).

In his revised and expanded version of *Ukiyo-e ruikō*, an early history of ukiyo-e, the scholar Saitō Gesshin (1804–78) wrote, "Hokusai produced ukiyo-e using the brush techniques of Ming painting. The master was the first to conceive of ukiyo-e in terms of Chinese painting" (Yura 1979, 139). In other words, more than any other ukiyo-e artist, Hokusai benefited from the vast reservoir of techniques found in Chinese painting. Hokusai probably did not have the opportunity to study Chinese paintings first hand, but he learned through studies of the illustrations in woodblock-printed Chinese books, either imported or reissued in Japan. He is known to have produced illustrations for works of Chinese literature, including *The Water Margin*, while his student Taito II produced designs for an edition of the *Romance of the Three Kingdoms*. Thus, Hokusai's strong connections with Chinese culture are evident. He painted this warrior when he was eighty-four years old, in the forceful style characteristic of his last years. NM

127 The Deity of the Big Dipper, Bunshōsei
1843
Signature: Hachijū-yon rō Manji hitsu (Painted by Manji, old man of eighty-four)
Seal: Katsushika (type three)
hanging scroll; ink and color on silk, 79.6 x 28.2 cm
Katsushika Hokusai Museum of Art, Tsuwano
Provenance: Kawanabe Kyōsai (1831-89).
Literature: Asahi 1993, no. 69; Nagata 2000, no. 110 (color).
(1-153)

128 Zhong Kui (Shōki) Riding a Chinese Lion
1844
Signature: Gakyō rōjin Manji hitsu, yowai hachijūgosai (Painted by Gakyō rōjin Manji, aged eighty-five years)
Seal: Katshushika (type three)
hanging scroll; ink and color on paper, 118.2 x 57.8 cm
Idemitsu Museum of Arts, Tokyo
Provenance: Takeoka Toyota collection; Hosomi collection.
Literature: Narazaki 1982, no. 34; Asahi 1993, no. 75; Nagata 2000, no. 116 (color); Nikkei 2005, cat. 481.
(1-137)

Bunshōsei is the name given to the six stars that make up most of the Big Dipper constellation, excluding the star at the end of the handle (called *yōkō* in Japanese). In China it is believed that the Sixth Celestial section (*ten no rokufu*), where Bunshōsei is located, regulates fortune and misfortune, illuminates the way of heaven, and controls all that is beneath heaven. In Edo-period Japan it was treated as equivalent to just the first star of the Big Dipper (*kaisei*), and it was a fashion among scholars to impress a seal cut with its design into the top-right corner of the page just inside the cover of their books. Bunshōsei took many forms. The dictionary *Daigenkai* (1932–37) contains the following description: "Beneath the constellation, a figure in the form of a devil (*oni*) carries a writing brush in his right hand and grasps a seal in his left. He is drawn with his left leg raised and he turns to look up at the six stars." The same dictionary quotes another source, (*Kakei shōwa*): "A figure in the form of a devil rides a flying dragon and raises a wooden rice measure (*masu*) high above his head."

The present painting follows these two descriptions almost exactly. Against the background of a full moon, the devil figure holds a rice measure in his right hand and a writing brush in his left. His body is red, and he is dressed in the costume of a monk. This form is reminiscent of Hokusai's many paintings of the demon-queller Zhong Kui (Japanese: Shōki; see cats. 1, 128, and 134) as well as one of the thunder god (cat. 132), painted when he was eighty-eight years old. Bunshōsei is imbued with a liveliness of spirit that belies the artist's advanced age of eight-four. Doubtless such a dynamic work reflects Hokusai's own personal belief in the cult of the constellation of the Big Dipper.

According to more popular belief, Bunshōsei was thought to be just one of the six stars of the constellation, the one that governed literature. Those who wished to pass the examinations to become a state official often worshiped him, and so there is also the possibility that the present painting was commissioned under such circumstances. AS

This dynamic painting depicts Shōki (Chinese, Zhong Kui), the heroic and stalwart figure admired in Asia since the mid-eighth century for his ability to expel demons. The brawny musculature of the arms is characteristic of the massive figural style that Hokusai adopted during his final years. The mythic figure's left hand grasps not a set of reins, but the lion's bristly mane, confirming his superhuman nature. The large-eyed and bearded Shōki appears awesome enough to drive away even the worst monster. With his gaze firmly fixed on a point in the distance, he might have descended from the heavens at that very moment. The lion, meanwhile, seems to be clawing through space at a furious rate.

Artists of the Edo period frequently depicted Shōki as a talisman against illness and misfortune. Ukiyo-e artists were no exception. But Hokusai in particular is known to have painted numerous versions of the subject, including a banner intended to ward off smallpox. This painting most likely had a similar purpose. It must have provided great comfort to the family lucky enough to see it hanging in their display alcove.

Completed when Hokusai was eighty-five years old, the scroll is famous among the group of paintings of gods and mythical animals that the artist produced during his final years. The powerful brushwork is characteristic of the artist's style at this time. Formerly in the collection of Takeoka Toyota, an important Japanese collector of ukiyo-e paintings, the work entered the collection of the Idemitsu Museum quite recently. The title of the work in this catalogue reflects an inscription on the box used to store the painting, but the word "lion" refers to the mythological lion known in Japanese as *shishi*.

Hokusai's figural style has many noteworthy features: For example, he made frequent use of intentional distortion. In this case, it is difficult to explain how the rear-right leg of the lion joins its body. Yet, this otherwise illogical detail was carefully calculated to give the whole of the powerful body a sense of solid form. The technical risks that Hokusai took result in images that have a strong impact on the viewer. This calculated risk lies at the heart of Hokusai's artistic genius. NM

129 Arhat
1846
Signature: Hachijū-nana rō Manji hitsu (Painted by Manji, old man of eighty-seven)
Seal: Katsushika (type three)
hanging scroll; ink and color on paper, 127.0 x 51.5 cm
Ōta Memorial Museum of Art, Tokyo
Literature: Ōta 1985, no. 577; Asahi 1993, no. 76 (color); Nagata 2000, no. 126; Nikkei 2005, cat. 483.
(1-136)

130 Wild Goose and Maple Leaves
1847
Signature: Hachiju-hachi rō Manji hitsu (By the brush of the eighty-eight year old man Manji)
Seal: Hyaku (One hundred)
hanging scroll; ink and color on silk, 85.1 x 35.3 cm
Private collection
References: Nagata 2000, no. 132 (color), 127 and 297; Nikkei 2005, cat. 486
(1-101)

Arhat is the final rank given to disciples of Hinayana Buddhism who have achieved enlightenment. In Japan, arhats are a common subject for Buddhist paintings and are typically shown in a group of sixteen, or even five hundred.

An arhat holds up a bowl, which emanates black smoke and radiates lightning. This suggests that a dragon will appear from the cloud of smoke, but the beast is not drawn here. The iconography of a dragon appearing from a bowl of water is associated with the Chinese immortal Chen Nan (Japanese: Chinnan), and alternatively with the bodhisattva Ryūjun (Sanskrit: Nagarjuna). However, in volume two of the *Hokusai manga* (published in 1815) there is a similar image with the title *Arhat Handaka (Handaka sonja)*. Also, in a picture of Shakyamuni and his

arhats in *Hokusai gashiki* (1819), there is one arhat who has a dragon coming out of his bowl—although his name is not given. It is likely that the present painting also depicts the arhat Handaka.

An earlier painting by Hokusai of the arhat Handaka, which is done in brilliantly fluid brushwork, has the signature "Hokusai Taito hitsu" (Tokyo National Museum). By comparison, this late work conveys the strong impact of the artist's obsessions with form, line, and color. Particularly unusual is the manner of depicting the smoke, which seems flung onto the paper. Also noteworthy is the way in which the figure is bent into a curved pose, apparently holding the smoke up. The highly inflected drapery is similar to that seen in *The Deity of the Big Dipper, Bunshōsei* (cat. 127). AS

A solitary wild goose turns its head to gaze upward toward a single maple leaf drifting toward the ground. The goose appears to call out into the empty sky. The somber coloration of the simple composition underscores the melancholy traditionally associated with the autumn season in Japanese poetry and art. Unusual hues of blended colors such as reddish browns and warm yellow-greens are distinctive characteristics of Hokusai's work. The bird's plumage is rendered in meticulous patterns, including one resembling fish scales on the back and graded tones of ink forming layers of long feathers on the wings and tail. Similar effects can be seen in *Ducks*

in Flowing Water (cat. 137) and in *Falcon in a Cherry Tree* (Nagata 2000, fig. 110 [color]).

The pose of the bird, with its back turned to the viewer, follows a formula that Hokusai often employed in his human figure compositions ranging from the alluring young women he painted in his youth to the contemplative figures like the *Traveler beside a Tree* (cat. 138) of his last years. Like many of Hokusai's late works, this painting focuses on a single subject, which projects a dignity and presence that exceeds the usual boundaries of a traditional motif. AY

131 Breaking Waves
1847
Signature: Hachijū-hachi rōjin Manji hitsu
(Painted by Manji, old man of eighty-eight)
Seal: Katsushika (type three)
hanging scroll; ink and color on silk, 126.0 x 46.2 cm
Freer Gallery of Art, Smithsonian Institution, gift of Charles Lang
Freer F1905.276
Provenance: Kobayashi Bunshichi, October 1905.
Literature: Stern 1960, no. 3; Forrer 1988, no. 439.
(1-108)

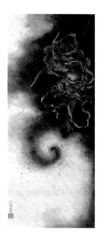

132 Thunder God
1847
Signature: Hachijū-hachi rō Manji hitsu (Painted by Manji, old
man of eighty-eight)
Seal: Hyaku
hanging scroll; ink and color on paper, 129.9 x 55.4 cm
Freer Gallery of Art, Smithsonian Institution,
gift of Charles Lang Freer F1900.47
Provenance: E. S. Hull, 1900.
Literature: Fenollosa 1901, no. 212; Stern 1973, no. 99; Stern and
Narazaki 1981, 16:no. 20; Nagata 1990, 5:no. 40; Nagata 2000,
no. 125 (color).
(1-161)

Waves rear up and break as they hit a rocky coastline topped with bushes and trees, and foam splinters and flies off in all directions. In the far distance cottages of a fishing village are lined up along the shore. Strong visual play is made between the echoing shapes of the main wave and the main outcrop of rock, and the repeating swirls of the drag tide introduce great depth. Brilliant blue and green mineral pigments dominate the landscape and white paint was energetically flicked across the surface of the painting to create sea spray. A pale blue wash is used for both sky and sea. What makes this image instantly recognizable as a late work by Hokusai is the eccentricity and drama of the treatment, but also the relative emptiness, even loneliness of the composition (compare, for example, *Traveler beside a Tree* [cat. 138], painted in the same year).

In the famous print "The Great Wave" (cat. 97) from the early 1830s, all the tentacles of foam are drawn so that they move essentially in one direction, with the monster wave poised to come crashing down onto the fishing boats. More similar waves are depicted in volume two of *One Hundred Views of Mount Fuji* (cat. 162), in which the spray also rises up, fragments, and flies off in all directions. Hokusai also experimented with

waves that form themselves into a kind of whirlpool—the so-called "male" and "female" waves he painted on the inside roof panels of the festival float for the Kamimachi neighborhood of Obuse (now the Hokusai Museum, Obuse, Nagano Prefecture). These two wave panels are thought to have been completed in the seventh month of 1845, and therefore they date from a couple of years earlier than the present painting (Nikkei 1982, 7:no. 38). The forms of the waves and whirlpools, the blue and green color scheme, the use of volumetric shading within each tentacle of foam, and the final flecking of white pigment are all aspects that the Obuse and Freer paintings share. The elemental power of the waves seen in these late works is treated as equivalent to mythological creatures such as the dragon and the phoenix; the waves are very much "alive."

The "Katsushika" (type three) seal is known on only one other work from Hokusai's eighty-eighth year, one entitled *Sunflower* (Cincinnati Art Museum; Nagata 2000, no. 127 [color]). This seems to represent the end of the period of use of this seal; subsequently Hokusai exclusively used the "Hyaku" (One hundred) seal on the paintings done up to the time of his death. TC

The wind god (Fūjin) and thunder god (Raijin) are deities in the form of demons who attend the bodhisattva Kannon (Sanskrit: Avalokitesvara), giving rise, respectively, to the wind and to the thunder and lightning. From ancient times they have been the subject of Buddhist paintings and sculptures. The pair of screens *Wind God* and *Thunder God* (Kennin-ji Temple, Kyoto) by Tawaraya Sōtatsu (fl. ca. 1600–40) is particularly famous.

The typical iconography for the thunder god depicts him with red body and horns, riding on a black cloud. He carries a ring of small drums on his back that he beats with sticks in both hands to conjure thunder and lightning. Here, Hokusai paints the thunder god with standard iconography, and yet manages to further imbue the deity with the miraculous sense of strength that rules the heavens, a power that pierces every-

thing and a gigantic presence that reaches to the limits of space. The figure of the red demon, grinding his teeth and smirking as he glares down to earth, might even be a representation of Hokusai himself. A small illustration of the thunder god is included in volume three of *Hokusai manga*. In the present painting, however, the figure is vividly human in appearance, but with an enhanced status as a deity. The combination of the skillfully gradated storm clouds and flicked black dots of ink serves to emphasize the atmosphere of mystery. Hokusai often used this technique for depicting dragons and clouds, such as those found in *The Chinese Immortal Yuzhi, Dragon with Qin* (cat. 19) and *Various Scenes* (cat. 45). It is also found in another work that Hokusai completed when he was eighty-eight years old titled *Apparition of the Seven-headed Dragon at Monk Nichiren's Sermon* (cat. 133). AS

133 Apparition of the Seven-headed Dragon
at Monk Nichiren's Sermon
1847
Signature: Hachijū-hachi rōjin Manji keihitsu
(Respectfully painted by Manji, old man of eighty-eight)
Seal: Hyaku
hanging scroll; ink and color on paper, 132.4 x 59.3 cm
Myōkōji Temple, Ibaraki
Literature: Narazaki 1982, no. 39.
(1-134)

134 Shōki
1847
Signature: Hachijū-nana rō Manji hitsu
(Painted by Manji, old man of eighty-seven)
Seal: Mount Fuji above clouds
hanging scroll; color on silk, 59.1 x 30.2 cm
Metropolitan Museum of Art, Charles Stewart Smith
Collection, gift of Mrs. Charles Stewart Smith, Charles Stewart
Smith, Jr., and Howard Caswell Smith, in memory of Charles
Stewart Smith 1914 (14.76.37)
Literature: Centre Culturel du Marais 1980, no. 238; Nagata
1990, 5:no. 103; Asahi 1993, no. 77; Calza 1994, no. 11.4; Nagata
2000, no. 123.
(1-132)

Hokusai was a devout follower of the Nichiren sect of Japanese Buddhism, which was founded by Nichiren Shōnin (1222–82). A sketch by one of his students, Tsuyuki Iitsu, shows that during his final years Hokusai even kept a portrait of Nichiren enshrined in his residence. He is also said to have made pilgrimages to several temples in Edo affiliated with Nichiren practice, including Hoshōji (dedicated to Myōken Bosatsu), Ikegami Honmonji, and Horinouchi Myōhōji. This painting is deeply connected with a religious faith driven by the desire for longevity, or more particularly, for the extended years that Hokusai hoped would allow him to advance as an artist.

The painting depicts an event associated with the period when Nichiren preached from a hut on Mount Minobu (in present-day Yamanashi Prefecture). Nichiren's followers at the event included a beautiful woman, who in fact was a snake goddess that resided in the great pond at nearby Mount Shichimen. Through the power of Nichiren's teachings, the woman realized that she would be reborn as an angel. She transformed herself into a dragon with seven heads (*shichimen*) and vowed to serve as the guardian deity of Mount Minobu. This painting depicts Nichiren in an atmosphere of great mystery, paying no heed

to the crowd of followers prostrating themselves in fear around him as he calmly confronts the dragon god. As a devout believer, Hokusai gave full expression to this famous episode in the life of the Venerable Patriarch (*Kōsō*), a name that followers of the sect used to refer to Nichiren. Hokusai was eighty-eight years old when he painted this work. In his later years, he produced many paintings of gods and mythical animals, as well as Buddhist subjects, such as Kōbō Daishi undergoing religious austerities (Nishiarai Daishi Sōjiji, Tokyo; Nagata 2000, no. 122 [color]).

This painting has long been in the collection of Myōkōji Temple (located in present-day Ibaraki Prefecture). The main devotional image of the temple is particularly famous, and one of Tokugawa Ieyasu's most important concubines, a woman named Oman, donated it to the temple. Oman gave birth to the founders of the Kii and Mito branches of the Tokugawa family. She was a fervent believer in the *Lotus Sutra* (a central text of the Nichiren sect), and she even climbed Mount Shichimen, despite a regulation barring women from the mountain. Hokusai may have known this aspect of the temple's history, when considering a subject appropriate for a work destined for its collection. NM

In this mesmerizing work, Zhong Kui (Japanese, Shōki), the mythical Chinese demon-queller stands forceful and erect, staring directly at the viewer. This hooded stare, coupled with the slight smile playing around his lips, is almost menacing. A wind passes through the painting from right to left, billowing the hem and sleeves of his scholar's robes and playing in the long mane of his hair and beard. But Shōki remains motionless and resolute, a mighty sword sheathed across his back.

Zhong Kui was a scholar of the Tang dynasty (618–907) who committed suicide after he failed his entrance exams for imperial civil service. He appeared in the feverish dreams of Emperor Xuanzong (r. 712–56) and loyally chased away the fearful demons that were troubling the ruler's sleep. In China and, later in Japan, where he is called Shōki, he has served as a talisman to ward off illness and evil. Banners and paintings of his image are displayed in Japan on Boys' Festival (fifth day of the fifth lunar month) together with kites of leaping carp. Painting his image in red was also thought to protect against the disease of smallpox, which killed many people in regular epidemics.

According to the artist Kunisada's widow (as told to Iijima Kyoshin), during his "Sōri" period (ca. 1795–98) Hokusai was living in poverty when he was commissioned to paint an image of Shōki in red. The patron was so delighted with the result that he rewarded Hokusai with two gold *ryō*, an enormous sum to one so impoverished (Iijima 1999, 9). In fact,

the earliest-known painting by Hokusai —with the "Shunrō" signature—is indeed a red Shōki, drawn in profile, with his mighty sword held vertical over the head of the cowering demon he grasps by the neck (cat. 1). In recent years, too, a hemp banner for the Boys' Festival, painted by Hokusai with a large figure of Shōki done in red, was rediscovered in the collection of the Museum of Fine Arts, Boston (Boston 2000, 3:no. 58). Hokusai continued to paint images of Shōki in both black and red, the last examples being the present painting and another in red (Nagata 2000, no. 124), both done in 1846 when Hokusai was eighty-seven years old.

A comparison between Hokusai's first (cat. 1) and last Shōki paintings demonstrates the extraordinary stylistic development that he achieved during the intervening period of more than forty years. The youthful work is dynamic and spirited and the forms expand almost to burst out of the confines of the scroll. By the time he was completing his last works, however, Hokusai steadily condensed his style to the point that tremendous forces seem to be contained within the menacing figure of Shōki. Extraordinary control is apparent in the crisp, articulated outlines of the drapery, and the transitions of tonality within the modulations of the facial features are so delicate that individual brushstrokes can no longer be detected with the naked eye. As with so many animal and mythological "portraits" from the last years, impressive emotional power radiates from the facial expression. TC

135 Minamoto no Yorimasa Aiming an Arrow
1847
Signature: Hachijū-hachi rōjin Manji hitsu (Painted by Manji, old man of eighty-eight)
Seal: Hyaku
hanging scroll; ink and color on silk, 99.0 x 42.2 cm
Private collection
Literature: Nagata 2000, no. 130.
(1-160)

136 Landscape with Boats and Mountain Village
1847
Signature: Hachijū-hachi rō Manji hitsu (Painted by the eighty-eight-year-old man Manji)
Seal: Hyaku
hanging scroll; ink and color on paper, 127.0 x 53.5 cm
The Hokusai Museum, Obuse
Literature: Hokusaikan 1985, no. 34; Nagata 2000, no. 133.
(1-158)

Minamoto no Yorimasa (1104–80) was a leading warrior of the late Heian period (794–1185) who came to prominence during the civil wars of the Hōgen (1156) and Heiji (1159) eras. In 1178 he was granted the court title "Sanmi," to which he had long aspired, and thus he is sometimes known as "Sanmi Yorimasa." The most famous tales about him, as recorded in later military epics such as Tales of the Heike (Heike monogatari, early thirteenth century), relate to incidents during the Ninpei (1151–54) and Ōhō (1161–63) eras, when he fired arrows at and subdued supernatural beings that were plaguing the emperor. One of these was the nue, a monstrous bird with "a head like a monkey, body like a tiger, and tail like a snake."

The painting shows the very moment when Yorimasa draws his bow and takes aim at the fearsome nue, which is expressed as a double band of lightning amid black clouds. Yorimasa is painted with vibrant red flesh and given the strong modeling of musculature and bones that is unique to Hokusai. The costume that envelops him is forcefully drawn, and the manner in which he looms out from the black clouds radiates an unusually powerful presence.

Yorimasa is usually shown with his cohort I no Hayata and the nue monster, but here he is depicted alone. A similar image by Hokusai is included in the illustrated book Warriors Classified by Family Name (Nagashira musha burui), published in 1841. AS

Hokusai was an ukiyo-e artist, and for that reason ranked as a painting artisan (gakō), producing his works for commission. On occasion, however, he created landscapes that seem to reveal an inner spiritual world. Painted from the imagination, this type of landscape was greatly admired in literati circles. Landscape paintings of this kind — and occasionally some of the printed views that appear in Hokusai's illustrated books — convey the essence not of a particular location but of a state of mind. They present harsh, strangely formed scenes reminiscent of Chinese painting, with trees growing from solid rock formations. As the scholar Saitō Gesshin wrote in Expanded Thoughts on Ukiyo-e (Zōho ukiyo-e ruikō, 1844), "Hokusai took as his basis the Chinese painting style and popularized it" (Yura 1979, 139). It thus appears that the artist always maintained a strong interest in China. Be that as it may, this somewhat austere scene might best be understood as a landscape from the artist's imagination. It was painted when Hokusai was eighty-eight years old. NM

137 Ducks in Flowing Water
1847
Signature: Yowai hachijū-hachi Manji (Manji, aged eighty-eight)
Seal: Hyaku
hanging scroll; ink and color on silk, 111.0 x 40.0 cm
The British Museum 1913.5-1.320, given by Sir W. Gwynne-Evans Bt
Provenance: Arthur Morrison.
Literature: Morrison 1911, 2:pl. XXVII; British Museum 1948, no. 172; Hillier 1955, no. 82; Forrer 1988, no. 441; Clark 1992, no. 103; Asahi 1993, no. 80; Calza 1994, no. 12.11; Nagata 2000, no. 131.
(1-159)

138 Traveler beside a Tree
1847
Signature: Hachijū-hachi rō Manji hitsu
(Painted by Manji, old man of eighty-eight)
Seal: Hyaku
hanging scroll mounted on panel; ink and color on paper, 126.2 x 52.3 cm
Freer Gallery of Art, Smithsonian Institution, gift of Charles Lang Freer F1904.186
Provenance: Kobayashi Bunshichi, 1904; Honma Kōsō.
Literature: Fenollosa 1901, no. 210; Nagata 2000, no. 289 (bw).
(1-157)

In this painting, the viewer seems to look down onto flowing water, where a pair of brightly plumed mallard ducks is swimming. One of the birds stares back alertly at us with almost human engagement, its head cocked slightly to one side. In a complex pose, the other up-tails and dives among the waterweed, its head and neck seen only in murky silhouette. Both lively creatures are testament to Hokusai's close and rigorous observation of the natural world. Just the following year, he published detailed instructions for painting a very similar mallard in his *Illustrated Manual on Color* (cat. 164).

Extraordinary care was taken to depict the changing appearances of the brilliant maple leaves as they start to sink into the water and also the waterweed, which fades away into the depths. The more one looks, a surprising amount of color

is apparent in the weeds. These varied optical effects are contained within the elegantly rhythmical arcs of the flowing water, which is also modulated with great sensitivity. All these elements combine to produce a work at once eccentric and sublimely calm, and with a grandeur of conception that is typical of Hokusai's last few years. Time, flow, change, light and reflection are all evoked in this work, but without a literal interpetation.

Hokusai used sweeping arcs across the composition and scattering maple leaves more than thirty years earlier to suggest a violent storm in his *Daoist Immortal Liezi in the Wind* (cat. 65). And a similar device of arcs done in carefully modulated printed blue was used to suggest flowing water over terrapins and pond weed in a large upright print of the 1830s (Nagata 1990, 1:no. 54). TC

In this work, a lone traveler stops on the road and looks back along the way by which he came. In black robes blown by the wind he presents a forlorn figure, posed so that he faces away from us and gazes off into a vast, undifferentiated space. A bundle is tied around his shoulders and a bag hangs from his sash at the back. His only companion in the composition is a single tree, its trunk evidently gnarled with age but still standing erect and tall. As with all the late paintings, Hokusai signed this one with his age (here eighty-eight) and applied a seal with the age to which he aspires (One hundred). It is impossible to read the image—if not literally, then at least metaphorically—as anything other than Hokusai's meditation on the long, and surely sometimes lonely, road he has traveled; as well as a statement of his determination to stay vigorous and strong. Every single dot of moss leaps out from the confines of the tree trunk, electric with life. Ernest Fenollosa, writing in 1900, commented on the complexity of the planes and wash describing the black robe: "the synthesis of line and mass in a single stroke, as if one could invent a new shape of brush for every

form of shadow nature presents." (Fenollosa 1901, no. 210).

Is this a traveling peddler or a priest? The answer depends on how one interprets what the figure is holding. Hokusai painted many tea-whisk peddlers in similar costume, but no tea-whisks are evident here. If the round object he holds is the end of a pair of traveling scales, then perhaps he is peddler of something else. Alternatively, if the implements are read as a metal gong and stick, then this suggests he is an itinerant follower of the sect of Monk Kūya, who would repeatedly dance and chant joyously an invocation to the Buddha (*Kūya nenbutsu*, or *hachitataki*). Irrespective of his exact identity, he carries the pathos of the painting.

Many pieces of paper were joined together to form the ground for this painting, suggesting that it is just a study for a more finished work that is now lost. However, by conscientiously applying his standard signature and seal for this year, Hokusai surely affirmed that it was a "finished work of art." Perhaps by this late stage in his life such distinctions seemed unimportant. TC

139 The Lute and White Snake of Sarasvati (Benten)
1847 (twentieth day, fourth month)
Signature: Kōka yon hinoto hitsuji shigatsu nijū nichi tsuchinoto mi no shirafude o kudasu, hachijū-hachi rō Manji (Old man Manji of eighty-eight, using [my] brush on the snake day, the twentieth of the fourth month in the sheep year, Kōka 4 [1847])
Seal: Hyaku
hanging scroll mounted on panel; ink and color on silk, 35.3 x 44.6 cm
Freer Gallery of Art, Smithsonian Institution, gift of Charles Lang Freer F1904.134
Provenance: Michael Tomkinson, London, 1904.
Literature: Stern and Narazaki 1981, 16:no. 117.
(1-167)

140 Fox Monk and Badger Monk
1848
Signature: Manji rōjin hitsu, yowai hachijū-kyū sai (Painted by old man Manji, aged eighty-nine years)
Seal: Hyaku
pair of hanging scrolls; ink and color on paper, each scroll: 122.5 x 56.8 cm
Private collection
Literature: Narazaki 1982, no. 35, 36; Nagata 2000, no. 135, 136 (color).
(1-165)

The *biwa*, a kind of lute played vertically on the lap with a plectrum, was an instrument particularly used as an accompaniment to chanting. Many of the most famous players were blind, often itinerant musicians such as the semilegendary Semimaru (see cat. 120). Here, the instrument lies on its back, wrapped in a luxurious and brilliantly colored brocade bag. The pattern of the brocade, a mixture of chrysanthemum roundels and white snowlike dotting, is drawn in a flat manner that contradicts the expected volume of the bag. Around the edge of the bag is a forceful and jagged outline, done in rich black ink. A white snake, each white scale of its pink-tinged body painstakingly differentiated, coils around the neck of the instrument and slithers its body across the flat front. The tasseled red cord of the bag is drawn in a manner that echoes the scales of the snake and seems almost animate itself; indeed the whole composition exudes a sense of mystery from this dynamic ten-

sion between the animate and the inanimate elements, as well as the unexpected presence of the white snake.

Hokusai added a long inscription to the signature that gives special prominence to the fact that he painted the work on a snake day (each day in the traditional lunar calendar was accorded one of the twelve zodiacal animals). The white snake and the *biwa* are both attributes of the Shinto-Buddhist deity Benzaiten (Benten), the only female among the Seven Lucky Gods (Shichifukujin). She is worshiped as a deity of good fortune and protector of music, scholarship, and the arts. Shrines to her are often located close to water (Benzaiten derived originally from the Indian river goddess Sarasvati). In the context of other late works by Hokusai that feature semi-mythological creatures, it can be imagined that the white snake may also have had some kind of talismanic meaning for him. TC

The fox and badger are featured in many of Japan's oldest folk tales. The two animals were believed to repay human beings for the good deeds or ill treatment they received from them. These paintings depict the animals in a similarly anthropomorphic manner.

Among the best-known tales about the fox (*kitsune*) is *The Master of the Sutra Storehouse (Hakuzōshū)*. The story concerns a priest during the Muromachi period (1333–1567) who, as a believer in the Shinto cult of Inari, captures three foxes, which are considered animal messengers of the Inari deity. The foxes turn out to have magical powers. The story inspired a famous *kyōgen* play, *Fox Bait (Tsuri-gitsune)* about an old fox who transforms into a priest in order to prevent other foxes from being snared in traps. Unfortunately, his priestly guise does not prevent the fox from being snared.

When it comes to the badger (*tanuki*), the best-known tale is probably "The Lucky Tea Kettle" (*Bunbuku chagama*). Many versions are told throughout Japan, but the most famous variant is associated with Morinji Temple in modern Gunma Prefecture. All versions describe the transformation of a badger into a teakettle.

In the tale, a temple has a kettle used during the tea ceremony. Curiously, no matter how much water is drawn from it, the kettle never empties. It turns out to be a badger that is several hundred years old. In another version, a man rescues a badger from a trap. The badger says that it will transform itself into a kettle, which it instructs the man to sell. The man does, then the badger reveals its true form and runs away. Or again, night after night a strange kettle transforms into a badger and dances. After being resold, the kettle is put on display, bringing good luck to all who view it. Hokusai's painting corresponds to yet another, slightly different version in which the priest who rescues the animal is actually a badger himself.

These two paintings depict the animals in an exceptionally human way, the badger as a priest beside a teakettle, and the fox revealing its true form as it approaches a trap set with a mouse. The pair make a grand and forceful composition, not least because Hokusai handled the ink masterfully, with just a few additional touches of color. The artist mobilized all his energies when he painted these works at the age of eighty-nine. NM

141 Demon Monk
1848, eighth day, sixth month
Signature: Kaei gan tsuchinoe saru nen rokugatsu hachi nichi
monjin Hokuyō shi okuru; yowai hachijū-kyū sai Gakyō rōjin Manji hitsu
Seal: Hakyu
Inscription: See below.
Inscription signature: Ikeda Gensai
hanging scroll; ink and color on paper, 52.8 x 56.2 cm
Sano Art Museum, Mishima
Literature: Asahi 1993, no. 83; Nagata 2000, no. 137 (color).
(1-164)

142 Fisherman and Woodcutter
1849
Signature: Kyūjū rōjin Manji hitsu (Painted by Manji, old man of ninety)
Seal: Hyaku
pair of hanging scrolls; ink and color on silk,
right: 113.4 x 39.6, left: 113.1 x 39.6 cm
Freer Gallery of Art, Smithsonian Institution,
gift of Charles Lang Freer F1904.181 and F1904.182
Provenance: Kobayashi Bunshichi, 1904; Honma Kōsō, 1892.
Literature: Fenollosa 1901, no. 217;
Stern 1960, nos. 7, 8; Stern 1973, nos. 100-01; Stern and Narazaki 1981, 16:nos. 55, 56; Forrer 1988, no. 447; Calza 1994, nos. 16.7, 16.8; Nagata 2000, nos. 293, 294 (bw).
(1-162)

In Buddhist iconography, the demon represents an evil force to be crushed by the Four Guardian Kings or by Zhong Kui (Japanese, Shōki). In Japan, however, certain demons, for example, were considered protective deities, symbolizing family ancestors or their ancient place of origin. Other demons represented the physical transformation of an individual under the influence of violent emotion. From the medieval period on, the demon became fully domesticated and, notwithstanding its spiritual character, even took on a familiar human aspect. Eventually in *Ōtsu-e* (Ōtsu pictures), a genre of folk art from the Edo period, the demon came to be depicted comically as an itinerant priest striking a gong and carrying a subscription list, a character known as the "Nenbutsu Demon" (Oni Nenbutsu). Ukiyo-e artists treated demons in a variety of ways, the most ordinary being appealingly humanized, like the Nenbutsu Demon. Hokusai and other artists occasionally depicted the Nenbutsu Demon in combination with the Wisteria Maiden, another stock figure in Ōtsu pictures.

The face of the figure here has lost much of its original red coloration, but the sagging mouth and lolling head suggest a state of inebriation. This demon is actually the very picture of drunkenness, making it likably human. The wine bottle, decorated with a scrolling vine pattern and the porcelain dish arranged with delicious raw fish together evoke the lifestyle of the ordinary people of Edo.

This painting is a minor masterpiece by an artist who often depicted deities and mythological creatures. Hokusai first presented the work to his student Hokuyō on the eighth day of the sixth month of 1848, at the age of eighty-nine. Hokuyō's diary indicates that he received the work at Hokusai's residence in Asakusa, Edo, upon returning from a trip to Nagasaki (Nagata 2000, 299). The lord of Shōnai domain, Ikeda Gensai, added the inscription later. It reads:

Yo no naka wa	Our world is such that
tora ōkami mo	"tiger" and "wolf" seem merely
na nomi nite	empty names beside
koromo o kitaru	the truly frightening vision
oni zo kashikoki	of a demon in priest's robes.

NM

Translation of inscription by Arthur Haft

Hokusai died on the eighteenth day of the fourth month, at the beginning of summer, in 1849 (Ka'ei 2). This pair of hanging scrolls is the most important work among the handful of paintings that have survived from his last few months, after he had reached the age of ninety. Beginning in the previous year he had been living in temporary lodgings at Henshō-in Temple, Asakusa, and during the spring of 1849 he was in ill health, attended by pupils, friends, and his daughter Ōi. So the final paintings were likely done just after the New Year, while he was still relatively strong.

True to the pervading ethos of his last works, Hokusai devised transcendent compositions in which both the fisherman and the woodcutter are shown in repose and with rapt expressions. Seated against rocks on the shore and with his basket placed beside him, the fisherman's legs are crossed or otherwise convoluted in a pose of apparent rapture as he gazes off into the empty space above the sea. This is the expression of a man — painted by a man — who contemplates eternity. The woodcutter has placed his bundles of brushwood on the ground and is smoking a pipe as he leans on the upturned handle of a great axe. His expression suggests deep content, maybe even inner contemplation. The strong, uncluttered compositions of the paintings are built around the contrast between sea and mountains, horizontal versus vertical.

In the literary culture of East Asia, fishermen and woodcutters are emblematic of those who live beyond the cares and concerns of everyday life. The theme of Hokusai's paintings is sometimes said indeed to derive specifically from the *Idle Conversations of the Fisherman and Woodcutter* (*Gyoshō kanwa*) by the famous Chinese Song-dynasty poet Su Dongpo (1036–1101; Nagata 2000, 299). But there seems to be more at work here. As Narazaki Muneshige has pointed out, the inclusion of the brilliant feathers in the fisherman's basket and the prominence of the gourd drinking vessel worn on the woodcutter's waist allude, respectively, to the ancient Japanese tales of *Cloak of Feathers* (*Hagoromo*) and *Nurturing the Aged* (*Yōrō*; Narazaki 1994, 272). Both of these well-known stories were adapted as *nō* plays in the medieval period. It is entirely typical of Hokusai, and particularly in his final years, that he manages to imbed such rich meanings into paintings that are nonetheless resolutely original and personal.

The outlines and folds of the robes of each figure are especially richly articulated, in often dryly brushed strokes that alternately speed, halt, broaden, and attenuate with apparently effortless control. Each and every line of the basket, leggings, straw apron, and brushwood bundles — as well as each limpet shell and mountain formation — has distinctive character. Light wisps of hair complement the highly sensitive modeling of the faces. Even just before his final illness, Hokusai gives no evidence of diminished powers. TC

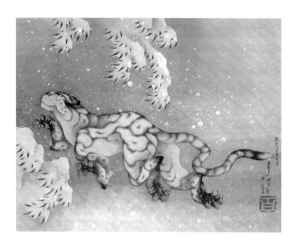

143 Tiger in Snow
1849
Signature: Ka'ei ni tsuchinoto tori-toshi tora no tsuki, Gakyō rōjin Manji rōjin hitsu, yowai kyūjūsai (Painted by Old Man Manji, the old man mad about painting, aged ninety years, in the first [tiger] month of the cock year, Ka'ei 2 [1849])
Seal: Hyaku
hanging scroll; ink and color on silk, 39.0 x 50.0 cm
Private collection
Provenance: Azabu Museum of Arts and Crafts.
Literature: Kobayashi 1995, 6:no. 60; Calza 1999, no. VI.28.
(1-163)

144 Five Fans
1849
Signature: Kyūjū rōjin Manji hitsu
(Painted by Manji, old man of ninety)
Seal: Hyaku
hanging scroll; ink and color on silk,
51.5 x 71.4 cm
Tokyo National Museum
Provenance: Yamatane Art Museum.
Literature: Asahi 1993, no. 84; Nagata 2000, no. 138.
(1-166)

145 Hotei and Chinese Child Acrobats
ca. 1840s
Inscription: *karako wa Hotei no ushiro e egakubeshi* ([You] should paint the Chinese children behind Hotei.)
ink on paper, 35.8 x 26.8 cm
Freer Gallery of Art, Smithsonian Institution, gift of Charles Lang Freer
F1904.213
Provenance: Kobayashi Bunshichi.
Literature: Asano 2005, fig. 54, 43.
(1-147)

This is not a real tiger but one that wanders through the empty sky with its gaze fixed on the heavens. One could even say that this represents Hokusai himself changed into a tiger, swimming calmly through space toward the great beyond. Bamboo leaves heavy with snow are painted in a spiky manner that echoes the shape of the tiger's claws, and the shell-white snow falls evenly on everything. Perhaps Hokusai realized that his death was near and chose to embody his life in a tiger from another dimension.

In his final years Hokusai favored supernatural subjects. Two other examples of tiger subjects are *Tiger Gazing at the Moon* (Katsushika Hokusai Museum,

Tsuwano), painted when Hokusai was eighty-five years old — similar in conception to *Tiger and Bamboo under the Moon* in the collection of the Edoardo Chiossone Museum of Oriental Art, Geneva, done in the 1810s — and *Tiger in the Rain* (Ōta Memorial Museum of Art, Tokyo), completed when Hokusai was ninety years old (Nagata 2000, no. 140). Both tigers are depicted as supernatural beings that have a human or even god-like aspect to them. It is certainly no mere coincidence that in volume thirteen of *Hokusai manga*, thought to have been published in the same year, there is a picture entitled *Running Tiger*, which shows the beast racing in the sky through a violent wind. AS

This work depicts the still-life composition of five scattered folding fans. Even for this conventional subject of Japanese painting, Hokusai created an original composition in which the fans are arranged as a dense pile. The fan at top left has what appears to be a Chinese-style poem written in gold on a dark blue ground, however it is impossible to read the characters. The back of a half-open red fan and a blue-gray fan with just one open fold are shown at the bottom of the composition, and one fan with a blooming morning glory and another with a barely blooming peony are placed above. The tonalities of the folds of the various fans are carefully and brilliantly modulated to suggest the fall of light and shadow. It is extraordinary that Hokusai was still able to do work of such technical perfection at the age of ninety. AS

This unsigned sketch portrays Hotei, the Zen Buddhist sage who became a popular deity. He gestures with his fan as a pair of Chinese acrobatic children perform behind him. To the right of the child who performs a handstand on the chest of his partner are brief instructions indicating that the Chinese children should be painted behind Hotei. This admonition suggests that the sketch was intended as a model for one of Hokusai's many followers. Asano Shūgō noted that this drawing also resembles a painting of Jūrōjin, the god of longevity, in the Museum of Fine Arts, Boston (Asano 2005, 43). AY

146 Boy Playing a Flute
ca. 1840
ink on paper, 11.4 x 15.9 cm
Freer Gallery of Art, Smithsonian
Institution, gift of Charles Lang Freer
F1904.254
Provenance: Kobayashi Bunshichi, 1904.
Literature: Stern 1960, cat. 16, 25; Stern
1973, cat. 104, 274–25.
(1-36)

One of the most endearing images by
Hokusai in the Freer Gallery of Art is this
small fragmentary unsigned sketch of a
young boy seated beside a basket and
playing a flute. Facing toward the viewer,
the child's arms and legs are delineated
with a few dry brushstrokes, while his
costume is rendered with broad, broken
strokes. Technically, this work corresponds closely to the paintings Hokusai
completed in his eighties, and the boy
recalls a famous painting in the Freer
collection in which a flute-playing boy
nestled on a willow-tree trunk is viewing
Mount Fuji (cat. 119). AY

147 Self-Portrait
1842
Signature: Hachijūsansai Hachiemon
(Eighty-three-year-old Hachiemon)
Seal: Manji
ink on paper, 26.9 x 16.9 cm
National Museum of Ethnology, Leiden
RMV 3513-1496
Provenance: Kaneko Fusui; F. Tikotin; F.
Lieftinick.
Literature: Hillier 1980, 73; Forrer 1988, 359;
Forrer 1991, cat. 111; Calza 2003, VI.17, 500;
Nikkei 2005, cat 473.
(1-1)

This self-portrait on a letter that was
likely written to an unnamed publisher
shows the aging artist smiling as he points
with his right hand. His letter reads:

The drawings on the scroll you mentioned were painted when this old man
was forty-one or forty-two. Moreover,
many copies of these pictures were
made. I compared them and recognize
one or two that are as they should be.
However, these are immature works
which I hope will amuse you.

—With best regards,
the 83-year-old Hachiemon
[seal] Manji

Of several self-portraits by Hokusai, this
one captures his energetic and lively personality best, although many paintings
created by Hokusai in his eighties seem
to have some implicit autobiographical
content. Hokusai lived for several years
under the assumed name Miuraya
Hachiemon, which he had taken, according to his own account, in order to
reduce the number of visits from those
seeking to commission additional work.
AY

Translation of letter by Takako Sarai

148 Daily Exorcisms
Nisshin joma
1843 (tenth and eleventh lunar months)
nine drawings; ink on paper
The Hokusai Museum, Obuse
Provenance: Honma Hokuyō.
Literature: Edo Tokyo Hakubutsukan 1995,
168–69; Calza 2003, 501–02.
(1-138)

a. Chinese Lion
tenth month, tenth day
31.8 x 23.2 cm

b. Chinese Lion
tenth month, eleventh day
31.9 x 23.3 cm

c. Lion Dance
tenth month, twenty-third day
32.0 x 22.9 cm

d. Lion Dance
tenth month, twenty-fifth day
31.7 x 23.0 cm

e. Lion Dance
tenth month, twenty-sixth day
31.5 x 23.0 cm

f. Lion Dance
eleventh month, fifth day
31.9 x 22.8 cm

g. Lion Dance
eleventh month, thirteenth day
29.7 x 23.3 cm

h. Lion Dance
eleventh month, eighteenth day
29.2 x 22.8 cm

i. Lion Dance
eleventh month, twenty-fifth day
30.4 x 23 cm

As he grew older, Hokusai became
increasingly preoccupied with living to
the age of one hundred or more, when
he believed that his art would embody
a divine spirit. Beginning in the eleventh
lunar month of 1842 and continuing to
the end of the next year, Hokusai began
each day by sketching a Chinese lion
(*karashishi*) or a masked and costumed
dancer performing a "lion dance"
(*shishimai*) while holding a fan and
a sword or wands with paper strips
attached, which are used in Shinto
purification rites. He inscribed each with
a date and intended with this daily act to
exorcise illness and death. More than

two hundred of the "daily exorcisms" are
known in various museum and private
collections. They are important records
of Hokusai's spiritual beliefs and practices, as well as clearly dated documents
of his informal brushwork at the ages of
eighty-three to eighty-four. In 1847,
Hokusai's daughter Ōi gave a group of
the drawings to Miyamoto Shinsuke, one
of Hokusai's patrons from Shinano
Province (modern-day Nagano
Prefecture), where Hokusai had lived for
a time. Hokusai gave other drawings,
including the ten sheets in the Hokusai
Museum, to his student, Honma Hokuyō
(1822–68). AY

149 Shōjō Lifting a Sake Keg
ca. 1840s
ink on paper, 31.3 x 17.4 cm
Freer Gallery of Art, Smithsonian
Institution, gift of Charles Lang Freer
F1904.255
Provenance: Kobayashi Bunshichi, 1904.
Literature: Stern 1960, cat. 20, 27; Stern
1973, cat. 108, 282–83.
(1-156)

Shōjō were red-haired mythical beings who possessed great strength and loved to drink sake. Hokusai's drawing portrays a *shōjō* lifting a sake cask over his head with one arm. The pose of the figure, viewed from the rear, convincingly captures his stance as he leans into his right leg to balance the thrust of the heavy sake cask. The style of this brush-and-ink drawing, with broad, broken brushstrokes defining the contours of the robe, corresponds closely to the artist's dated paintings produced when he was in his eighties. During this period, Hokusai's paintings often portrayed supernatural subjects in dynamic poses and delineated with energetic brushwork. This drawing was one of a large group by Hokusai that Freer purchased from the Japanese art dealer Kobayashi Bunshichi. AY

Final Drawings (*hanshita-e*) for the Print Series, *One Hundred Poets, One Verse Each, as Explained by the Nurse*

Hokusai's long-standing interest in classical Japanese poetry inspired him to design a series of one hundred prints based on the anthology *One Hundred Poets, One Verse Each, as Explained by the Nurse* (*Hyakunin isshu*). The eminent scholar, critic, and poet Fujiwara no Teika (1162–1241) compiled the anthology, which is arranged to represent Japanese poetry from the seventh century to Teika's own time, beginning with Emperor Tenji (626–71; Mostow 1996, 1). Hokusai added the words "uba ga etoki" (as explained by the nurse) to the title of the series, which was widely familiar in Edo-period Japan through illustrated printed books and even card and shell-matching games based on the verses. Traditionally, the poets themselves were represented, following the conventions of portraying immortals of poetry *(kasen)* in simple architectural or landscape settings. Hokusai's recasting of the series by introducing the intermediary of explanations by an *uba* (a wet nurse for an infant or an old woman), gave him a wide scope for novel and at times humorous images, many of which depart completely from the refined, elite world of the Japanese imperial court (Morse 1989, 7). Visual and verbal puns are abundant in these images, which draw upon the wordplay and intentional challenge to the strict rules of classical poetry that were common in contemporary *kyōka*. Nishimuraya Yohachi, who had published Hokusai's most famous print series and many of his books, began publication in 1835 and Ise Sanjirō

continued it (ibid. 1989, 14–16). Twenty-seven designs are known from prints published at the time, one from a keyblock proof, and four from publication based on surviving drawings.

The majority of the unpublished designs for Hokusai's "One Hundred Poets" print series are known from final drawings for keyblocks *(hanshita-e)*, forty-one of which are in the Freer Gallery of Art. Freer purchased thirty-three of the drawings from the English collector Michael Tomkinson. A red seal on the reverse of most of the surviving drawings suggests that the artist Kawanabe Kyōsai (1831–89), who admired Hokusai, may have owned them; the drawings reached Paris, where Japanese art enthusiasts including the collector and writer Edmond de Goncourt viewed them in 1885 (ibid. 1989, 17). Since *hanshita-e* survive only when prints remain unpublished, they offer a rare insight into the artist's draftsmanship and working methods. Hokusai's *hanshita-e* for this series reveal the extraordinary care with which he worked out the composition, linear and textural renderings, and other details of his print designs. Patches of paper were carefully inserted in some designs to make corrections to figure placement or other details. Drawn mainly with a very fine brush on thin, translucent paper, these images encompass a wide range of subjects, many of which have a complex and indirect relationship to the original poem. AY

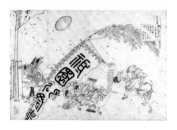

150 One Hundred Poets, One Verse Each, as Explained by the Nurse: Fun'ya no Yasuhide
mid-1830s
Hyakunin isshu uba ga etoki: Fun'ya no Yasuhide
Signature: saki no Hokusai Manji
ink on paper; *hanshita-e*, 25.3 x 37.2 cm
Freer Gallery of Art, Smithsonian Institution, gift of Charles Lang Freer F1907.551
Provenance: Michael Tomkinson; Ernest Hart.
Literature: Morse 1989, 64-65; Mostow 1996, 206-08.
(1-73)

The late-ninth-century court poet Fun'ya no Yasuhide composed the poem on this work. Yasuhide was included among the Six Immortals of Poetry (*rokkasen*) and the Thirty-six Immortals of Poetry. The poem reads:

fuku kara ni	As soon as it blows,
aki no kusaki no	the autumn trees and grasses
shiwoureba	droop, and this must be why,
mube yamakaze wo	quite rightly, the mountain wind
arashi to ifuramu	is called "the ravager."

The poem focuses on the Chinese character as a rebus that combines the characters for "mountain" and "wind," to form a single ideograph meaning "storm," "tempest," or the verb *arasu* (to ravage). In Hokusai's image, a gust carries a traveler's hat away and a banner for the Gion Festival is nearly blown over. Men struggle to restrain a book and scroll while a woman holds her kimono against the wind. Visually echoing the imagery of the poem and the illustration, the calligraphy is broken into two sections as if blown apart by the wind, and the poem reads from right to left in the upper section and from left to right in the lower section, changing direction like the gusty wind. AY

Translation of poem from Mostow 1996, 207

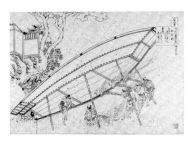

151 One Hundred Poets, One Verse Each, as Explained by the Nurse: Ki no Tomonori
Hyakunin isshu uba ga etoki: Ki no Tomonori
mid-1830s
Signature: saki no Hokusai Manji
ink on paper; *hanshita-e*, 25.3 x 37.2 cm
Freer Gallery of Art, Smithsonian Institution, gift of Charles Lang Freer F1907.553
Provenance: Michael Tomkinson; Ernest Hart.
Literature: Morse 1989, 84–85; Mostow 1996, 240–41.
(1-74)

152 One Hundred Poets, One Verse Each, as Explained by the Nurse: Fujiwara no Asatada
Hyakunin isshu uba ga etoki: Chūnagon Asatada
mid-1830s
Signature: saki no Hokusai Manji
ink on paper; *hanshita-e*, 25.3 x 37.2 cm
Freer Gallery of Art, Smithsonian Institution, gift of Charles Lang Freer F1907.556
Provenance: Michael Tomkinson; Ernest Hart.
Literature: Morse 1989, 104–05; Mostow 1996, 272–73.
(1-76)

153 One Hundred Poets, One Verse Each, as Explained by the Nurse: Monk Shun'e
Hyakunin isshu uba ga etoki: Shun'e Hōshi
mid-1830s
Signature: saki no Hokusai Manji
ink on paper; *hanshita-e*, 25.3 x 37.2 cm
Freer Gallery of Art, Smithsonian Institution, gift of Charles Lang Freer F1907.572
Provenance: Michael Tomkinson; Ernest Hart.
Literature: Morse 1989, 175–76; Mostow 1996, 392–93.
(1-77)

The poet Ki no Tomonori (ca. 850–905) assisted his younger cousin Ki no Tsurayuki (ca. 872–945) in compiling the *Collection of Ancient and Modern Poems (Kokinshū)*, the first collection of Japanese poetry to be compiled by imperial decree. Tomonori is included among the Thirty-six Immortals of Poetry. The poem representing Tomonori in the later "One Hundred Poets" anthology was included in the *Kokinshū*. It reads:

hisakata no	In these spring days
hikari nodokeki	with the tranquil light encompassing the four directions
haru no hi ni	why should the blossoms scatter
shizu-kokoro naku	with uneasy hearts?
hana no chiruramu	

In Hokusai's illustration, the phrase "haru no hi," meaning "days of spring," seems to have been interpreted as "fires of spring." Both day(s) and fire(s) have the same sound, "hi," in Japanese (Morse 1989, 84). With cherry blossoms falling like snow from the tree above, Hokusai illustrates workers heating the pitch applied to seal the bottoms of boats brought ashore for the winter. Seasonal imagery and scenes, including smoke, light, and fire are among many of Hokusai's designs for the "One Hundred Poets" series. AY

Translation of poem from Mostow 1996, 240

Fujiwara no Asatada (910–61) held the office of Chūnagon (middle counselor) in the Great Council of State (Dajōkan), the highest governing body of the Heian-period imperial court. He is included among the Thirty-six Immortals of Poetry. The following poem is included in the early eleventh-century imperial anthology *Collection of Gleanings (of Japanese Poems) (Shūishū)*:

afu koto no	If there were no such thing
taete shi naku ha	as ever having met her, then,
naka-naka ni	contrary to all expectations
hito wo mo mi wo mo	neither her coldness nor my pain
uramizaramashi	would I have to resent!

The poem reflects on the longing for a woman who has yet to consent to receive the author as a lover. Hokusai's drawing portrays a woman appearing to Abe no Yasuna, who had sheltered a fox from hunters years before. Some time later, a beautiful woman, Kuzunoha, who was really the fox disguised as a human, came to him, gave birth to a son, and died (or disappeared). Later she revealed her true identity to Yasuna in a dream (Morse 1989, 104). The pose of the woman who appears before Yasuna and his son, and the sweep of her long kimono echo the forms of the foxes who gather on the plain, breathing fire as they gather on the last day of the year. The woman's figure appears on a patch of paper attached to the main sheet at its edges. This represents a correction of this key figure by Hokusai, who from his earliest works paid close attention to the placement of figures in his designs. AY

Translation of poem from Mostow 1996, 272

The Buddhist priest Shun'e (b. 1113) was the son of the poet Minamoto no Toshiyori (Shunrai), who is also included among the "One Hundred Poets." Shun'e was a prominent poet whose residence was called Karin'en (Garden in the poetic woods), where a circle of poets often gathered. The poem by Shun'e reads:

yomosugara	All through the night
mono-omofu koro ha	recently, as I dwell on things
akeyaranu	even the gap between the doors
neya no hima sahe	of my bedroom, which does not lighten,
tsurenakarikeri	seems cruel and heartless to me.

Although the voice in the poem is often interpreted to be that of Shun'e, it is described as a love poem, and can be interpreted as the voice of a woman who waits in vain throughout the night for a lover who never arrives. Hokusai's illustration departs from the usual convention of portraying the priest gazing out into the night and instead shows a woman looking out into a garden that is dimly lit by a crescent moon. AY

Translation of poem from Mostow 1996, 392

154 One Hundred Poets, One Verse Each, as Explained by the Nurse: Monk Saigyō
Hyakunin isshu uba ga etoki: Saigyō Hōshi
mid-1830s
Signature: saki no Hokusai Manji
ink on paper; *hanshita-e*, 25.3 x 37.2 cm
Freer Gallery of Art, Smithsonian Institution, gift of Charles Lang Freer
F1907.573
Provenance: Michael Tomkinson; Ernest Hart.
Literature: Morse 1989, 178; Mostow 1996, 395-96.
(1-78)

155 One Hundred Poets, One Verse Each, as Explained by the Nurse: Sarumaru Dayū
Hyakunin isshu uba ga etoki: Sarumaru Dayū
ca. 1835-36
Signature: saki no Hokusai Manji
Censor seal: *Kiwame*
Publisher: Ise Sanjirō
color woodblock print; *ōban*, 25.2 x 37.0 cm
Honolulu Academy of Arts, gift of James A. Michener, 1987 (20,082)
Literature: Morse 1989, 34-35; Mostow 1996, 155-57; Calza 2003, VI.12, 497.
(1-70)

156 One Hundred Poets, One Verse Each, as Explained by the Nurse: Abe no Nakamaro
Hyakunin isshu uba ga etoki: Abe no Nakamaro
1835
Signature: saki no Hokusai
Publisher: Ise Sanjirō
Censor seal: *Kiwame*
color woodblock print; *ōban*, 26.0 x 37.8 cm
Honolulu Academy of Arts, gift of James A. Michener, 1987 (20,083)
Literature: Morse 1989, pl. 7; Forrer 1991, pl. 79; Edo Tokyo Hakubutsukan 1995, 172; Mostow 1996, 161-63; Calza 2003, VI.12.1A, 498.
(1-67)

Saigyō (1118–90), who was born to a warrior family, became a Buddhist priest and one of the most esteemed Japanese poets from his own lifetime to the present day. His poem reflects on whether it is the moon or his own thoughts that preoccupy him. It reads:

nagete tote	"Lament!" does it say?
tsuki ya ha mono wo	Is it the moon that makes me
omohasuru	dwell on things? — No, and yet,
kakochi-gaho naru	look at the tears flowing down
wa ga namida kana	my reproachful face!

In Hokusai's drawing, the full moon appears among clouds high in the sky, while the poet gazes upward. The diagonal frame of the roofline of Saigyō's dwelling reinforces the strong visual relationship between the priest and the moon. A patch of paper on which the priest is drawn indicates that Hokusai revised the drawing at least once. Hokusai's admiration for Saigyō may have led him to portray the poet as an elderly man with facial features not unlike his own. AY

Translation of poem from Mostow 1996, 395

An autumnal poem attributed to the eighth-century poet Sarumaru inspired this scene of women carrying pack baskets down a mountain path toward their home village. Clouds fill the valleys with mist, and red maple leaves fan out against the sunset. The lines, forms, and empty space at the center of the composition focus on the silhouettes of two deer on a distant peak. The plaintive cry of the stag seems to cause one woman to look in his direction, and reflects the loneliness that the poem expresses. It reads:

oku yama ni	When I hear the voice
momijihi fumi-wake	of the stag crying for his mate
naku shika no	stepping through the falling leaves
kowe kiku toki zo	deep in the mountains — then is the time
aki ha kanashiki	that autumn is saddest.

AY

Translation of poem from Mostow 1996, 155

The poet Abe no Nakamaro (710–90) traveled to China at the age of sixteen. He served the emperor Xuanzong and became a friend of the famous Chinese poets Li Bo and Wang Wei. He was shipwrecked off the coast of Annam in Southeast Asia and returned to China, where he died. Nakamaro's poem refers to the familiar and scenic landscape of Nara, the capital of Japan and his home. It reads:

ama no hara	As I gaze out, far
furi-saki-mireba	across the plain of heaven,
kasuga naru	ah, at Kasuga,
mikasa no yama ni	from behind Mount Mikasa,
ideshi tsuki kamo	it's the same moon that came out then!

Hokusai portrays Nakamaro standing at the top of a hill, surrounded by Chinese soldiers who defer to him as he composes his poem. He gazes eastward toward his distant homeland and contemplates the moon, wondering if it is the same moon that rose behind Mount Mikasa. Hokusai's earlier prints of the subject referred to a legend that the Chinese emperor had imprisoned Nakamaro in a tower when he was suspected of espionage. Here Hokusai creates an unexpected and subtler scene, in which the moon appears only as a reflection in water rather than in the expected position high in the sky. A rough preparatory drawing for this print shows the moon in the sky above the boats. The calligraphy of the poem on the square cartouche, which is divided into two parts separated by open space, reflects the distance separating Nakamaro from his home. AY

Translation of poem from Mostow 1996, 161

157 One Hundred Poets, One Verse Each, as Explained by the Nurse: Ariwara no Narihira
Hyakunin isshu uba ga etoki: Ariwara no Narihira
1836
Signature: saki no Hokusai Manji
Censor seal: *Kiwame*
Publisher: Ise Sanjirō
color woodblock print; *ōban*, 26.2 x 37.6 cm
The Art Institute of Chicago, Clarence Buckingham Collection 1928.1094
Literature: Morse 1989, 54–55; Forrer 1991, cat. 78; Mostow 1996, 192–93;
Calza 2003, VI.12.3, 498.
(1-68)

158 One Hundred Poets, One Verse Each, as Explained by the Nurse: Minamoto no Muneyuki
Hyakunin isshu uba ga etoki: Minamoto no Muneyuki Ason
1836
Signature: saki no Hokusai Manji
Censor seal: *Kiwame*
Collector seal: Wakai
Publisher: Ise Sanjirō
color woodblock print; *ōban*, 25.8 x 37.6 cm
The Mann Collection, Highland Park, Illinois
Provenance: Wakai Kenzaburō; Le Véel.
Literature: Morse 1989, 76–77; Forrer 1991, cat. 80; Ōta 1994, cat. 84; Mostow 1996, 226–27;
Calza 2003, VI.12.4, 498.
(1-72)

Ariwara no Narihira (825–80) was one of the most famous Japanese poets, and he is included among the Six Immortals of Poetry and the Thirty-six Immortals of Poetry. He is also understood to be the protagonist of the tenth-century *Tales of Ise* (Mostow 1996, 192). The poem in the "One Hundred Poets" anthology also is included in the *Kokinshū* anthology in which a headnote explains that a painted screen showing autumn leaves floating on the Tatsuta River inspired it. The poem reads:

chihayaburu	Unheard of
kami-yo mo kikazu	even in the legendary age
tatsuta-gaha	of the awesome gods:
kara kurenawi ni	Tatsuta River in scarlet
midzu kuguru to ha	and the water flowing under it.

Translation of poem from Mostow 1996, 192

Interpretations of the imagery of this poem vary. In one version, the last two lines would be translated as:

Tatsuta River, tie-dyed the deepest Chinese scarlet
(Mostow 1996, 192).

In this interpretation, the leaves float on the blue water as if a blue cloth had been tied here and there and dipped in scarlet. Hokusai's illustration shows people crossing a steeply arching bridge across the scenic Tatsuta River south of Nara. A servant accompanies the woman at center, and two samurai tug at a bundle as they ascend from the bank. A peasant couple carrying heavy packs climbs from the opposite shore. Below, red maple leaves float on the blue river. Unusual colors like the warm tones of the mist are characteristic of Hokusai's choices for the prints in this series. AY

Minamoto no Muneyuki (d. 939) was a prominent poet who often exchanged verses with Ki no Tsurayuki. His poem, composed on the subject of winter, was in response to an erudite debate over whether autumn or winter evoked the greatest sadness. It reads:

yama-zato ha	In the mountain village,
fuyu zo sabishisa	it is in winter that my loneliness
masarikeru	increases most,
hito-me mo	when I think how
kusa mo	both have dried up,
karenu to omoheba	the grasses and people's visits

Hokusai's image of hunters gathered around a fire near a crude shelter is one of the most famous prints in the "One Hundred Poets" series. Contrasts between movement and stillness, light and darkness are devices that Hokusai often used to heighten the impact of his most successful print designs. Light, warmth, and billowing smoke from the lifesaving fire and human activity dominate the center of the picture, which is surrounded by the desolation, darkness, and stillness of the landscape in the dead of winter. The hunters seem to have dispelled for the moment the austerity and loneliness of the cold and lifeless season. AY

Translation of poem from Mostow 1996, 226

159 One Hundred Poets, One Verse Each, as Explained by the Nurse: Fujiwara no Yoshitaka
Hyakunin isshū uba ga etoki: Fujiwara no Yoshitaka
1836
Signature: saki no Hokusai Manji
Censor seal: *Kiwame*
Publisher: Ise Sanjirō
color woodblock print; *ōban*, 26.2 x 37.5 cm
Honolulu Academy of Arts, gift of James A. Michener, 1991 (21,926)
Literature: Morse 1989, 112-13; Forrer 1991, cat. 82; Mostow 1996, 290-91; Calza 2003, VI.12.7.
(1-69)

The poet Fujiwara no Yoshitaka (954–74) died in his youth of smallpox. He left a collection of poetry, including this poem to a woman with whom he had just spent his first night:

kimi ga tame	Even the life that
woshikarazarishi	I'd not have been sorry to lose
inochi sahe	just to meet you once,
nagaku mogana to	now, having met, I think:
omohinuru kana	"I want it to last forever!"

Hokusai chose to illustrate guests enjoying the view across a lake from a bath-house. The relationship between the emotions expressed by the poem and this scene are somewhat difficult to interpret, but the steam rising from the bath suggests the warmth that the poem's writer must have felt for the woman he had longed for and finally embraced. AY

Translation of poem from Mostow 1996, 290

160 One Hundred Poets, One Verse Each, as Explained by the Nurse: Fujiwara no Sadaie
Hyakunin isshū uba ga etoki: Gon chūnagon Sadaie
1836
Signature: saki no Hokusai Manji
Censor seal: *Kiwame*
Publisher: Ise Sanjirō
color woodblock print; *ōban*, 25.1 x 37.3 cm
Honolulu Academy of Arts, gift of James A. Michener, 1971 (16,146)
Literature: Morse 1989, pl. 97; Calza 2003, no. VI.12.
(1-71)

Fujiwara no Teika (Sadaie, 1162–1241) was a master poet and compiler of the anthology *Hyakunin isshu*. He chose a love poem to represent himself in the "One Hundred Poets" anthology:

konu hito wo	For the man who doesn't come
matsuho no ura no	I wait at the Bay of Matsuo
yufu-nagi ni	in the evening calm
yaku ya mo shiho no	where they boil seaweed for salt,
mi mo kogaretsutsu	I, too, burn with longing!

Hokusai's image focuses on the reference to Matsuo Bay, where a group of workers boils seaweed to extract salt. Smoke printed in beautifully gradated color rises from the furnace where kelp is burned. Slender women assist in unbundling the kelp and carrying away buckets of ash. Their presence in Hokusai's picture may refer to the earlier poem from the anthology (*Manyōshū*) on which Teika composed his variation. The *Manyōshū* poem describes fisher-maidens who gather seaweed in the morning calm and boil it for salt in the evening calm. Teika transforms the imagery into a poem of longing. AY

Translation of poem from Mostow 1996, 427

161 One Hundred Poets, One Verse Each, as Explained by the Nurse: Mibu no Tadamine
Hyakunin isshū uba ga etoki: Mibu no Tadamine
mid-1830s
Signature: saki no Hokusai Manji
keyblock proof, ink on paper; *ōban*, 26.4 x 37.8 cm
Honolulu Academy of Arts, gift of James A. Michener, 1991 (21,928)
Provenance: Chandler Collection.
Literature: Morse 1989, 78-79; Mostow 1996, 232-33; Calza 2003, no. VI.12.
(1-75)

The last print in progress for Hokusai's "One Hundred Poets" series is this picture of a nobleman leaving a woman's house in the early morning. Two farmers, beginning their day of labor, appear startled to encounter him, and one adjusts his sandal to avoid meeting the man's eye. The poem refers to the *ariake*, the late-rising moon that remains visible at dawn. It reads:

ariake no	There is nothing so depressing
tsurenaku mieshi	as the break of day and
wakare yori	leaving you after
akatsuki bakari	having seen the heartless
uki mono ha nashi	morning moon.

The keyblock, carved from a drawing pasted face down as a guide, would have printed the black lines of the final print, and the marks at the bottom would have guided placement of the color blocks. The print was never completed, and publication of the "One Hundred Poets" series to which Hokusai had devoted much thought and effort, was suspended, apparently abruptly, and never resumed. AY

Translation of poem from Mostow 1996, 232

162 One Hundred Views of Mount Fuji
Fugaku hyakkei
3 volumes
volume 1, 1834
volume 2, 1835
volume 3, 1849
Signature: Nanajūgo rei, saki no Hokusai Iitsu aratame Gakyō rōjin Manji hitsu (volume 1); nanajūroku rei, saki no Hokusai Iitsu aratame Gakyō rōjin Manji hitsu, (volume 2)
Seal: The shape of Mount Fuji (volumes 1 and 2)
Engraver: Egawa Tomekichi
Publisher: Nishimuraya Yohachi (volumes 1 and 2); Eirakuya Tōshirō (volume 3)
woodblock printed book; *fukurotoji*, 22.4 x 25.6 cm
Smithsonian Institution Libraries, Freer Gallery of Art and Arthur M. Sackler Gallery Library, Special collection NE1325.K3 A64 1834
Literature: Oka 1974, no. 218-19; Hillier 1980, 213-25; Edo Tokyo Hakubutsukan 1995 180-81; Calza 2003, 492.
(1-128)

The constantly changing appearance of Mount Fuji, which could be seen from most parts of Edo, fascinated the people of Edo and held them in awe. From ancient times, the mountain was regarded as sacred. Hokusai's illustrations in volumes one and two of *One Hundred Views of Mount Fuji* are masterpieces of woodblock printing. The master engraver Egawa Tomekichi carved the blocks, and Hokusai specifically requested Tomikichi when he wrote to his publisher regarding the commission. No one else had the skill, Hokusai insisted, to carve the blocks to the standard required to capture the nuances of his brush for these great printed pictures. Designed on single or double pages, the illustrations in these volumes include many remarkable and occasionally humorous designs. As in the highly successful color prints in the *Thirty-six Views of Mount Fuji* series, the mountain is shown from near and distant viewpoints, framed by a wave

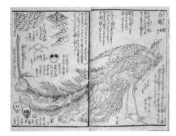

and plovers, or reflected in a sake cup. The quality and printing of the "One Hundred Views" transcends all but a few of the famous color prints.

Hokusai, who probably worked as a block carver in his teens, had an exceptional understanding of the aesthetic potential of woodblock printing. The superior quality of printing in this book achieves subtle effects of delicate, perfectly even gray tones that even the most skillful painter could not achieve with brush and ink. AY

163 Illustrated Book of Leaders of China and Japan
Wakan ehon sakigake
1 volume
1836
Signature: saki no Hokusai aratame Gakyō rōjin
Seal: Mount Fuji
Publisher: Kitajima Junshirō
woodblock printed book; *fukurotoji,*
23.0 x 16.0 cm
Smithsonian Institution Libraries, Freer Gallery of Art and Arthur M. Sackler Gallery Library, Special collection NE1325.K3 A78 1836
Literature: Toda 1930, 263; Hillier 1980, 227–44.
(1-141)

Tales of warriors were a long-standing tradition in Japan, beginning with recitations of the lengthy and deadly battles between the Taira and Minamoto clans in the late twelfth century. By Hokusai's lifetime, Chinese warrior tales had also become popular, and as an illustrator he became familiar with many of them. His warrior images are imaginative and powerful. Hokusai's highly developed skills in composition heighten the dramatic tension of the scenes. In the small space of an open book, he manipulated the placement of the figures to maximize their forceful confrontations. AY

164 Illustrated Manual on Color
Ehon saishiki tsū
2 volumes, *edehon*
1848
Signature: Gakyō rōjin Manji hitsu
Publisher: Izumiya Ichibei and others
woodblock printed book; *fukurotoji,*
19.3 x 13.0 cm
The British Museum 1979.3-5.0465 JH 465
Literature: Hillier 1980, 227–44; Edo Tokyo Hakubutsukan 1995, 194; Calza 2003, 502
(1-96)

Near the end of his life, Hokusai created an instruction manual on colors, which provides detailed information on pigments and painting methods. He included sample details to guide the painting of birds and their feather patterns, insects, flower petals, the patterns of fur on animals, water in motion, and expansive lakes. AY

165 IIllustrated Book of the Glories of China and Japan
Ehon wakan no homare
1 volume
1850
Signature: saki no Hokusai Gakyō rōjin Manji hitsu
Publisher: Kamiya Tokuhachi
woodblock printed book; *fukurotoji,*
23.0 x 16.2 cm
Smithsonian Institution Libraries, Freer Gallery of Art and Arthur M. Sackler Gallery Library, Special collection NE1325.K3 A639 1850
Literature: Hillier 1980, 227–44; Edo Tokyo Hakubutsukan 1995, 190.
(1-52)

This book was designed when Hokusai was seventy-six years old, according to the inscription accompanying the illustration of Kamata Matahachi writing the title with a brush held at the end of a rolled mat. However, the colophon gives the date of publication as 1850, and no earlier editions are known, so *Illustrated Book of the Glories of China and Japan* was first printed after Hokusai's death. In one remarkable illustration, Hokusai depicts the warrior Minamoto no Yoshisada praying to the god of the sea to allow him to retreat via water. The form of the god with a serpentlike tail appears to dissolve in the hollow of the wave. AY

CONCORDANCE (Volume 1 to Volume 2 catalogue numbers)

VOL. 1	VOL. 2	VOL. 1	VOL. 2	VOL. 1	VOL. 2	VOL. 1	VOL. 2
1	147	43	27	85	44	127	77
2	17	44	43	86	72	128	162
3	2	45	126	87	106	129	19
4	35	46	80	88	105	130	65
5	121	47	82	89	113	131	28
6	122	48	63	90	114	132	134
7	41	49	89	91	115	133	1
8	64	50	61	92	84	134	133
9	48	51	62	93	95	135	47
10	34	52	165	94	29	136	129
11	16	53	59	95	87	137	128
12	18	54	8	96	164	138	148
13	26	55	66	97	71	139	31
14	22	56	23	98	116	140	58
15	68	57	60	99	6	141	163
16	36	58	69	100	83	142	37
17	42	59	92	101	130	143	38
18	33	60	93	102	32	144	74
19	52	61	94	103	50	145	75
20	51	62	57	104	86	146	13
21	45	63	21	105	85	147	145
22	117	64	53	106	118	148	125
23	55	65	108	107	30	149	39
24	10	66	109	108	131	150	104
25	11	67	156	109	124	151	103
26	73	68	157	110	88	152	79
27	9	69	159	111	81	153	127
28	7	70	155	112	56a	154	3
29	5	71	160	113	56b	155	4
30	119	72	158	114	56c	156	149
31	67	73	150	115	70	157	138
32	91	74	151	116	107	158	136
33	90	75	161	117	97	159	137
34	78	76	152	118	96	160	135
35	40	77	153	119	99	161	132
36	146	78	154	120	98	162	142
37	49	79	24	121	100	163	143
38	76	80	14	122	102	164	141
39	25	81	46	123	101	165	140
40	20	82	54	124	110	166	144
41	12	83	123	125	112	167	139
42	120	84	15	126	111		

GLOSSARY OF JAPANESE TERMS

benizuri-e   Color print in safflower red (*beni*) and green printed from separate blocks.

bijin   Beautiful women, occasionally handsome young men.

bijinga   Prints or paintings of beautiful women or men.

bunjinga   Literati painting practiced by Edo-period artists who followed Chinese artistic methods and models and often adopted the ideals of Chinese scholar-painters.

edehon   Illustrated handbook of artistic models.

egoyomi   Picture calendars issued for the New Year that often incorporated allusions to the year of publication, such as animal signs associated with the zodiac or embedded characters indicating the cyclical year.

ehon   Picture book.

fūzokuga   Genre pictures illustrating activities of contemporary life.

gesaku   Edo-period popular literature.

gofun   Shell white, a mineral pigment.

haikai   A poem or series of linked verses composed in a nonstandard or comic style.

hanamichi   A raised walkway from which kabuki actors enter or leave the stage.

hanashibon   Short, humorous stories.

hanshita-e   Preliminary sketches for woodblock prints.

ichimai-e   Commercially published single-sheet prints.

jōruri   Plays with narration accompanied by music.

kachōga   Bird-and-flower painting.

kabuki   A type of popular Japanese theater developed from the early seventeenth century onward. Kabuki actors were a major subject of Japanese prints.

kasen   Immortals of Poetry. Groups of famous poets of the past selected for the merit of their poetry.

kibyōshi   "Yellow covers," or "yellow-backs," inexpensive woodblock-printed editions of illustrated contemporary fiction popular from the mid-1770s.

kyōka   "Mad verse," a type of witty poetry based on the form of the classical thirty-one syllable *tanka* or *waka*, but often breaking the rules of classical diction and composition.

kyōka ehon   Albums combining illustrations and *kyōka* poems.

machi-eshi   Town (or city) painters who earned their livelihood by selling their paintings.

manga   "Random sketches," a term used in the title of Hokusai's most popular series of books of miscellaneous illustrations.

mitate-e   Often translated as "parody pictures," *mitate-e* usually recast classical literary or historical subjects in modern settings.

musha-e   Warrior pictures.

nishiki-e   "Brocade prints," a term describing full-color woodblock prints that were first published in 1775.

nō   A type of Japanese theater performed by masked actors.

orihon   Folding albums.

rokkasen   Six Immortals of Poetry. See *kasen*.

sekiga   Impromptu paintings. Paintings done quickly for patrons or the public.

senryū   A poetic form usually of stanzas of five, seven, and five syllables. Originally, these were composed to follow a topic (*dai*) or foundation stanza (*maeku*; Miner 1985, 296).

sharebon   "Smart" or "clever" books popular around 1764–88.

shogakai   Gatherings of artists to produce painting and calligraphy.

surimono   Luxurious prints employing high-quality materials and techniques and published in limited numbers, usually for private circulation.

tanzaku   Long, narrow paper used for inscribing poetry. Also the format of similar proportions for prints.

uki-e   "Perspective picture," prints or paintings employing Western principles of perspective.

ukiyo   "Floating world," a term describing the transient and illusory pleasures of the great cities of the Edo period.

ukiyo-e   "Pictures of the floating world," a term describing both woodblock prints and paintings of popular subjects such as courtesans, actors, landscapes, nature studies, warriors, ghosts, and legends.

wakashu   Young, elegant men.

yakusha-e   Actor prints.

yomihon   "Reading books," extended fictional narratives often based on historical subjects that became popular in the early nineteenth century. *Yomihon* were often published in serial editions with illustrations by well-known artists to improve their sales.

BIBLIOGRAPHY

Ann Arbor Art Association. *Exhibition of Oriental and American Art.* 2d ed. Detroit: J. Bornman & Son, 1910.

Anderson, William. *The Pictorial Arts of Japan.* London: Sampson Low, Marston, Searle and Rivington, 1886.

Asahi Shimbunsha, ed. *Dai Hokusai ten* (Great Hokusai exhibition). Tokyo: Asahi Shimbunsha, 1993.

Asakura, Musei. "Ukiyo-e shigon." *Ukiyo-e* 43 (1918).

Asano, Shūgō. "Hokusai no nikuhitsuga no inshō ni tsuite" (Seals on Hokusai's paintings). In *Hokusai and His Age: Ukiyo-e Painting, Printmaking and Book Illustration in Late Edo Japan,* edited by John T. Carpenter. Amsterdam: Hotei Publishing, 2005. Originally published in *Siren, Bulletin of Chiba City Museum of Art,* no. 1 (March 1994).

_____. *Katsushika Hokusai: Shunga no sekai* (Katsushika Hokusai: The world of erotic art). Tokyo: Yōsensha, 2005.

_____. "*Surimono* Art and Literary Circles: The *Genroku kasen kai awase and Umazukushi* Series." In Hokusai, by Gian Carlo Calza. London and New York: Phaidon Press, 2003.

_____. "Ukiyo-e hanga no sankeitai: ichimai-e, surimono, hanpon" (Three types of ukiyo-e prints: *Ichimai-e, surimono,* and woodblock books). In *Nihon bijutsu zenshū.* Vol. 20. Tokyo: Kōdansha, 1991.

Asano, Shūgō and Timothy T. Clark, eds. *Kitagawa Utamaro.* Tokyo: Asahi Shimbunsha, 1995.

Asano, Shūgō and Yoshida Nobuyuki, eds. *Hokusai. Ukiyoe wo yomu* (Reading ukiyo-e prints). Vol. 4. Tokyo: Asahi Shimbunsha, 1998.

British Museum. *The Work of Hokusai.* London: British Museum, 1948.

Calza, Gian Carlo. "Imitations, Copies and Fakes after Paintings by Hokusai." In *Hokusai and His Age: Ukiyo-e Painting, Printmaking and Book Illustration in Late Edo Japan,* edited by John T. Carpenter. Amsterdam: Hotei Publishing, 2005.

_____. *Hokusai.* London and New York: Phaidon Press, 2003.

_____. *Hokusai: il vecchio pazzo per la pittura.* Milan: Electa, 1999.

_____, ed., with the assistance of John T. Carpenter. *Hokusai Paintings: Selected Essays.* Venice: International Hokusai Research Centre, University of Venice, 1994.

Carpenter, John T., ed. *Hokusai and His Age: Ukiyo-e Painting, Printmaking and Book Illustration in Late Edo Japan.* Amsterdam: Hotei Publishing, 2005.

Centre Culturel du Marais. *Le fou de peinture: Hokusai et son temps.* Paris: Centre Culturel du Marais, 1980.

Clark, Timothy. *One Hundred Views of Mount Fuji.* London: British Museum, 2001.

_____. *Ukiyo-e Paintings in the British Museum.* Washington, D.C.: Smithsonian Institution Press, 1992.

_____. "Paintings by Hokusai in the British Museum." *Orientations* 21, no. 8 (August 1990): 37-44, 145.

Croissant, Doris. "Hokusai and Takahashi Yuichi: Changing Concepts in Still-life Painting." In *Hokusai and His Age: Ukiyo-e Painting, Printmaking and Book Illustration in Late Edo Japan,* edited by John T. Carpenter. Amsterdam: Hotei Publishing, 2005, 216–233.

Edo Tokyo Hakubutsukan, ed. *Katsushika Hokusai ten.* Tokyo: Edo Tokyo Hakubutsukan, 1995.

Fenollosa, Ernest F. *Catalogue of the Exhibition of Paintings of Hokusai, Held at the Japan Fine Art Association, Uyeno Park, Tōkio, from 13th to 30th January, 1900.* Tokyo: Bunshichi Kobayashi, 1901.

_____. *The Masters of Ukioye: A Complete Historical Description of Japanese Paintings and Color Prints of the Genre School.* New York: The Knickerbocker Press, 1896.

_____. *Museum of Fine Arts. Department of Japanese Art. Special Exhibitions of the Pictorial Art of Japan and China. No. 1. Hokusai, and His School. Catalogue.* Boston: Alfred Mudge & Son, 1893.

_____. *Review of the Chapter on Painting in Gonse's "L'Art Japonais."* Boston: J. R. Osgood and Company, 1885.

Fitzhugh, Elisabeth West. "A Pigment Census of Ukiyo-e Paintings in the Freer Gallery of Art." *Ars Orientalis* 11 (1979): 27-38.

Fitzhugh, Elisabeth West, John Winter, and Marco Leona. *Studies Using Scientific Methods: Pigments in Later Japanese Paintings.* Washington, D.C.: Freer Gallery of Art, Smithsonian Institution, 2003.

Forrer, Matthi. *Hokusai: Prints and Drawings.* Munich: Prestel-Verlag, 1991; distributed in the U.S. and Canada by Neues Publishing.

_____, with texts by Edmond de Goncourt. Hokusai. New York: Rizzoli, 1988.

Freer Papers. Freer Gallery of Art and Arthur M. Sackler Gallery Archives.

Fujikake, Shizuya. *Ukiyo-e no kenkyū.* 3 vols. Tokyo: Yūzankaku, 1943.

Goncourt, Edmonde de. *Hokousaï.* Paris: Bibliothéque Charpentier, 1896.

Gonse, Louis. *Collection Louis Gonse.* Paris: Impr. G. Petit, 1926.

_____. *L'Art Japonais.* Vol. 2. Paris: A. Quantin, 1883.

Hashimoto Masakuni. "Kobikichō edokoro" (Kobikichō bureau of painting). *Kokka,* no. 3 (1889): 15-19.

Hayami, Akira. *Rekishi jinkō-gaku de mita nihon* (Japan as seen through historical demography). Tokyo: Bungei Shunjū, 2001.

Hillier, Jack. *The Art of Hokusai in Book Illustration.* London: Sotheby Parke Bernet; Berkeley: University of California Press, 1980.

_____. *Catalogue of the Japanese Paintings and Prints in the Collection of Mr. & Mrs. Richard P. Gale.* London: Routledge & Kegan Paul, 1970.

_____. *Hokusai Drawings.* London: Phaidon Press, 1966.

_____. *Hokusai: Paintings, Drawings, and Woodcuts.* London: Phaidon Press, 1955.

Hokusaikan, ed. *Nikuhitsu Katsushika Hokusai* (Paintings by Hokusai). Obuse, Japan: Hokusaikan, 1989.

Ihara, Toshirō. *Kabuki nenpyō* (Chronology of kabuki). Vol. 4. 2d ed. Tokyo: Iwanami Shoten, 1973.

Iijima, Kyoshin. *Katsushika Hokusai den* (Biography of Katsushika Hokusai). 1893. Reprint, Tokyo: Iwanami Shoten, 1999.

Ikeda, Yasaburō, ed. *Nihon meisho fūzoku zue.* 19 vols. Tokyo: Kadokawa Shoten, 1979-88.

Imahashi, Riko. *Edo kaiga to bungaku: byōsha to kotoba no Edo bunkashi* (The art of describing in Tokugawa Japan: Painting and literature). Tokyo: Tokyo University Press, 1999.

Inoue, Kazuo. "Hokusai kenkyū dampen 2." *Ukiyo-e shi,* no. 2 (1929): n.p.

Itō, Megumi. "Teisai Hokuba no shoki sakuhin to seibotsunen ni tsuite" (Concerning the life dates and early work of Teisai Hokuba). *Hokusai kenkyū,* no. 34 (2003): 72-76.

Kaneko, Fusui. *Ukiyoe nikuhitsu gashū.* 3 vols. Tokyo: Ryokuen Shobō, 1964.

Katsushika, Hokusai. *Ehon saishiki tsū* (Illustrated manual on color). Edo: Yamaguchiya Tōbei, 1848.

_____. *Fugaku hyakkei.* Edo: Nishimuraya Yūzō, 1834.

Katsushika Hokusai Museum, ed. *Katsushika Hokusai ten.* Tokyo: Ota Memorial Museum of Art, 2004.

Kerlen, H. *Catalogue of Pre-Meiji Japanese Books and Maps in Public Collections in the Netherlands.* Amsterdam: J. C. Gieben, 1996.

Keyes, Roger S. "The Dragon and the Goddess: Using Prints to Date, Identify and Illuminate Hokusai's Early Paintings." In *Hokusai and His Age: Ukiyo-e Painting, Printmaking and Book Illustration in Late Edo Japan,* edited by John T. Carpenter. Amsterdam: Hotei Publishing, 2005.

_____. "The Young Hokusai." In *Hokusai,* by Gian Carlo Calza. London and New York: Phaidon Press, 2003.

Kikuchi, Sadao. "Hokusai." *Nihon no bijutsu* 74 (July 1972): 27.

Kobayashi, Bunshichi. *Ukiyo-e tenrankai hinmoku* (Ukiyo-e exhibition list). Tokyo: Kobayashi Bunshichi, 1892.

Kobayashi, Tadashi, ed. *Nikuhitsu ukiyo-e taikan* (Survey of ukiyo-e painting). Vol. 5. Tokyo: Kōdansha, 1996.

_____, ed. *Nikuhitsu ukiyo-e taikan.* Vol. 2. Tokyo: Kōdansha, 1995.

_____, ed. *Nikuhitsu ukiyo-e taikan.* Vol. 4. Tokyo: Kōdansha, 1994.

_____, ed. *Hizō Nihon bijutsu taikan.* 12 vols. Tokyo: Kōdansha, 1992.

Kobori, Sakae. "Kusamura wo nanotta gakō." *Ukiyo-e kai,* no.4-2 (1939): n.p.

Kōdansha, ed. *Hizō ukiyo-e taikan.* Vol 1. Tokyo: Kōdansha, 1987.

Kōeki shoka jinmei roku (Directory of outstanding persons). Vol. 2. Edo: 1842.

Kōeki shoka jinmei roku. Vo1. 1. Edo: 1836.

Kokuritsu Kokkai Toshokan, ed. "*Kyokutei raikanshū.*" *Kokuritsu Kokkai Toshokan Shozō kichōsho kaidai* (Bibliography of rare books in the National Diet Library). Vol. 12. Tokyo: Kokuritsu Kokkai Toshokan, 1982.

Kubota, Kazuhiro. "Katsushika Hokusai to Edo kyōka no kenkyū." *Kashima bijutsu kenkyū,* no. 12 (1995): 4.

Kyoto Teishitsu Hakubutsukan. *Ukiyoe shūei.* Kyoto: Kyoto Teishitsu Museum, 1923.

Lambourne, Lionel. *The Aesthetic Movement.* London: Phaidon Press, 1991.

Lane, Richard. "Love's Labours Found: the Erotic Art of Hokusai." In *Hokusai,* by Gian Carlo Calza. London and New York: Phaidon Press, 2003.

_____. *Hokusai: Life and Work.* New York: E. P. Dutton, 1989.

Lawton, Thomas, and Linda Merrill. *Freer: A Legacy of Art.* Washington, D.C.: Freer Gallery of Art, Smithsonian Institution, 1993.

McCullough, Helen Craig. *Brocade by Night: "Kokin wakashū" and the Court Style in Japanese Classical Poetry.* Stanford: Stanford University Press, 1985.

McKee, Daniel. *Japanese Poetry Prints: Surimono from the Schoff Collection.* Ithaca, NY: Herbert F. Johnson Museum of Art, Cornell University, 2006.

Meech, Julia. "The Early Years of Japanese Print Collecting in North America." *Impressions: The Journal of the Ukiyo-e Society of America, Inc.* New York: The Ukiyo-e Society of America, 2005.

_____. *The Matsukata Collection of Ukiyo-e Prints: Masterpieces from the Tokyo National Museum.* New Brunswick: The Jane Voorhees Zimmerli Art Museum, Rutgers, the State University of New Jersey, 1988.

Miner, Earl, Hiroko Odagiri, and Robert E. Morrell. *The Princeton Companion to Classical Japanese Literature.* Princeton: Princeton University Press, 1985.

Mirviss, Joan B. *Masterpieces of the Art of Surimono.* New York: Joan B. Mirviss, 2003.

_____. *Amerika no 3-josei ga atsumeta Bunka, Bunsei no shugyoku no surimono* (Jewels of Japanese printmaking: Surimono of the Bunka-Bunsei era 1804-1830). Tokyo: Ōta Memorial Museum of Art, 2000.

Morrison, Arthur. *The Painters of Japan.* 2 vols. London and Edinburgh: T.C. and E.C. Jack, 1911.

Morse, Peter. *Hokusai: One Hundred Poets.* New York: George Braziller, 1989.

Mostow, Joshua S. *Pictures of the Heart: The Hyakunin Isshu in Word and Image.* Hawaii: University of Hawaii Press, 1996.

Murasaki Shikibu. *The Tale of Genji.* Translated by Edward G. Seidensticker. New York: Alfred A. Knopf, 1977.

Museum of Fine Arts, Boston. *Bosuton Bijutsukan nikuhitsu ukiyo-e* (Ukiyo-e paintings Museum of Fine Arts, Boston). 4 vols. Tokyo: Kōdansha, 2000-01.

Nagata, Seiji, ed. *Hokusai nikuhitsuga taisei* (Compilation of paintings by Hokusai). Tokyo: Shōgakukan, 2000.

_____. "Katsushika Hokusai nikuhitsu kanshō 57: Shōki zu and 58: Kōraku gaeri no zu." *Hokusai kenkyū* 25 (1998): 75-76.

_____. "Hokusai sakuhin no in'ei ni tsuite" (Seal impressions on Hokusai's paintings). *Hokusai kenkyū* 23 (1997).

_____. *Hokusai: Genius of the Japanese Ukiyo-e.* Tokyo: Kodansha International, 1995.

_____. *Hokusai bijutsukan.* 5 vols. Tokyo: Shūeisha, 1990.

_____. "Katsushika Hokusai nikuhitsu kanshō 16: Futamata daikon to Daikoku zu ippuku." *Kobijutu* 83 (July 1987): 128-29.

_____. *Katsushika Hokusai nenpu* (Chronology of Katsushika Hokusai). Tokyo: Sansai Shinsha, 1985.

Naitō, Masato. "Manipulation of Form in Hokusai's Paintings of Beauties." In *Hokusai and His Age: Ukiyo-e Painting, Printmaking and Book Illustration in Late Edo Japan,* edited by John T. Carpenter. Amsterdam: Hotei Publishing, 2005. Originally published in Idemitsu Bijutsukan kenkyū kiyō (Tokyo: Idemitsu Museum of Arts, 1995).

_____. *Ukiyo-e saihakken:Daimyōtachi ga medeta ippin·zeppin* (Rediscovery of ukiyo-e: Masterpieces of art admired by the daimyō). Tokyo: Shōgakukan, 2005.

_____. "Kaiga no rakkan ni kuwaeru kaō no shiyō ni tsuite." *Idemitsu bijutsukan kiyō,* no. 6 (2000): 109.

Narazaki, Muneshige. "Paintings of Hokusai's Final Years." In *Hokusai Paintings: Selected Essays*, edited by Gian Carlo Calza. Venice: International Hokusai Research Centre, University of Venice, 1994.

_____, ed. *Nikuhitsu ukiyo-e.* Vol. 7. Tokyo: Shūeisha, 1982.

_____, ed. *Zaigai Nihon no shihō.* Vol. 7. Tokyo: Mainichi Shimbunsha, 1980.

_____, ed. *Zaigai hihō: Nikuhitsu ukiyo-e.* Vol. 3. Tokyo: Gakushū Kenkyūsha, 1969.

_____. *Hokusai. Genshokuban bijutsu raiburari* (Library of color-illustrated art). Vol. 117. Tokyo: Misuzu shobō, 1957.

_____. *Hokusai ron.* Tokyo: Atorie sha, 1944.

Naruse Fujio. *Shiba Kōkan: shōgai to gagyō.* 2 Vols. Tokyo: Yasaka Shobō, 1995.

Nihon Art Center, ed. *Hiroshige II. Meihin soroimono Ukiyo-e.* Vol. 11. Tokyo: Gyōsei, 1991.

Nihon Keizai Shimbun (Nikkei), ed. *Hokusai ten* (Hokusai). Tokyo: Nihon Keizai Shimbun, 2005.

_____. *Hokusai: Bridging East and West.* Tokyo: Nihon Keizai Shimbun, 1998.

_____, ed. *Matsui korekushion: Ippin ni miru ukiyo-e 25nen.* Tokyo: Koshikawa Ukiyo-e bijutsukan and Nihon Keizai Shimbun, 1998.

_____, ed. *Nikuhitsu ukiyo-e.* Vol. 7. Tokyo: Shūeisha, 1982.

_____. *Hokusai ten.* Tokyo: Nihon Keizai Shimbun, 1967.

Oka, Isaburō, ed. *Hokusai, Ukiyo-e taikei.* Vol. 8. Tokyo: Shūeisha, 1960.

Oka Isaburō. *Hokusai. Ukiyo-e taikei,* Vol. 8. Tokyo: Shūeisha, 1974.

Ōta Memorial Museum of Art, ed. *Katsushika Hokusai ten.* Tokyo: Ōta Memorial Museum of Art, 2004.

_____, ed. *The Mann Collection.* Tokyo: Ōta Memorial Museum of Art, 1994.

_____, ed. *Katsushika Hokusai ten.* Tokyo: Ōta Memorial Museum of Art, 1985.

Revon, Michel. *Étude sur Hoksaï.* Paris: Lecène, Oudin et cie, 1896.

Rosenfield, John M. "Hokusai and Concepts of Eccentricity." In *Hokusai Paintings: Selected Essays,* edited by Gian Carlo Calza. Venice: International Hokusai Research Centre, University of Venice, 1994.

Saitō, Gesshin. *Suiyo sōko* (Literary pursuits upon awakening). 24 vols. Edo: 1862.

_____. *Bukō nenpyō* (Chronology of Edo). 8 vols. Edo: 1850.

_____. *Zōho ukiyo-e ruikō* (Expanded thoughts on ukiyo-e). Edo: 1844.

Sandara Hōshi, ed. *Kyōka tsurane awase onna shinasadame.* Edo: 1794.

Sandler, Mark Howard. "The Yomihon Illustrations of Katsushika Hokusai." Ph.D. diss., University of Washington, 1977. University Microfilms, 78-970.

Setchūsha Sanchō. *Gakujo gōshi.* Edo: 1775.

Shikitei Sanba. Postscript to *Ukiyo-e ruikō.* Edo: 1821.

Shimizu, Yoshiaki. "An Individual Taste for Japanese Painting." *Apollo* 118, no. 258 (1983).

Shirai, Kayō. *Gajō yōryaku* (Brief history of artists). Kyoto: 1831.

Shugio, Hiromichi, ed. *Japanese Art Folio.* Part 4. Tokyo: Ogawa shashin seihansho, 1898.

Smith, Bradley. *Japan: A History in Art.* New York: Simon and Schuster, 1964.

Smith, Henry D., II. *Hokusai: One Hundred Views of Mount Fuji.* New York: George Braziller, 1988.

Stern, Harold Phillip. *Ukiyo-e Painting.* Washington, D.C.: Freer Gallery of Art, Smithsonian Institution, 1973.

_____. *Hokusai: Paintings and Drawings in the Freer Gallery of Art.* Washington, D.C.: Freer Gallery of Art, Smithsonian Institution, 1960.

Stern, Harold Phillip, and Muneshige Narazaki. *Ukiyo-e shūka.* Vol. 16. Tokyo: Shōgakkan, 1981.

Suzuki, Jūzō. *Ningen Hokusai.* Tokyo: Ryokuen Shobō, 1963.

Takeoka Toyota, ed. *Yamato-e.* Kyoto: Gabundō, 1919.

Takeuchi, Makoto. *Bijuaru gaido Edo jidaikan* (Visual guide to the Edo period). Tokyo: Shōgakukan, 2002.

Toda, Kenji. *Descriptive Catalogue of Japanese and Chinese Illustrated Books in the Ryerson Library of the Art Institute of Chicago.* Chicago: The Lakeside Press, R. R. Donnelley & Sons, 1931.

Tokyo Toritsu Bijutukan. *Daiei hakubutsukan hizō Edo bijutsu ten* (Exhibition of secret treasures of Edo art in the British Museum). Tokyo: Tokyo Toritsu Bijutukan, 1990.

Tsuji Nobuo. "In a Fantasy World: Hokusai's Late Works." In *Hokusai,* by Gian Carlo Calza. London and New York: Phaidon Press, 2003.

Uchida, Kinzō. "Kuwagata Keisai hitsu Edo meisho zue to sono shūhen: Kinsei fūkeiga no tenkai no naka de" (Edo famous places and environs by Kuwagata Keisai). In *Kuwagata keisai Kōto meisho zue no sekai* (A world of pictures of Edo famous places). Tokyo: Ōzorasha, 1993.

White, Julia M., Reiko Mochinaga Brandon, and Yoko Woodson. *Hokusai and Hiroshige: Great Japanese Prints from the James A. Michener Collection, Honolulu Academy of Arts, 1998.* San Francisco: Asian Art Museum of San Francisco, 1998.

Yamaguchi, Keizaburō, ed. *Masterpieces of Ukiyo-e from the Irma Grabhorn-Engel Collection.* Tokyo: Bun You Associates, 1995.

Yasuda, Gōzō. *Gakyō Hokusai.* Tokyo: Arimitsu Shobō, 1971.

Yonemura, Ann. *Masterful Illusions: Japanese Prints in the Anne van Biema Collection.* Washington, D.C.: Arthur M. Sackler Gallery, Smithsonian Institution; Seattle: University of Washington Press, 2002.

Yura, Tetsuji. *Sōkō Nihon ukiyo-e ruikō* (A comprehensive edition of Thoughts on Ukiyo-e). Tokyo: Gabundō, 1979.

INDEX

CONTRIBUTORS

ASANO SHŪGŌ is chief curator at the Chiba City Museum of Art. After serving as editor of *Genshoku Ukiyo-e dai hyakka jiten* (Color Encyclopedia of Ukiyo-e), he participated in establishing the Chiba City Museum of Art, which opened in 1994. He is currently researching the history of early modern Japanese painting, especially ukiyo-e and genre painting (*fūzokuga*). His publications include *The Passionate Art of Kitagawa Utamaro* (with Timothy Clark, 1995), *Nishiki-e wo yomu* (Reading color woodblock prints, 1997–98), *Hishikawa Moronobu ten* (with Kobayashi Tadashi and Tsuji Nobuo, 2001), and *Edo no shunga: Katsushika Hokusai shunga no sekai* (Edo erotic art: Katsushika Hokusai's world of erotic art). He was a contributing author to *Hokusai ten* (Hokusai exhibition, 2005), the catalogue of the Hokusai exhibition at the Tokyo National Museum.

TIMOTHY CLARK is head of the Japanese section in the department of Asia at The British Museum. He has organized or co-organized many exhibitions, most recently *Kabuki Heroes on the Osaka Stage, 1780–1830* (with Professor Drew Gerstle of SOAS, University of London), which has been shown at The British Museum, Osaka Museum of History, and Waseda University Theatre Museum, Tokyo. His publications include: *Ukiyo-e Paintings in the British Museum* (1992), *Demon of Painting: The Art of Kawanabe Kyōsai* (1993), *The Actor's Image: Ukiyo-e Prints of the Katsukawa School in the Clarence Buckingham Collection* (with Ueda Osamu, 1994), *The Passionate Art of Kitagawa Utamaro* (with Asano Shūgō, 1995), *One Hundred Views of Mount Fuji* (2001), *The Dawn of the Floating World: Early Ukiyo-e Treasures from the Museum of Fine Arts, Boston 1650–1765* (with Louise E. Virgin, Anne Nishimura Morse, and Allen Hockley, 2001), and *Kazari: Decoration and Display in Japan, Fifteenth–Nineteenth Centuries* (edited by Nicole Coolidge Rousmaniere, 2002). His research interests include the Maruyama-Shijō school of painting and the development of the art market and exhibitions in premodern Kyoto.

KOBAYASHI TADASHI is professor in the department of art history at Gakushuin University in Tokyo and director of the Chiba City Museum of Art. He is a specialist of the history of paintings in the Edo period. He has edited major reference series such as *Nikuhitsu ukiyo-e taikan* (Ukiyo-e paintings in Japanese collections, 1994–97) and has written on Edo art and artists in such publications as *Edo kaigashi ron* (Essays on the history of Edo painting, 1985), *Edo no gakatachi* (Artists of Edo, 1987), and *Ukiyo-e no rekishi* (History of ukiyo-e, 1998), as well as monographs on Edo artists. He was guest curator for *An Enduring Vision: Seventeenth–Twentieth Century Japanese Painting from the Gitter-Yelen Collection* (2002) and was a contributing author to the exhibition *Hokusai ten* (Hokusai Exhibition, 2005) at the Tokyo National Museum.

NAGATA SEIJI is deputy director of the Ōta Memorial Museum of Art in Tokyo and director of the Katsushika Hokusai Museum of Art in Tsuwano, Japan. An authority on Hokusai, he has published many books, including *Katsushika Hokusai nenpu* (Chronology of Katsushika Hokusai, 1985), *Hokusai edehon* (Hokusai's art manuals), *Hokusai manga* (Hokusai's random sketches), *Hokusai bijutsukan* (Hokusai Art Museum, 1990) and *Hokusai nikuhitsuga taisei* (Compendium of paintings by Hokusai, 2000). He was guest curator of the exhibition, *Hokusai ten* (Hokusai exhibition, 2005) at the Tokyo National Museum.

NAITŌ MASATO is chief curator of the Idemitsu Museum of Arts in Tokyo. He has served as executive director of the International Ukiyo-e Society. He received a Kajima Art Foundation award for a study of the *Hokusai manga* in 1993. He is currently researching the history of paintings in the Edo period, especially ukiyo-e and the Rinpa school. He has published numerous books, including *Ukiyo-e saihakken* (Rediscovering ukiyo-e) and *Utagawa Kuniyoshi* (1998). He co-authored the exhibition catalogue, *Rimpa Art from the Idemitsu Collection* (1998) with Yamane Yūzō and Timothy Clark.

ANN YONEMURA is senior associate curator of Japanese art at the Freer Gallery of Art and Arthur M. Sackler Gallery, Smithsonian Institution. She has organized or co-organized exhibitions on subjects ranging from *Ancient Japan* (1992) to modern Japanese prints, and she has edited and contributed to many exhibition catalogues and scholarly publications. She conducted research on Japanese Buddhist and Shinto paintings as visiting scholar at the Nara National Museum in 2004. Among her recent publications are *Masterful Illusions: Japanese Prints in the Anne van Biema Collection* (2002) and an essay on Charles Lang Freer's collection of paintings by Hokusai in *Hokusai ten* (Hokusai exhibition, 2005), the catalogue of the exhibition at the Tokyo National Museum. She is curator of *Hokusai* (2006) at the Arthur M. Sackler Gallery, Smithsonian Institution, and is editor and contributing author of the catalogue.